SUPERVISION
as a
PROACTIVE
PROCESS

SUPERVISION
as a
PROACTIVE
PROCESS

John C. Daresh
Ohio State University

Longman
New York & London

Supervision as a Proactive Process

Longman Inc., 95 Church Street, White Plains, N. Y. 10601

Associated companies:
Longman Group Ltd., London
Longman Cheshire Pty., Melbourne
Longman Paul Pty., Auckland
Copp Clark Pitman, Toronto
Pitman Publishing Inc., New York

Executive editor: Naomi Silverman
Development editor: Virginia L. Blanford
Production editor: Marie-Josée A. Schorp
Cover design: Paul Agule Design
Text art: Hal Keith
Production supervisor: Judith Millman

Library of Congress Cataloging-in-Publication Data

Daresh, John C.
  Supervision as a proactive process.

  Bibliography: p.
  Includes index.
  1. Supervision of employees.   I. Title.
HF5549.12.D37   1989   658.3'02   88-8465

ISBN 0-8013-0025-8

89 90 91 92 93 94 9 8 7 6 5 4 3 2 1

To the memory of my parents, George and
Anne Daresh, and to
the ultimate clients of more effective
supervision: Children in our schools,
the Sunshine in our live . . .

Contents

Foreword   xiii

Acknowledgments   xv

INTRODUCTION   1

**PART I.   EDUCATIONAL SUPERVISION: TRADITION
AND CONTEXT**   5

Chapter 1.   In Search of a Definition   7
  The Earliest Stage: Supervision as Inspection   8
  The Next Stage: Supervision as "Science"   11
  The Era of Emphasis on Human Relations   14
  Where Are We Now? Current Perspectives   17
  What Is Supervision?   20
  Summary   21
    Suggested Activities   *21*
    References   *22*
    Additional Readings   *22*

Chapter 2.   Personal Assumptions Guiding Supervisory Practice   **23**
  Beliefs, Attitudes, and Values   24
  McGregor's Assumptions   26
  Individual Action Planning   29

Summary   36
Suggested Activities   *37*
References   *37*
Additional Readings   *37*

Chapter 3.   Continuing Controversies   **38**
Controversy 1: Is There Such a Thing as "a" Supervisor?   38
Controversy 2: Is There a Difference between Administration
    and Supervision?   42
Controversy 3: Can Supervisors Ever Really Get Anything Done?   45
Summary   47
Suggested Activities   *47*
References   *48*
Additional Readings   *48*

PART II.   THEORY INTO PRACTICE   **49**

**Chapter 4.   The Role of Theory in Improving
                Supervisory Practice**   **51**
Definition of Theory   51
Functions of Theory   53
Steps in Theory Development   54
Characteristics of "Good" Theory   56
Restrictions on the Use of Theory   58
Distinctions between Formal Theory and Personal Philosophy   58
Summary   60
Suggested Activities   *61*
References   *61*
Additional Readings   *61*

Chapter 5.   Organizational Analysis   **62**
Formal Analysis: Hage's Axiomatic Theory of Organizations   63
Formal Analysis: Getzels's Social Systems   69
Morgan's Organizational Metaphors   72
Informal Analysis: Mile's Organizational Health   75
Informal Analysis: Organizational Climate   78
Summary   79
Suggested Activities   *82*
References   *82*

Chapter 6.   Leadership   **83**
Alternative Definitions   84
Descriptive versus Normative Views   85
Historical Development of Leadership   86
Alternative Descriptive Models   90

Alternative Normative Models   91
Emerging Issue: Instructional Leadership   97
General Comments about Leadership   101
Summary   102
    Suggested Activities   *103*
    References   *103*

Chapter 7.   Motivation   **105**
Definition of Motivation   105
Alternative Conceptualizations of Motivation   106
Equity Theories of Motivation   109
Reinforcement Theories of Motivation   110
Expectancy Theories of Motivation   111
Individual Professional Philosophy and Approaches to Motivation   112
Summary   113
    Suggested Activities   *114*
    References   *114*
    Additional Reading   *114*

**PART III.   THE REALITIES OF SUPERVISION: COMMUNICATION,
              CHANGE, POWER, AND CONFLICT**   **115**

Chapter 8.   Communication   **117**
Definition of Communication   117
Functions of Communication   118
Forms of Communication   123
Potential Barriers to Communication   125
Skills to Improve Communication   127
Summary   127
    Suggested Activities   *128*
    References   *128*

Chapter 9.   Change Processes   **129**
Alternative Conceptual Models of Change   130
Barriers to Organizational Change   137
Phases of Change   140
Overcoming the Barriers   142
Summary   143
    Suggested Activities   *143*
    References   *144*

Chapter 10.   Exercising Power and Authority   **146**
Alternative Definitions   147
Characteristics of Power   148
Characteristics of Authority   150

Implications for Supervisors   152
Summary   152
    Suggested Activities   *153*
    References   *153*

Chapter 11.   Conflict as a Supervisory Reality   **154**
What Is Conflict?   155
Types and Sources of Conflict   156
Conflict-Handling Styles   161
Summary   163
    Suggested Activities   *163*
    References   *164*
    Additional Readings   *164*

**PART IV.   WORKING WITH PEOPLE:
           PROCESS AND EVALUATION**   **165**

Chapter 12.   Groups   **167**
Definitions of a Group   167
Basic Considerations of Groups   169
Group Effectiveness   175
Applications to Supervision   176
Summary   177
    Suggested Activities   *177*
    References   *177*

Chapter 13.   Teachers and Supervisors   **178**
Who Are Teachers?   179
Why Do People Become Teachers?   182
What Do Teachers Do?   184
So What Can Supervisors Do?   190
Summary   193
    Suggested Activities   *193*
    References   *194*
    Additional Readings   *194*

Chapter 14.   Evaluation   **195**
Types of Evaluation   196
Objectives of Evaluation   198
Current Problems and Issues in Evaluation   201
Summary   211
    Suggested Activities   *211*
    References   *212*

PART V.   MODELS FOR SUPERVISION: NOW AND THE FUTURE   213

Chapter 15.   Clinical Supervision   215
Underlying Assumptions of Clinical Supervision   215
Developing an Appropriate Climate   218
Stages of the Clinical Supervision Model   219
Limits of Clinical Supervision   228
Summary   230
   Suggested Activities   *230*
   References   *230*
   Additional Readings   *231*

Chapter 16.   Emerging Models of Supervision   232
Developmental Supervision   232
Differentiated Supervision   237
Summary   248
   Suggested Activities   *248*
   References   *249*
   Additional Readings   *250*

**Chapter 17.   Supervision as Effective Staff Development and
                Inservice Education   251**
Finding a Definition   252
Research Related to Inservice and Staff Development   253
Important Missing Ingredients   258
Promising Practices   265
Summary   266
   Suggested Activities   *267*
   References   *267*

Chapter 18.   Future Trends and Issues in Supervision   269
Continued Call for Reforms   269
Increased Professionalism of Supervisors   270
More Professional Opportunities   271
Summary   271

Index   *273*

Foreword

You are about to read a book that could help to change the nature of administration in schools. The importance of supervision is given lip service by teachers and administrators alike, but changes in current practice have been regarded by both groups as nearly impossible to accomplish. John Daresh says it isn't so.

Supervision is often described as little more than a formal exercise used to fulfill contractual obligations. Some see it as an administrative ritual undertaken to enforce adherence to prescribed curriculums, to decide who to hire, fire or promote, or to convince outsiders that rigorous evaluations of instruction are part of school life. Unfortunately, in most schools, supervision is no more than a principal or curriculum supervisor entering a teacher's classroom to sit through a prearranged observation. After watching the teacher conduct a lesson, the supervisor meets with the teacher at some later point to discuss what happened, to fill out a uniform checklist, and to reach agreement on some sort of rating.

Albert Shanker recalls meeting with a group of administrators and supervisors and asking them if they recall a time when they as teachers were formally observed. All in the audience raised their hands. When asked how many of them found that the observation procedure helped them to become better teachers, almost no hands were raised. When asked how many of them formally observe teachers in their own roles as administrators and supervisors, all hands were once again raised.

This, then, is what passes for supervision in most schools and although both teachers and administrators are quick to distance themselves from the usefulness of such exercises, few seem able to deliver alternative models.

John Daresh offers those alternatives and along with them he provides the theoretical and evidential arguments that insist there is not only a better way, but it can be done in any setting.

This book is guided by simple, yet powerful, assumptions. The first is that supervision is a process of overseeing the ability of people to meet the goals of the organization in which they work. The second is that supervision is a process, and the third is that supervision is proactive.

Professor Daresh is a man with a point of view. Supervision, he says, is not a neutral, reactive, or haphazard process. Good supervision changes people and their organizations for the better. Good supervision is a radical action.

To make his arguments, Dr. Daresh presents his case for proactive supervision in five parts. Part I focuses on the importance of one's values, attitudes, and assumptions to good supervision. Part II presents and analyzes a series of theories that underlie the supervisory process. Specific components of the supervisory process—communication, change, conflict, and power—are the focus of Part III. Part IV explores specific strategies for working with teachers and groups, and discusses the evaluative nature of supervision. Finally, specific models of supervision are examined in Part V.

Effective schooling will not be accomplished unless we improve supervision in schools. Readers of this book will find practical tools that can make a difference.

Charol Shakeshaft,
Hofstra University

Acknowledgments

This first effort to complete a sole-authored book has been an exciting learning activity. But I must admit that, despite the fact that there is but one name printed on the front of this book, many others deserve special recognition for their assistance in helping me to move toward the goals I have set. This, by the way, represents an example of the spirit of proactive supervision and support that goes well beyond many of the examples used in the text.

My first acknowledgment goes to my editor at Longman, Naomi Silverman. Along with the educational consultant for this series, Joel Spring, Naomi has consistently asked the questions that I needed to answer, provided the deadlines that I needed to meet (and occasionally did), and given directions that have helped a neophyte move through this process with a minimum of discomfort. Another major contributor to this effort was Virginia Blanford, Longman's developmental editor, who spent many hours transforming the "professorese" writing of the original drafts into a considerably more readable and useful volume.

Others have helped considerably during the preparation of this book and deserve not only a mention here but also my continuing thanks. Marsha Playko, my administrative assistant, has kept my other responsibilities on track, prodded me into action, provided insightful feedback, and, most importantly, always been a friend throughout a most stressful and busy year. James LaPlant, my former colleague at the University of Cincinnati, continued to ask the tough questions and to provide the ongoing collegial support that has been typical of his role as my mentor. Robert Franz of Ohio Dominican College, and Sharon Pape of Southern Illinois University, reviewed early draft chapters and provided me with helpful comments and suggestions. Others who have been a source of constant support throughout the year include my colleagues at the Danforth Foundation Program for the Preparation of Principals, particularly Donn Gresso, Jack Greer, Curtis Sellers, Dick Andrews, Bruce Barnett, Bob Sinclair, Dan Duke, and Frank MacQuarrie. Each of these individuals has given me the feedback and support needed to complete this project.

I would also like to recognize the contributions of my current colleagues in the College of Education at Ohio State who also took interest in this project. Among the many who have helped, I express special thanks to Donald Anderson, Jim Altschuld, Virgil Blanke, Brad Mitchell, Bob Donmoyer, Ken Howey, Nancy Zimpher, Vern Cunningham, Charles Galloway, Bill Wayson, Gail McCutcheon, Don Cruickshank, Mary Ann Sagaria, and Jack Hough for their comments that were so helpful at various points in the writing process. In addition, I want to thank the many students who have been enrolled in my Fundamentals of Supervision classes at both Ohio State University and the University of Cincinnati.

Special recognition is also owed to Alice Ray and Kathy Shonkwiler, extraordinarily talented secretaries to the Educational Administration program faculty, who kept my work on schedule by doing so many things so well and so often as this work was proceeding. I express my thanks to my colleagues in the field across Ohio who so often modeled the best leadership practices of talented superintendents, principals, and supervisors. These gifted individuals all provided evidence of the fact that effective, proactive supervision is a possibility, not an unattainable dream.

Finally, special acknowledgment and thanks are due to my wife, Stephanie, and daughter, Bridget, who provided critical understanding and support while I worked on this effort. Stephanie spent hours typing the initial drafts of the chapters in this volume, and my little Bridget spent hours doing what she could do to help by understanding why her mommy and daddy were always so busy. This book would not have been possible, and the rest of these acknowledgments could not have been written, without their constant support, understanding, and involvement.

Introduction

Imagine two different supervisors or school administrators facing the same question: What is required to encourage veteran teachers to explore the new research on effective teaching strategies? The first supervisor announces a plan for all teachers to study the topic in inservice workshops, and the experienced teachers immediately and clearly voice their resistance—the program will mean more work, and besides, they are competent and effective teachers already. The supervisor reacts to this resistance by hastily putting an inservice program together, hiring an outside consultant to run it, and requiring the entire faculty to attend the sessions.

The second supervisor approaches the problem differently. In fact, the task may not become problematic in the first place, for this supervisor has taken time throughout the year to talk with all the teachers on a one-to-one basis. As a result, the supervisor is neither surprised nor frustrated when some teachers express little interest in the plan to acquaint them with new research on teaching. This second supervisor already knows where probable sources of dissatisfaction exist among the teachers and constructs the inservice agenda to accommodate this fact. Expert teachers are consulted and given leadership roles; workshops are geared to actual needs; potential resistance is defused.

This brief example illustrates two very different approaches to the exercise of supervisory responsibilities. The first supervisor approaches the job *reactively*. As long as the school seemed to be moving along reasonably well, the supervisor left things alone; but conflict erupted suddenly and unexpectedly when experienced teachers were presented with an inservice agenda for which they were unprepared and which they felt was being forced

1

on them. This supervisor, who believed in the need for teachers to keep up with research, was no doubt angry and frustrated because plans for good, professional inservice training had been "sabotaged."

The second supervisor practices *proactive* supervision. Through constant involvement with staff throughout the year, even when everything was running smoothly, this supervisor could anticipate and plan for negative reactions to a particular decision. In fact, the second supervisor would probably have avoided making a unilateral decision about a topic for inservice training in the first place and instead would have spent considerable time during the year getting to know the *people* in the organization and the *nature* of the organization. As a result, the supervisor could *proactively* anticipate problems in advance and minimize their negative consequences for the organization.

In this book, which emphasizes the development of skills, knowledge, and attitudes consistent with proactive supervision, we make a number of fundamental assumptions about the nature of supervisory responsibilities in general. First, we assume that our understanding of educational supervision must be based on a knowledge of historical definitions and perspectives. Second, we assume that supervision today represents a blend of many earlier as well as current perspectives. As a result, we begin in Chapter 1 by reviewing the development of educational supervision in the United States and some of the most important trends that have guided that development. Finally, and most importantly, we assume that the most productive and effective way to define educational supervision today is as a *proactive process*. This central assumption underlies virtually all of the arguments advanced in this text.

What do I mean by proactive supervision? I believe that there are six major components to this view of leadership practice in schools. To be an effective proactive supervisor, you need to:

1. Know your own beliefs.
2. Understand the nature and characteristics of organizations.
3. Understand that supervision is not an event or a series of events; it is an ongoing *process.*
4. Examine and understand alternative perspectives, even those that you do not fully accept.
5. Be consistent in your own behavior.
6. Be capable of analyzing the people in your organization and their patterns of behavior.

The chapters in this text are not designed to teach you each of these characteristics independently. Rather, these six concepts are woven into a total pattern of supervisory behavior, throughout the 18 chapters of this book. I believe, and stress throughout this volume, that effective supervisors look at their responsibilities *holistically* and not as a series of tasks and responses to the various emergencies that arise in the life of a school or a district. The effective proactive supervisor must develop a total understanding of what is being done, to whom, and with what likely consequences.

Supervision, as you will discover by reading this book, is not a neutral or reactive process where things simply "happen." Rather, *good* supervision changes people and their organizations for the better. Supervision is a critical responsibility in schools, and effective supervision can be extremely rewarding to the educator who chooses to follow this career route. I hope this book will assist you in deciding if in fact you *want* to follow the supervisory path and, if you do select educational supervision as your career, I hope that this text will help you be as good an educational supervisor as you can be.

PART I

Educational Supervision: Tradition and Context

The single most important attribute for any educator, and particularly for those educators who engage in supervisory practices, is an understanding of his or her own basic attitudes, values, and assumptions concerning both supervision and education. This understanding can derive only from a knowledge of history and context—how supervision has developed in American education—and of theories of educational supervision.

CHAPTER 1

In Search of a Definition

Educational supervision is a field in search of a definition. Although supervision has been a normal school-based activity for as long as there have been public schools in America, no real consensus has ever been reached concerning what supervision should be or what educational supervisors should do. Attitudes about schools, teachers, and learners have changed periodically since the 17th century. As a result, views of what constitutes proper and effective supervisory practice have also shifted.

In this chapter we will review the major changes that have occurred, as well as the approaches to supervisory practice that have paralleled changing perceptions of public education and educational management and that serve as examples of the transitory nature of definitions. To clarify the particular approaches that dominated specific historical periods of supervisory practice, we will note some of the basic assumptions, characteristics, and definitions typical of each period and provide some examples of how supervisory practice has been affected by the predominant definitions and assumptions. Before beginning this review, however, we should make an important point: Although this chapter appears to describe an orderly, sequential, and basically rational development of the field of supervision, in fact, the history of supervision has never really been as clear-cut as it might seem. Overlaps exist from one period to another, and features of most of the "old" views of supervision are still alive and very much with us today.

One important assumption underlies this review of alternative definitions and serves also as a crucial foundation for the concept of proactive supervision that is espoused throughout this text. The field of educational supervision is greatly influenced by the ways in which individuals and groups define that field on a day-to-day basis. A brief review of perspectives from the past enables us to see how supervision has developed over time, and how some of our present practices and beliefs got their start. This understanding of history will help you make consistent choices about "proper" supervisory behavior—an important component of the authenticity that must underlie proactive supervisory practice.

Throughout this book I will suggest that effective supervisors are *proactive* in their approach to supervisory responsibilities. What I mean by this, simply, is that they *plan ahead* and *anticipate* proper ways of behaving in advance, before little problems become major crises. *Proactive supervision* is leading, not simply reacting after a situation forces you to respond. It is an easy concept to define, but as the chapters ahead will show, a difficult one to put into action.

THE EARLIEST STAGE: SUPERVISION AS INSPECTION

The issue of providing supervision for teachers in American schools is as old as the history of formal education in this country. In fact, the year 1642, when the first Massachusetts School Law was enacted, also marks the beginning of educational supervision in American schools. This first stage of supervisory development lasted until approximately the conclusion of the Civil War, in 1865.

During these years, supervisors were primarily engaged in *inspection* (or, as some call it, "snoopervision")—an approach based on the assumption that an educational supervisor's job was to find out all the wrong things that teachers were doing in their classrooms. While this description seems rather harsh, we need to recall some historical facts before judging 17th- and 18th-century supervisors as insensitive ogres who lacked compassion or basic respect for teachers. The fact is that during the earliest days of American education, teachers often were not well-educated and frequently stayed only a step or two ahead of their students in basic skills. Teachers in those years often needed monitoring to make certain that at least minimally acceptable levels of performance were being maintained in classrooms and schools. Individual supervisors did not always agree with these responsibilities. In fact, the judgmental nature of supervision during this time rested in job descriptions, not in personal interpretations.

The first stage of supervisory practice (roughly 1642–1865) can be further subdivided into two distinct eras: The first of religious control, and the second of a more secular nature. The first years of American public education were characterized, particularly in the New England colonies, by the assumption of community religious leaders that public schools were necessary to ensure that local religious beliefs and values would be both preserved and transmitted from generation to generation. Supervision, then, was defined largely in religious terms. The Massachusetts Bay Colony of 1642 provides the earliest known description of educational supervision:

> This Court, taking into consideration the great neglect of many parents and masters in the training up of their children in learning and labor, and other implyments which may be proffitable to the common wealth, do hereupon order and decree, that in every town ye chosen men appointed for managing the prudentiall affaires of the same shall henceforth stand charged with the care of the redress of this evill . . . and for this end, they, or the greatest number of them, shall have the power to take into account from time to time of all parents and masters, and of their children, especially of their ability to read and understand the principles of religion and the capitall laws of this country. (Massachusetts School Law, 1642)

These "chosen men" were typically either ordained ministers or elders in local congregations—an understandable phenomenon in light of the fact that the teaching and learning they went out to review was tied directly to matters of religion. If students were not learning how to read, they were not learning how to read the Bible; if they were not learning how to read the Bible, their paths to eternal salvation were blocked because they would never be able to gain insights into the Scriptures and to learn about their God.

After the American Revolution, the duty of monitoring what was taking place in classrooms was increasingly entrusted to committees of laymen who were not associated with any specific religious group. This switch no doubt occurred as part of the general secularization of American society taking place at this time. As the years went on, school officials placed less and less emphasis on the supervisor's responsibility to verify the quality of religious instruction, and more on the supervisor's responsibility to oversee the quality of secular instruction. What remained constant, however, was the assumption that teachers lacked basic competency. Two popular definitions of supervision illustrate this shift in focus. Theodore Dwight (1835) noted:

> Visitation and careful examination are necessary to discover the teacher's merits in teaching and governing the attention, deserts, and improvements of the children. To render a teacher, in the first place, to convince him that he can, are the principal objects to be offered by a friend of education. (p. 21)

About 30 years later, James Wickerman (1864) provided another view of what supervisors were supposed to do, in which supervisors are no longer referred to as "friends of education."

> Such visitations (by supervisors) are necessary to secure the caretaking of the grounds, buildings, furniture, and apparatus; necessary to secure the

most rapid progress on the part of the pupils; necessary to encourage competent teachers and to detect incompetent ones; in short, necessary to insure the well-working of the whole school machinery. (p. 9)

As these definitions show, the religious orientation in educational supervisory practice had given way to a more worldly, secular view by the mid-19th century. On the other hand, these definitions continue to demonstrate some striking similarities derived from a common set of assumptions held by educators throughout the first stage of supervisory development in American education.

Assumptions and Related Practices of the Early Stage of Supervision

1. Teachers were not to be trusted. Perhaps the most basic premise of the earliest descriptions of supervision was simply that teachers were, for the most part, incompetents who could not be trusted to do their assigned jobs. At first, this assumption suggested a lack of trust in teachers' abilities to provide instruction in religion. The supervisor's responsibility, then, was to be present in classes as often as possible and to be a safeguard against the spread of any religious heresy, either intentional or unintentional. Instruction was monitored closely, not so much to guarantee proper methods of teaching, but rather to make certain that proper interpretation of the Bible was maintained. Even when this religious focus became blurred and finally disappeared, however, teachers were still viewed as essentially incompetent employees who needed to be carefully watched.

2. Supervisors had the right to intervene directly in the classroom. During these early years, supervisors often engaged in activities that were disruptive in their own right; they deliberately tried to "catch" teachers making mistakes. Supervisors made frequent, usually unannounced, classroom visits, which typically were carried out in a way that intimidated even the most confident or competent of instructors. Supervisors of the time frequently entered a classroom while a lesson was in progress, and then openly and defiantly debated with the teacher about the accuracy of the information he or she was imparting.

3. Supervisors were meant to be inspectors. Supervisors were expected not only to monitor instructional processes and correct incompetent teachers in the midst of leading their classes; they were also generally expected to review the characteristics of the total school, not as consultants or facilitators, but solely as inspectors. They performed a "quality control" function, overseeing the upkeep of school buildings, instructional materials, and equipment. They were supposed to make sure, for example, that the school-house roof did not leak, that the fire in the stove was well stoked, and that there were sufficient slates and benches for all the students.

THE NEXT STAGE: SUPERVISION AS "SCIENCE"

From approximately the end of the Civil War until soon after World War I (around 1920), teaching procedures and educational practices in general were greatly influenced by experts whose interest was primarily the improvement of organizational efficiency. Much of what they believed was affected by the views of various writers on corporation management, particularly Frederick W. Taylor (1916) whose "scientific management principles" were advocated as the way to ensure good practice in industrial organizations. A review of Taylor's major tenets provides a context for our discussion of this second period of supervisory thought and practice. The essential points of Taylor's views include the following:

1. *Time-study principle.* All productive effort should be measured by accurate time study and a standard time established for all work done in the shop.
2. *Piece-rate principle.* Wages should be proportional to output and their rates based on the standards determined by time study. As a corollary, a worker should be given the highest grade of work of which he is capable.
3. *Separation-of-planning-from-performance principle.* Management should take over from workers the responsibility for planning the work and making the performance physically possible. Planning should be based on time studies and other data related to production, which are scientifically determined and systematically classified; it should be facilitated by standardization of tools, implements, and methods.
4. *Scientific-methods-of-work principle.* Management should take over from workers the responsibility for their methods of work, determine scientifically the best methods, and train the workers accordingly.
5. *Managerial-control principle.* Managers should be trained and taught to apply scientific principles of management and control (such as management by exception and comparison with validated production standards).
6. *Functional principle.* The strict application of military principles should be reconsidered and the industrial organization should be so designed that it best serves the purpose of improving the coordination of activities among the specialists. (Villers, 1960, p. 78)

These principles of scientific management imply that certain features of organizational life are so predictable that specific laws can be formulated to guide behavior in virtually every circumstance, and that outcomes are also highly predictable in organizational settings. In educational as well as corporate supervision during this period, the belief reigned that behavioral formulae, when faithfully followed, would necessarily and automatically lead to predictable outcomes and products.

William Payne's 1875 definition of supervision reflects this notion of precision and certainty of performance in schools:

> The theory of school supervision . . . requires the superintendent to work upon the school through the teachers. He is to prepare plans of instruction and discipline, which the teachers must carry into effect; but the successful working out of such a scheme requires constant oversight and constant readjustments. Hence arises the necessity for conference, instruction in methods, and correction of errors. The teachers of a graded school should be under continual normal instruction. (p. 4)

In 1914, E. C. Eliot offered this view:

> Supervisory control is concerned with what should be taught, when it should be taught, to whom, how, and to what purpose. (p. 23)

Both these views of supervision strongly imply that there is a single "right way" of doing things in education, and that once this path is identified, it is the supervisor's responsibility to ensure that teachers know and follow it. The supervisor is also charged with the responsibility of *planning*—that is, of finding the most efficient and economical ways to attain organizational goals.

Scientific management principles clearly influenced the development of educational supervision during this period, but other factors also played a role. For example, many schools grew rapidly in both size and complexity, to the extent that larger organizational arrangements—districts and systems— were established across the nation, particularly in urban centers in the North and East. This increased organizational complexity was a major factor in the creation of a more *segmented* view of educational supervision. Larger school systems began hiring two individuals—a *business manager* as well as a *supervisor of instruction*—who would function as equal partners in the hierarchical structure of the school district. Both were responsible to a third person in another newly created role, the *superintendent of schools.* This concept of dual administration (business and instruction) greatly influenced the development of modern administrative and supervisory practice. One product of this era in educational history, then, was the beginning of what might be called the institutionalization and professionalization of the educational supervisor's role. In later chapters, we will look at the problems this separation of functions has created.

Assumptions and Related Practices of the "Scientific" Period of Educational Supervision

1. Great faith was placed in educational "laws." Many educators sincerely believed that scientific research would provide the answer to virtually any problem. Organizations throughout society were awakening to the possibility that rules and principles could be established to guide practice. School administrators in particular were open to this line of thinking, because at this time schools were emerging from over two centuries of rather confused development. The notion that the educational practices of the past could be understood and even improved upon if some key "facts" and laws were learned was indeed tempting.

The outcome of this view, in terms of supervisory practice, was that increasingly, the educational supervisor became a *quality control reviewer* who checked to see if employees conformed to procedures; the supervisor's job was to make sure that the "scientific" rules of schooling were being followed. Thus, the emphasis in supervision was on the maintenance of acceptable teaching behaviors, and particularly on ensuring that these were carried out efficiently.

2. The supervisory staff of a school system would determine the proper methods of instruction. This "scientific" approach to supervision emphasized a "top-down" orientation to defining and communicating information concerning instructional practices. The supervisory personnel of a school or district were viewed as the legitimate experts in the field of instruction, to the extent that such experts could reasonably be expected to define precisely what constituted proper performance. Scientific management principles urging separation of management from employee control made unthinkable the possibility that teachers would work together to influence or define proper instructional techniques. Quite simply, teachers were viewed as the implementors of administrators' policies, and supervisors were around to make certain that the policies were being implemented faithfully.

To summarize, the overriding aim of educational supervision as it was practiced during this era was to develop teachers to be as "professionally efficient" as possible at all times. Professional efficiency was narrowly defined as competence in such things as self-analysis, self-criticism, and self-improvement—at least in terms of teachers' abilities to conform to stated standards of performance. Those standards were determined at higher levels of the school district organization and then transmitted to the teachers. A primary activity of educational supervisors, then, was to provide either condemnations or commendations after classroom visits. Compromises between these two extremes were not possible.

THE ERA OF EMPHASIS
ON HUMAN RELATIONS

One consequence of the "scientific" era of supervisory practice was the tendency to value organizational goals more than the interests and needs of the people who worked in the organization. Scientific management often emphasized the notion that all organizational components—employees included—were best understood as replacement parts: "One teacher is just as good as another" could have been a motto of the time. Predictably, a vigorous reactive movement eventually emerged. In the "human relations" era from approximately 1920 to 1960, a supervisory philosophy emerged that placed primary emphasis on developing the individuals who worked in schools and on satisfying their personal interests. Widespread support developed for cooperative group efforts as both an end and a means for change in schools.

Supervisors were encouraged to use every means possible for stimulating and encouraging classroom teachers, with the assumed outcome being more effective instruction. Characteristic terms found in the literature describing supervision during this era include such words as "coordinating," "integrating," "creativity," "stimulation," and "democratic relationships." Again, a glance at some definitions from the time provides insights to guide our understanding of the era. For example, the National Education Association (NEA) in 1930 stated:

> [The following is a] . . . fundamental philosophy of supervision: Supervision is a creative enterprise. It has for its objective the development of a group of professional workers who attack their problems scientifically, free from control of tradition and actuated by the spirit of inquiry. Supervision seeks to improve an environment in which men and women of high professional ideals may live a vigorous, intelligent, creative life. (p. 47)

What is truly remarkable about this definition, when compared to those in the earlier era of "scientific supervision," is the sudden shift in emphasis toward allowing employees to work together to define organizational goals and to create appropriate activities to meet those goals. The "top-down" emphasis of supervisory control has given way to a more democratic process. Two additional definitions support this view. Cox (1934) observed:

> The supervisory function is described not so much toward teachers and their methods as it is toward practices of advisement, student activities, pupil control of defensible subject matter, and personality adjustments of pupils and teachers. (p. 33)

Several years later, Briggs and Justman (1952) defined supervision in these terms:

In general, to supervise means to coordinate, stimulate, and direct growth of teachers in the power to stimulate and direct the growth of every pupil through the exercise of his talents toward the richest and most intelligent participation in the society and world in which he lives. (p. 21)

Any review of the human relations approach to educational supervision would be incomplete if it did not include at least a brief description of the work of Kimball Wiles, often characterized as the chief advocate for this perspective. In 1967, Wiles wrote the following description of what supervisors should do:

They [the supervisors] are the expediters. They help establish communication. They help people hear each other. They serve as liaison to get people into contact with others who have similar problems or with resource people who can help. They stimulate staff members to look at the extent to which ideas and resources are being shared, and the degree to which persons are encouraged and supported as they try new things. They make it easier to carry out the agreements that emerge from evaluation sessions. They listen to individuals discuss their problems and recommend other resources that may help in the search for solutions. They bring to individual teachers, whose confidence they possess, appropriate suggestions and materials. They serve, as far as they are able, the feelings that teachers have about the system and its policies, and they recommend that the administration examine irritations among staff members. (p. 11)

Clearly there is a great difference between the perspective of this *human development* era of supervision and those of the *inspection* and *scientific* eras. In the first two centuries of American education, very little concern was expressed about the individual needs of teachers and others in school systems. In Wiles's words, on the other hand, we find little or no concern for the priorities and needs of the organization. The focus had shifted from things to people.

Assumptions and Related Practices
of the Human-Relations Era

1. If people are happy, they will be productive. This is the fundamental premise of this era, and it is the key ingredient of any approach to supervisory or managerial practice that endorses the fulfillment of human needs. If we truly believe that happy employees will be better, more effective employees, then the primary task for supervisors must be to focus on whatever they determine are the needs and interests of the workers. Educational supervisors must then spend a good deal of time seeking input from teachers and staff members concerning working conditions and other issues related to the quality of life in the organization. Human relations supervisors and administrators frequently go out of their way to make workers comfortable through notes of praise ("Smile-O-Grams") in teachers' mail boxes, staff parties ("TGIF"), and so forth. More substantively, such supervisors also emphasize discussion groups, shared decision-making activities, and group-process skill development.

2. The improvement of the psychosocial climate of the school is a legitimate concern of supervisors. The human relations movement, which emerged quite forcefully during the 1920s and 1930s, was heavily influenced by the research and theory bases that were increasingly popular in the social sciences. Gestalt psychology and other views that emphasized the need for organizational process development had a strong impact on the prevailing notions of supervision. The result of this psychological "intrusion" into supervisory practice, however, was not simply that a particular perspective was considered more valid than others. Rather, the overall tenor of supervision was altered; it became acceptable for educational leaders to expend energy toward trying to change the "feel" of an organization. Previously, only the measurable outcomes of organizations were considered to be the legitimate concerns of supervisors and administrators.

3. The supervisor is an "in-between" person in school systems. Whether it was a conscious modification or not is unclear and probably quite unimportant, but during this period the formal role of the supervisor changed drastically from that of an authority figure to that of a process helper and consultant. In contrast with earlier periods of supervisory development when supervisors were either inspectors or efficiency experts, supervisors became supporters, facilitators, and consultants to teachers. Two reasons might explain this shift. First, educational organizations and curricula were becoming more complex, and increasing specialization took place in many professional roles. The job of the supervisor probably reflected this change more than any other. Increasing demands for more varied curricula in school districts created the need for subject area specialists—one frequent conceptualization of the role of supervisors—to work with teachers and provide expert assistance to help solve classroom instructional problems.

Second, a prevailing philosophical orientation of human relations management was that teachers and other workers needed supportive people to help them with their jobs. The supervisor's role was ideally suited to that function.

The nature of the supervisor's role continues to be debated. In Chapter 3 we will see how supervisors are often found in a "neither-fish-nor-fowl" situation characteristic of many ambiguous roles.

WHERE ARE WE NOW?
CURRENT PERSPECTIVES

Supervisory thought and practice today in some ways result from all three of these earlier perspectives, but in many ways bear no resemblance to any of them. Some educators today lean toward supervisory practices that are actually a return to the earlier "inspection" and "scientific" supervision; others have built on the concept of human relations to develop an approach often referred to as *human resource development.* In the remainder of this chapter we will visit each of these stances briefly to provide you with the information about alternative definitions of educational supervision that you need to understand if you are to practice proactive supervision.

Return to Inspection

You would not expect to hear any modern supervisor openly suggesting that most teachers in his or her district are incompetent, and that the supervisor's job is to "catch" people teaching incorrectly or providing incorrect information to their pupils. Yet this approach to supervision persists, frequently veiled in such jargon as "getting tough with those teachers who aren't performing." When school districts are faced with the unhappy need to reduce teaching staffs because of declining enrollment, budget shortages, or other environmental pressures, there is often talk about the need to lay off "incompetent" teachers—not just those who happen to be the most recently hired. This kind of rhetoric can lead to a climate where virtually all teachers feel threatened, and supervisors and administrators feel compelled to look for the worst, rather than the best, characteristics of their staffs.

The increasing acceptance of competency tests for teachers, which are required in a number of states and local school districts, is a very real manifestation of this approach. The unstated belief behind the calls for such testing is clearly that some teachers—an undetermined number—are doing a poor job, and that these ineffective individuals must be "weeded out" from the ranks of public school teachers. The best way to do this, say proponents of competency testing, is to subject *all* teachers to an assumption of inadequate professional performance by requiring them to take tests or else lose their teaching certificates. Letters to newspaper editors across the nation each day attest to the fact that a percentage of the American public accepts this assumption.

In some school systems, the perception of widespread teacher incompetence has led supervisors and administrators to define their jobs once again as those of inspectors. Such educators are likely to engage in behaviors indicating a general lack of trust in the teaching staff. They may call for unannounced supervisory classroom visits to gather information about classroom activities, for example. Discussions of procedures that require a collaborative relationship between teachers and supervisors become pointless. Clinical supervision, a model that requires open communication (see Chapter 15), would be impossible.

Return to Scientific Supervision

A blind faith in the certainty that "scientific" laws can guide educational practice is by no means dead and buried. While the pontifications of disciples of scientific management like Frederick Taylor may seem foolish over-statements today, many educators do believe that educational practice can be understood according to predictable relationships among predictable variables. If we know how to mix six chemicals to produce compounds in life-saving medicines, why can't we know exactly which six ingredients to mix to form children who can read, write, and cipher?

The press for a return to scientific management in education comes from many sources. School boards, whose members often have strong ties to the private business world that is still heavily influenced by the heritage of scientific management, wonder why educators do things so "inefficiently," while those in the private sector more effectively change raw materials into finished products. There is a great desire to find predictability in educational practice; counting of products becomes an indicator of organizational effectiveness, and the assumption is often made that "more is better."

Educational supervisors who agree with the assumptions of this approach would probably attempt to produce more visible signs of productiveness in their schools, possibly in the form of higher scores on standardized achievement tests. A conception of teaching influenced by Eisner's or Rubin's "artistic" views (see Chapter 15) would be unacceptable.

Human Resource Development

Rather than an outright return to human relations supervision equivalent to the revivals of inspection and scientific supervision, proponents of this approach have incorporated the basic assumption of human relations (namely, that people in an organization hold the key to a more effective supervision or management) into a variation known as *human resource development* (HRD). If any single view can truly be called dominant in supervision today, it would be this one.

As its name implies, human resource development suggests that the most important activity of a supervisor is to help people within an organization—its "human resources"—become as skillful and effective as possible. The organization will be improved because its most important features—its employees—will be more effective.

There is a good deal of overlap between human relations and human resource development. Both approaches place tremendous emphasis on the needs of the people who work in an organization, and both views hold that organizational effectiveness is a desirable outcome of the intervention by a supervisor. In addition, both views suggest that the key to organizational effectiveness is the extent to which workers can feel satisfied with their jobs.

Some important differences, however, keep human resource development from being a mere rehash of the earlier concept. Human relations advocates believed that emphasizing the happiness of an organization's employees would almost automatically guarantee that those employees would work harder, thereby increasing the overall effectiveness and productivity of the organization: "Happy people are productive people." The principal duty of the supervisor, manager, or administrator, then, would be to make certain that the conditions of employment guaranteed that workers would be content and satisfied with the workplace, and would therefore want to work much harder in the future. In school settings, the supervisor would engage in those activities that would ensure that teachers had what they wanted in terms of supplies and equipment, and that they were reasonably satisfied with the ways in which others were treating them. By contrast, the human resource development approach advocates that employees will be happier, more satisfied, and ultimately more productive only if they are first satisfied through working in a productive organization: "Happy employees are productive employees if they work in a productive place." Thus, the supervisor becomes primarily interested in bringing about greater organizational effectiveness, thereby creating a setting where employees can feel satisfied through their association with productivity. In many ways, then, human resource development supervision is an outcome of the human relations movement. The key distinction is in the emphasis selected by the supervisor.

Proponents of human resource development criticize the earlier human relations perspective as highly manipulative, because it assumed that a supervisor could be nice to employees and thereby make them "buy into" organizational goals without hesitation. Human relations believers, on the other hand, suggest that, because of its emphasis on organizational productivity, human resource development is but a thinly disguised return to scientific management. The real distinction seems to be more subtle, however. In human relations supervision, the desire is to satisfy people's needs as an immediate goal and outcome; organizational effectiveness is a by-product. Such an approach shows more immediate results; people tend to be comfortable in a human relations environment. The human resource development advocates, however, claim that people will *eventually* be happy if the organization is productive, even though the immediate impression may be that the supervisor is ignoring individual needs, and that the results will be longer lasting. In fact, meeting the concerns of employees is a long-term goal for human resource supervisors, who believe that immediate energy needs to be directed toward organizational effectiveness.

WHAT IS SUPERVISION?

In this chapter I have provided a general review of the development of educational supervision over the years. We noted that the field has been influenced by the tendency to find the worst in people, and later by the assumption that people are the most important component in any organization. Currently, several perspectives on the roles and responsibilities of those charged with supervisory duties compete for our attention. Numerous definitions have been offered, but none was endorsed without reservation.

You may find a bias in this book toward the basic belief that human resource development is a reasonable perspective in most cases. An even more fundamental view here, however, is that the *best* way for anyone with supervisory responsibilities to behave is to understand as many alternative views as possible and then to choose a perspective that is most consistent with one's own basic set of values and philosophy to guide personal practice. The most important thing to do after making an initial selection of an acceptable perspective, then, is to *behave in a fashion that is faithful to that orientation.* As we noted in the introduction to this section, a key ingredient in the process of proactive supervision is the maintenance of *authentic* and *consistent* behavior. While there are clear strengths and weaknesses inherent in all orientations to supervision, there is probably nothing more damaging to supervisory effectiveness than to pretend to have a particular perspective, and then to act in a way that suggests an entirely different view. Time and again teachers report great frustration with what they perceive to be inconsistent or inauthentic behavior on the part of administrators and supervisors. While it is probably true that few teachers would be overjoyed with the prospect of working for someone who espoused the beliefs of the inspection era, such a condition would be more acceptable than one where a new supervisor claimed to be a human relations proponent, but actually was a "closet inspector." People value predictable, consistent, and authentic behaviors.

One additional comment needs to be made. There are probably times and situations in the life of any organization that make different supervisory practices more (or less) acceptable and effective. Supervisors as inspectors—and the inherent assumption that teachers are not competent—is not typically attractive; on the other hand, there *are* times when incompetent teachers require careful scrutiny. Human relations supervision may be criticized as manipulative; but there might be a time—after a particularly autocratic administrator has just departed, for example—when an overemphasis on human relations would be both effective and important.

Is there, then, a single, acceptable definition of supervision? The ones that we have introduced thus far have faults, although they may be useful from time to time. The answer to this question, particularly in this volume's context of proactive supervision, is not easy. If proactive supervision calls for *you* to select a perspective and "stick with it," then my espousal of a single definition of supervision that is tied too closely to one set of assumptions will contradict a fundamental value of this text. The basic definition presented here represents an attempt to go beyond the educational settings and focus on essential features of supervision as it might be carried out in *any* situation. The following simple definition will be used here: **Supervision is the process of overseeing the ability of people to meet the goals of the organization in which they work.**

A key feature of this definition is its suggestion that supervision needs to be understood as a *process,* and not as a specific professional role. It is also related to the concept of *proactive supervision* that serves as the foundation of this book. That concept simply holds that the best supervision is based on a set of fundamental values and assumptions possessed by the individual serving in a supervisory capacity. The major problem of current school supervisory behavior is its undue emphasis on *reactive* performance—doing things as a result of a crisis orientation rather than through careful, logical planning and preparation. Remaining chapters of this text are devoted to suggesting that effective supervision is based on the development of a more predictable strategy to guide action, and that strategy must emerge regardless of an individual's definitions, philosophy, or overall orientation.

SUMMARY

In this chapter we reviewed several alternative perspectives of supervisory practice to enable you to question your own personal assumptions regarding the "proper" definition of supervision. The hope is that you will be able to begin formulating a *personalized,* but *authentic* perspective of effective supervisory behavior. Further, we pointed out that the development of a personalized understanding of supervision is the first step forward in *proactive,* rather than *reactive,* supervision.

SUGGESTED ACTIVITIES

1. Interview at least four different supervisors or school administrators to determine their predominant views of supervision. You might start by asking for their definition of supervision. Propose a supervisory situation, such as "reasons for evaluating staff." Interpret responses according to the historical views presented in this chapter. Were there any responses that came from the "inspection" era? From "scientific" supervision? From the "human relations" era?
2. Look at the job descriptions of supervisors in two or more different school districts. Can you determine if there are any prevailing views of what supervisors are "supposed to act like," according to the historical definitions reviewed in this chapter?

REFERENCES

Briggs, Thomas H., & Justman, Joseph. (1952). *Improving instruction through supervision.* New York: Macmillan.

Cox, Philip W. L. (1934). *High school administration and supervision.* New York: American Book Company.

Cubberly, Ellwood P. (1916). *Public school administration.* Boston: Houghton Mifflin.

Dwight, Theodore. (1835). *The school-master's friend of the committee-man's guide.* New York: Roe Lockwood.

Eisner, Eliot W. (1979). *The educational imagination.* New York: Macmillan.

Eliot, E. C. (1914). *City school supervision.* New York: World Book Company.

Massachusetts Bay Company in New England: Records of the Governor and the Company. (1642). (Vol. II.)

National Education Association, Department of Superintendence. (1930). *The superintendent surveys supervision.* (Yearbook 8). Washington, DC: The Association.

Payne, William H. (1875). *Chapters on school administration.* New York: Wilson Hinkle and Company.

Rubin, Louis J. (1985). *Artistry in teaching.* New York: Random House.

Taylor, Frederick W. (1916). The principles of scientific management. *Bulletin of the Taylor Society.*

Villers, Raymond. (1960). *Dynamic management in industry.* Englewood Cliffs, NJ: Prentice-Hall.

Wickerman, James P. (1864). *School economy: A treatise on the preparation, organization, employments, government, and authorities of schools.* New York: Lippincott.

Wiles, Kimball, & Lovell, John T. (1967). *Supervision for better schools.* Englewood Cliffs, NJ: Prentice-Hall.

ADDITIONAL READINGS

Glickman, Carl D. (1985). *Supervision of instruction: A developmental approach.* Boston: Allyn & Bacon.

Sergiovanni, Thomas J. (Ed.). (1982). *Supervision of teaching.* Yearbook of the Association for Supervision & Curriculum Development. Alexandria, VA: Association for Supervision & Curriculum Development.

CHAPTER 2

Personal Assumptions Guiding Supervisory Practice

Several important concepts underlie the process of proactive supervision. In Chapter 1, for example, we introduced the notion that the effective supervisor reviews and considers many different perspectives concerning supervision, but ultimately selects one point of view and remains true to it. Such adherence to a particular perspective is to be encouraged, even if your stance reflects an approach to supervision based on scientific management or some other relatively unpopular view. Of course, you will change or modify a position from time to time, depending on a wide array of reasons. However, your authenticity and your clarity in espousing a particular supervisory philosophy are the first important ingredients of effective proactive supervision.

Even more crucial in developing a framework for successful supervisory practice is an ability to analyze your own personal beliefs, attitudes, and values, as components of a clear philosophy of education. The practitioner of educational supervision who is unable to articulate basic thoughts concerning professional issues will find successful leadership difficult. Equally important, without the capacity to *reflect* on the beliefs that form the basis of a personal educational philosophy, you will be unable to provide your staff and teachers with modeling and leadership to help them grow and develop in their own roles.

In this chapter we will examine how supervisors build efficient practice on personal assumptions. First, we review fundamental concepts such as attitudes, values, and beliefs. Second, we develop the concept that an educational philosophy clarifies action planning. Third, we briefly examine the emerging concept of reflective practice as it relates to individual philosophy formulation. Finally, we consider the practical implications of individual philosophy building and action planning.

BELIEFS, ATTITUDES, AND VALUES

An important first step in defining your personal philosophy is to become more familiar with the meaning of such frequently used words as *attitudes, beliefs,* and *values,* and to understand how these affect the ways in which you behave. In the long run, this serves several different important objectives.

First, if you are aware of values in general and how they affect human behavior, you will become more appreciative of your own views on a given issue. In other words, even the activity of *talking about values* tends to make us more sensitive to them and the role they play in shaping our behavior. Just thinking about the fact that people have attitudes, beliefs, and values that differ from our own is the first step toward accepting those differences.

Second, supervisors must examine the issue of values because, as educational leaders, they will be called upon to analyze the values of the people who work in, around, and with schools. Developing personal competency in how to "read" the values, attitudes, and beliefs of the people associated with any organization is a critical skill; a supervisor who is unable to sense those things that people hold dearest to them will almost certainly be an ineffective leader. All people in all organizations have absolute points beyond which they will not compromise or change. Attempting to push people beyond those limits is a serious blunder. Appreciating the value orientations of others is necessary for perceiving those "nonnegotiable" issues.

Third, and perhaps most directly related to the overall concept of proactive behavior, supervisors need insights into value orientations. Organizational leaders are often the most visible people in the organizations; as such, they represent to many people, not only their personal value systems but also the orientation of the entire school or district. Frequently we think not of "the elementary school down the block," but of "Mr. X's school," where Mr. X is the principal. The leader, a values witness, provides the members of the organization with an implicit identity and a sense of "what's right," or "what we do around here."

We now turn to defining more precisely the terms so often used to describe that sense of "what's right": beliefs, attitudes, and values.

Beliefs

The primary component in a general system of values is a belief or set of beliefs, or what Milton Rokeach (1971) has defined as "any simple proposition, conscious or unconscious, inferred from what a person says or does, capable of being preceded by the phrase 'I believe that' " (p. 61). We all have hundreds, perhaps thousands of beliefs about an equally large number of things, places, people, or ideas. These notions are often short-lived because we find out that they are not correct, or because we simply do not find them important enough to hold onto for very long. A person may wake up in the morning, for example, "believing" that the weather outside is hot, cold, or any one of dozens of other adjectives. That belief may be shed as soon as the radio reports the day's temperature or the person actually goes outside or gets sufficiently absorbed in some other "belief" that the temperature outside becomes unimportant. In schools, much of what teachers and others do is based on beliefs. Teachers are quick to explain their approaches to classroom management issues in terms related to the ways in which they "believe" students will act under certain circumstances.

Attitudes

Attitudes are, in a sense, the next step in a hierarchy. Again, note Rokeach's definition (1971): "An attitude is a relatively enduring organization of beliefs around an object or situation predisposing one to respond in some preferential manner" (p. 180). Attitudes are clusters of individual beliefs that survive the immediate moment. The belief that it is hot or cold outside may be fleeting, but our belief about temperature generally may create a particular *attitude* about the weather. Some people are happy to believe that it is cold outside because their attitude toward cold weather, built on personal history, is positive.

We can certainly have incorrect attitudes based on false beliefs; this does not make the potency of the attitude any less real, however. Consider, for example, a belief acquired as a child, based on an image in a movie or on television, that Spanish-speaking people are lazy. As the child grows, the belief may unite with other incorrect beliefs to form an attitude of prejudice toward Hispanics in general. The attitude may be *wrong,* but it is *real* and may continue to influence the person for a long time unless a deliberate effort is made to change it.

Values

Rokeach (1971) defines values as "types of beliefs, centrally located within one's belief system, that address how one ought or ought not to behave, or about some end state of existence worth or not worth attaining" (p. 202). In many ways, values represent our more or less permanent view of reality, formed and fashioned out of more temporary beliefs and attitudes as well as the beliefs and attitudes of others in our family, neighborhood, or larger societal environment.

Awareness of some unique characteristics of individual values can increase our understanding of this concept. First, although values are generally more permanent than attitudes or beliefs, a hierarchical order exists among our personal values. This order is based on the relative potency, durability, and stability of values, as we can see by looking at the values that exist within a particular society and culture. For example, Jacob Getzels suggests that certain *sacred* values at the core of American society constitute stable ideals—"democracy," "individualism," "human perfectability." Related to, yet hierarchically below these, are *secular* values that are more likely to shift over time. Americans once expressed an affinity for rugged individualism and pioneering spirit, for example, but in more recent years we have seen a shift toward conformity and self-satisfaction. In the future, no doubt other secular values will emerge. In addition to secular and sacred values, *operational* values represent the individual ways in which each person behaves in accordance with the larger values of society.

The existence of operational values suggests a second important concept, namely that values are abstract ideals that may be positive or negative and are not necessarily tied to specific objects or situations. For example, a person can save money because saving is a valued practice. The act of saving, however, does not imply that the money put aside will be used for a good or bad purpose. Values represent a person's beliefs about ideal modes of conduct. We can form short-lived beliefs or attitudes about a single person or thing, but we usually do not form a complete value system. A person may be a Christian, for example, because his or her value system is modeled after the value system exemplified by Jesus Christ.

A third characteristic of values is that, contrary to beliefs and attitudes, values are not typically articulated directly by their bearers. More often than not, our behavior is the strongest demonstration of our values. As shown in Chapter 8, what is not stated but rather can be inferred from our behavior is normally a more honest representation of our values than what we say. Because values reflect the most fundamental elements of our thoughts, we rarely state them openly. Because they are so central in our lives, however, they play an extremely important and influential role in determining our outward behavior. We cannot "hide" our values for very long. Thus, supervisors who try to display to others values that do not reflect what they truly believe will probably not succeed.

One final observation: Each of us acquires hundreds, even thousands, of beliefs and attitudes about a variety of subjects, but ultimately we acquire only a few lasting values. Supervisors must be aware of their own values and communicate those values openly and honestly to others, because, in large measures, our values represent who we are.

McGREGOR'S ASSUMPTIONS

In Chapter 1 we considered a number of definitions of and perspectives on educational supervision. At different times, supervision has been viewed as a means to correct incompetent teachers, to promote better human relations in schools, or to increase the measurable productivity of schools. In this book I do not espouse any of these three views, but I do recognize that, because each is based on a *total value system* supported by some people in supervisory roles, each is a legitimate way of thinking. I also suggest that a critical responsibility of those of us in supervisory positions is to examine our personal values and determine how they align with one or another perspective. We must do this openly, so that people who work in the school are aware of where we are "coming from." Most of us *like* to work with others who hold similar values; most of us *can* work with others with whom we *openly* disagree; but no one can work effectively with those who attempt to hide their true value orientations.

A useful framework for analyzing individual values regarding supervisory responsibility is Douglas McGregor's (1960) "Theory X/Theory Y," which is often used to illustrate how people in organizations can be motivated. A review of McGregor's basic assumptions is a good starting place for the supervisor intent on forming a personal and honest view of what supervision implies.

Theory X Assumptions

1. People are naturally lazy; when faced with a choice, they normally prefer to do nothing.
2. People work mostly for money and status rewards.
3. The main force keeping people productive in their work is fear of being demoted or fired.
4. People remain children grown larger; they are naturally dependent as learners.
5. People expect and depend on direction from above; they do not want to think for themselves.
6. People need to be told, shown, and trained in proper methods of work.
7. People need supervisors who will watch them closely enough to be able to praise good work and reprimand errors.
8. People have little concern beyond their immediate material interests.
9. People need specific instruction on what to do and how to do it; larger policy issues are none of their business.
10. People appreciate being treated with courtesy.
11. People are naturally compartmentalized; work demands are entirely different from leisure activities.
12. People naturally resist change; they prefer to stay in the same old ruts.
13. Jobs are primary and must be done; people are selected, trained, and fitted to predefined jobs.

14. People are formed by heredity, childhood, and youth; as adults they remain static.
15. People need to be "inspired" through pep talks; they must be pushed or driven.

Theory Y Assumptions

1. People are naturally active; they set goals and enjoy striving to attain them.
2. People seek many satisfactions in work: pride in achievement; enjoyment of process; sense of contribution; pleasure in association; stimulation of new challenges, and so forth.
3. The main force keeping people productive in their work is desire to achieve their personal and social goals.
4. People normally mature beyond childhood; they aspire to independence, self-fulfillment, and responsibility.
5. People close to the situation see and feel what is needed and are capable of self-direction.
6. People who understand and care about what they are doing can devise and improve their own methods of doing work.
7. People need a sense that they are respected as capable of assuming responsibility and self-correction.
8. People seek to give meaning to their lives by identifying with nations, communities, companies, or causes.
9. People need ever-increasing understanding; they need to grasp the meaning of the activities in which they are engaged; they have cognitive hunger as extensive as the universe.
10. People crave genuine respect from others.
11. People are naturally integrated; when work and play are too sharply separated both deteriorate.
12. People naturally tire of monotonous routine and enjoy new experiences; in some degree everyone is creative.
13. People are primary and seek self-realizaton; jobs must be designed, modified, and fitted to people.
14. People constantly grow; it is never too late to learn; they enjoy learning and increasing their understanding and capability.
15. People need to be encouraged and assisted.

We can make two general observations about the pairs of items shown in the above lists. First, most people will not agree with *every* item under either Theory X or Theory Y; one list will be preferable, but a few statements from the other list will probably seem more accurate. Second, our true feelings about a particular item may not be reflected in the statements of *either* list; we might prefer a middle ground. Very few of us could be classified as "absolute" Theory X- or Theory Y-type supervisors. However, we can gain considerable insight into our own values by determining which of these items seem more accurate and acceptable. Such insight is the first step toward developing a personal educational philosophy.

INDIVIDUAL ACTION PLANNING

Each of us has an established set of beliefs and attitudes that shape our values. The next step is to put these concepts together into a meaningful statement to guide behavior in a supervisory role. In this section, I suggest some ways to assemble your most important value statements into a working *personal philosophy,* one that can be translated into an individual *action plan.*

Construct Theory

The assumptions that underlie individual action planning come from a body of theory that has recently emerged in preservice teacher education, called *Construct Theory.* Developed by G.A. Kelly (1965) as a way to explain actions in terms of mental constructs, it attempts to explain how people derive *signs* used in making decisions about how they conduct their lives. Antoinette Oberg (1986) says of Construct Theory:

> It is the major premise of Construct Theory that people's actions are based on the ways in which they anticipate future events . . . Future events are differentiated on the basis of constructs, which are the attributes or qualities the events are expected to exhibit. (p. 121)

Construct Theory can help us understand why effective supervision is not always "knowing all the answers," but rather developing a way of thinking through problems and asking the right questions. Donald Schon (1983), in *The Reflective Practitioner,* observes that the critical responsibility of a professional is often to recognize the nature of problems, and not always to determine "perfect" solutions to all dilemmas.

Construct Theory and the concepts of reflection-in-action described by Schon are important bases for the development of personalized guides to supervisory action.

Educational Platform Development

The supervisor's *educational platform,* developed by Thomas Sergiovanni and Robert Starratt (1988), is a model designed to help professional educators assess their views about a series of educational issues by stating their views in a straightforward manner, akin to the platform statements made by political candidates in an election campaign. The major difference between a politician's and an educator's platform is that the latter is structured to communicate the educator's deepest and truest attitudes, values, and beliefs, even if these are contrary to the sentiments of "the public." (An individual educational platform is very similar to a personal, informal theory, a concept explained in greater detail in Chapter 3.)

Sergiovanni and Starratt's model for formulating a supervisor's educational platform includes 12 major elements. Ten of these deal with general educational themes, and, as a result, they can serve as the basis for any professional educator's platform. The last two are linked specifically to the role of a supervisor.

1. The aims of education.
2. The major achievements of students this year.
3. The social significance of the student's learning.
4. The supervisor's image of the learner.
5. The value of the curriculum.
6. The supervisor's image of the teacher.
7. The preferred kind of pedagogy.
8. The primary language of discourse in learning situations.
9. The preferred kind of teacher-student relationship.
10. The preferred kind of school climate.
11. The purpose or goal of supervision.
12. The preferred process of supervision.

The following excerpts from one particularly well-developed statement prepared by a classroom teacher contemplating a change to a supervisory position in her school system illustrate how writing a platform helps define personal views.

Aims of Education
The aims of education are threefold. First, the schools must help each student to acquire a sense of self-fulfillment and self-worth in which all children can discover and realize their own unique talents, gifts, and abilities. . . . Secondly, the schools must help students create and maintain meaningful relationships with others. They must help students learn how to communicate . . . their needs, attitudes, concerns, and appreciations. . . . Finally, educators should enable students to become productive, responsible citizens in our society. Schools need to impart the basic knowledge, develop creative expression, and provide a variety of experiences that will enable each individual to assume a role within one's community, one's country, and one's world. . . .

Major Achievements of Students this Year
The major achievements I would hope to have my children display by the end of the year include both academic achievements and personal achieve-

ments. As a first-grade teacher, I hope that my children will acquire the basic skills, concepts, and information that they will need in order to continue in their educational pursuit. . . . Along with an ability to receive and absorb specific facts, concepts and skills, I hope that my children will achieve the necessary work habits that they will need in order to accomplish their present and future goals. . . . In order to meet the personal objectives that I deem important for my children I hope to create a safe and comfortable environment in which they can explore and discover themselves.

Social Significance of the Students' Learning
Our children are our future. Therefore, student learning profoundly affects us in that students' views of the world begin to take shape during the school years. Out of the student population will come the future leaders and decision makers of our country. Thus, the future quality of life in our society is directly related to the quality of education we provide for our students today.

The Image of the Learner
Children are unique. Therefore, their ability to acquire and retain new knowledge and skills is unique. One method of instruction, although it may be appropriate for a percentage of the children within a classroom, cannot adequately meet the individual needs and learning styles of the remainder of the children. Thus, in order to motivate children to greater degrees of personal success, it is necessary to provide a variety of learning strategies within a classroom. . . .

Value of the Curriculum
In essence, the curriculum is a composite of all experiences, planned and unplanned, that constitute the learning of the individual. These learnings occur both within and outside of the classroom. Those experiences which children encounter through the interaction with their families and peers, through the mass media such as television, radio, magazines, and newspapers, and through their social and religious organizations strongly impact the curriculum that is presented in the schools. Therefore, in designing and developing curricula for schools, this "hidden" curriculum needs to be recognized, acknowledged, and planned for specifically. In so doing, the teacher can be proactive rather than reactive in providing the optimal learning experiences for each child. . . .

The Image of the Teacher
A teacher is an individual with a specific purpose or mission. A teacher with a mission has a deep underlying belief that students can grow and attain self-actualization. Teachers believe that they have something of significance to contribute to other people, especially students, and believe with every fiber of their being that they can "make a difference." Teachers believe that children can learn and want to learn and are driven from within to find the

technique or strategy that will assist that child to learn. . . . Teachers also receive high personal satisfaction and inner joy from the growth of their students. They seek out the resources necessary to stimulate and activate learning within the student and are excited when students think, respond, and learn. . . . A teacher is also a contributing member of the larger school setting and should value working closely with the principal and other staff personnel.

Preferred Kind of Pedagogy
As a first-grade teacher, I employ a multitude of ideas, materials, and experiences when helping my children to learn. Because of the age, experiences, and socialization of first-graders, at the beginning of the year I find it is necessary to assume a more directive role within my particular classroom. I feel that this is appropriate and necessary in order to help six- and seven-year-olds feel safe and secure in their new environment, and to help them make a transition from a more home-centered world into a more school-centered world. . . . As I work within my classrooms encouraging children to higher degrees of personal and academic achievement, I also utilize the larger resources of the school. These include students, the principal, the media specialist, the special area teachers . . . the guidance counselor, the psychologist, and our teacher aides. I believe that it takes many caring and concerned individuals to help a child learn and grow into a healthy, productive adult. . . .

Primary Language of Discourse in Learning Situations
Children learn best when they are involved and when the material presented is relevant to their interests and needs. Therefore, the language within the classroom should foster communication. This communication can take many forms: discussion, lecture, questions and answers, dialogue, and role-playing. But whatever form that it takes, it should have at its base the interests and needs of the child. . . .

Preferred Kind of Teacher-Student Relationship
The relationship established between the teacher and the student has a profound effect upon the child's ability to function and to learn to his or her optimal level. A teacher's priority is to foster a safe environment in which each child feels a sense of belonging, importance, and acceptance. If this is established, the child is able to channel his or her energy into positive learning rather than withdrawing from the learning situation in a negative way. . . . It is important for the teacher to understand that each child is unique and that a teacher's expectations for one student may not be the same expectations that one may have for another student. . . .

The Preferred Kind of School Climate
An atmosphere of trust and safety must be created within a classroom. Within this environment, each child's unique needs and interests can be met. Because all students are different, they have different requirements for

openness and structure, for movement and control, for an opportunity to work in groups or the need to work alone. It is important to meet these differences and to help children create an awareness and understanding of the similarities and differences that they share. . . . A teacher needs to realize that no one best environment will meet the needs of every student. . . . A positive climate is essential throughout the total school building and should be realized districtwide. . . .

Allowing for and appreciating the special needs, interests, and styles of our colleagues—feeling valued and important as professionals and as people—ultimately transfers itself into an atmosphere that profoundly affects children and stimulates their capacity to learn.

Purpose of Supervision
The purpose of supervision is to maximize children's learning. This is accomplished by directly improving the quality of a teacher's instruction within the classroom. A supervisor, therefore, is an individual whose responsibility and desire is to help teachers recognize and capitalize on their strengths. A supervisor must also understand and assume responsibility for the goals and priorities of the organization as a whole. This requires that the supervisor must often bridge the gap between the interests and needs of the teachers and those of the administration. Thus, the supervisor's role is often one of effective communication and advocacy—advocacy of the teacher and advocacy of the administrator.

The supervisor must clearly visualize how each separate part of the organization fits together for the benefit of the whole and be able to take the steps necessary to accomplish this end. Thus, the supervisor must be genuinely concerned and comfortable with each group and be able to effectively merge their varied concerns and transcend the difficulties to a level of greater excellence for the total organization. In order to accomplish this, supervisors must clearly understand their personal platforms. This has the potential of creating a climate of trust and credibility between supervisors and all parties involved. When this is achieved, the needs of the child are enhanced, and that is our primary focus as educators.

Preferred Process of Supervision
As I grow in my understanding of supervision and the various modes of supervisory practice, I believe that there is no one best way to supervise. I realize that each situation is different and that each individual is unique. It is my responsibility as a supervisor to evaluate and to respond to each condition by gathering and accessing the data surrounding that particular situation.

I respond to the inherent worth and value of each individual, and this belief will be a strong guide within me as I interact with my colleagues. I believe that growth is attained most completely when the strengths of an individual are determined and those strengths are developed and encouraged. By identifying and developing strengths, I believe that the personal dignity of the individual is preserved and that this is the foundation upon which change and growth can occur. I feel that as I direct and encourage teachers to utilize their strengths to their greatest potential, they will, in turn, direct their abilities to more productive instruction of the children.

I realize that, at times, I will find it necessary to supervise a staff member who is minimally effective with children. I hope, by identifying that person's strengths with him or her, that might increase the person's sense of self-worth and, possibly, minimize any confusion or anxiety that may be hindering the individual's effectiveness in the classroom. If it becomes apparent that this person's strengths could be utilized more appropriately in a different direction, working together with him or her to explore possible alternatives would be appropriate. I am aware that a high degree of trust needs to be established before this is even possible.

I see myself applying the human resources philosophy. When members of an organization understand the goals of that organization, and become the agents by which those goals are achieved, then growth within those members is attainable to a higher degree. Personal self-attainment is energizing, both to the individual and to the organization, and creates an atmosphere of good will, trust, and greater cooperation. This has a cyclic effect. Within the organization, participation should be encouraged at the level at which an individual is capable: understanding that each person has his or her own "timing" and will develop accordingly. It is necessary to stimulate learning for each staff member by offering many opportunities for personal and professional growth, such as inservices, workshops, conference attendance, and involvement in specific interest and support groups. Staff who had interest and skills in a particular area would be encouraged to share them, formally or informally, with their peers. In this fashion, a network of in-house expertise is developed for the recognition and the evolution of the presenter, the growth of the staff, and the benefit of the children. In this manner, supervisors can, by acknowledging the control of the growth of their teachers with their colleagues, internalize and expand the ownership of the goals of the district.

I have provided only excerpts for the first 10 issues, but the last two topics, "Purpose of Supervision" and "Preferred Process of Supervision," are quoted in their entirety. The "author" of this platform, like most readers of this text, is a classroom teacher who was thinking about pursuing a professional career in a supervisory position. As a result, her statements in the last two sections are best understood as an attempt to find a personal vision of leadership or supervision.

Sergiovanni and Starratt's notion of the educational platform is useful for a number of reasons. First, writing a formal educational platform requires you to articulate many of the things that you may take for granted as you go about your business in a particular role. It is not unusual to hear highly experienced teachers praise the platform-writing process simply because it is a *disciplined* way to express sets of values, beliefs, and attitudes they may have forgotten over the years. Second, writing a platform results in a formal agenda that allows you to see and then confront ideas that are rarely stated.

A third benefit of preparing a platform is that it allows you to make your values more visible to others. Although we don't recommend circulating copies of a personal platform as a standard practice, a well-prepared platform can be a useful tool for sharing important personal feelings with others who need to know your beliefs. In sum, a formal statement can help you gain greater insights into your fundamental "nonnegotiable" or "sacred" values.

Everyone who works in any organization wonders from time to time whether or not to stay in a particular position. Sometimes an organization changes to the extent that it no longer seems to represent values that were once appealing. A formal platform statement is a visible and constant reminder of what an educator holds in greatest esteem. Its real value may be to help you answer the question, "What is *so important* to me that I would quit rather than compromise?"

Action Plan

Articulating an individual educational platform is an extremely powerful activity for reviewing professional and personal values, but it is little more than an exercise unless it is combined with an *action plan*. An action plan need not be a formal statement with a predetermined number of "elements" like the platform, but it should list actions that will allow you to put to use the platform's critical concepts. The action plan will enable you to look at your present role to determine how personal behavior actually matches both the platform and the characteristics of the job.

The elementary teacher quoted earlier moved from the initial platform statement to a statement of analysis, and finally to a personal action plan.

Platform Analysis
The writing of my platform has been a challenging and a valuable undertaking. I feel these beliefs and assumptions, but have never articulated them until now. This has been an affirming exercise, but, at the same time, I realize that I am also in process. I am not the same person today that I was yesterday. Nor will I be the same person tomorrow as I am today. . . . I know that should I ever step out of the process, I will stop growing as an individual and will lose any effectiveness that I might have as a teacher and a supervisor. . . . I found as I placed my thoughts on paper that there was an element of interrelatedness among the different themes. In order to achieve one aspect of my platform, I needed to build upon the others. As a result, I sense a unified direction for myself. It is as though I have developed

a focus, and that the confusion that accompanies indecision is removed. As a teacher, I know what I'm about and feel that what I do is valuable. Yet, as I began to express my thoughts concerning supervision, I found myself searching for clarity. My experience in personnel, in facilitating both student and adult groups . . . has given me a background of understanding. There are still gaps in this understanding. This is what is directing me to gain a better understanding of the field of supervision.

Personal Action Plan
I plan:

1. To exercise my belief that learning is a lifelong adventure. This would include my present goals. . . .
2. To become a more effective classroom teacher, and to continually seek the resources that will permit children to reach their greatest potential.
3. To encourage and assist in the development of the staff within my particular school and within the district. To plan and implement with my principal a specific plan for staff support and supervision.
4. To plan and implement my field experience study. To evaluate my growth and needed areas of growth with my supervisors and the participants involved in my experience.
5. To continually clarify my educational platform by asking the question, "What is best for children?"

This teacher's action plan allows her to examine the major "nonnegotiable" issues described in her original platform statement and to select a series of important objectives. Action planning allows the teacher to come full cycle from original statement of philosophy to a statement of action.

SUMMARY

This chapter introduces the most critical and basic aspect of supervision as a proactive process: *To be most effective, supervisors must be aware of their personal assumptions, attitudes, beliefs, and values.*

Attitudes and beliefs change frequently during our lives; values are more permanent. However, values can also be modified over time. Personal values can be put together in a coherent statement to guide supervisory practice, using procedures developed by Sergiovanni and Starratt, involving two separate but related tools: an individual educational platform and an action plan. Writing these as a formal activity helps individual educators to understand and to demonstrate their most important values. Becoming aware of our personal values benefits both us individually and the organizations in which we work. Excerpts from the educational platform and action plan of one elementary teacher illustrate how formulation of a personal statement can guide future practice.

SUGGESTED ACTIVITIES

1. Formulate your own educational platform, according to the guidelines provided by Sergiovanni and Starratt. As preservice students, many of you will not be able to address every element of the list, but try to define your feelings about as many elements as possible. What do you consider to be the primary aims of education? What is your image of the learner? What pedagogical methods do you prefer? What kind of student-teacher relationship and school climate do you favor? What do you consider the purpose or goal of supervision?
2. Review the educational platform that you have developed. In what ways can your values and beliefs about education be put into action in supervisory practice? Make a brief, informal list of actual behaviors or objectives that translate your beliefs into actions.

REFERENCES

Kelly, G. A. (1965). *A theory of personality: The psychology of personal constructs.* New York: Norton.

McGregor, Douglas. (1960). *The human side of enterprise.* New York: McGraw-Hill.

Oberg, Antoinette. (1986). Using construct theory as a basis for research into teacher professional development. *Journal of Curriculum Studies, 19*(1), 55–65.

Rokeach, Milton. (1971). *Beliefs, attitudes, and values: A theory of organization and change.* San Francisco: Jossey-Bass.

Schon, Donald A. (1983). *The reflective practitioner: How professionals think in action.* New York: Basic Books.

Sergiovanni, Thomas J., & Starratt, Robert J. (1988). *Supervision: Human perspectives* (4th ed.). New York: McGraw-Hill.

ADDITIONAL READINGS

Argyris, Chris. (1982). *Reasoning, learning and action: Individual and organizational.* San Francisco: Jossey-Bass.

Raven, J. (1981). The most important problem in education is to come to terms with values. *Oxford Review of Education, 7*(2), 253–272.

Sanders, Donald P., & McCutcheon, Gail. (1986). The development of practical theories of teaching. *Journal of Curriculum and Supervision, 2*(1), 50–67.

Schon, Donald A. (1987). *Educating the reflective practitioner.* San Francisco: Jossey-Bass.

Sergiovanni, Thomas J. (1987). *The principalship: A reflective practice perspective.* Boston: Allyn & Bacon.

CHAPTER 3

Continuing Controversies

In this chapter we will review and examine some major, continuing controversies that typically surround discussions about the nature of supervision in schools. Understanding these controversies will help you clarify your own view of educational supervision.

CONTROVERSY 1: IS THERE SUCH A THING AS "A" SUPERVISOR?

There is an old saying that goes, "If you say something often enough and with enough conviction, whatever you say will eventually become true—or at least, believed to be true by a lot of people." A little of this same logic has crept into discussions concerning educational supervision. The literature has generally treated supervision as if it were a field with clear boundaries and well-accepted definitions and assumptions. In truth, supervision is a highly ambiguous field of which no clear view is generally held. Supervision is not easy to define.

We can see the vague and fluid nature of education supervision by comparing and contrasting two different educational roles, those of the school principal and the supervisor. Most people recognize and understand what a "school principal" is. We may even have an image of what a principal looks like, how his or her office is arranged, what he or she usually does, how students and teachers interact with a principal, and so forth. Furthermore, tremendous similarities exist in the principal's role from school to school, district to district, state to state, or even nation to nation. Rural, suburban, and urban school principals lead very different lives in many ways, but their basic job descriptions appear very similar. In addition, the public perceptions of what or who a principal is remain fairly stable: We have generally had enough encounters with individuals who are called "principals" to lead us to believe that we know what they do.

By contrast, there is no similar automatic or universal recognition of what supervisors "usually" do for several reasons. First, what supervisors do in Chicago may not at all be what supervisors do in Boston. Second, those who carry out supervisory duties in one school district may have substantially different job titles than those in similar positions in other settings. And third, many school districts have no formal supervisory positions at all. A number of people who have spent a lot of time around schools have simply never met anyone who holds the title "supervisor." We could not, in all likelihood, find anyone who had never encountered a principal.

When supervisors do exist, they are responsible for a wide variety of tasks. The following list indicates the responsibilities assigned to individuals who are specifically designated as *supervisors* in five different school districts across two states. Clearly, no single person could be expected to undertake all the prescribed activities, and we might even ask if all these duties should really be considered "supervisory" in nature. The fact is, however, that these tasks are all listed in the formal job descriptions of people who needed state certification as "supervisors" in order to get their jobs.

The supervisor of instruction . . .

1. assists in assessing needs at the local school and citywide levels.
2. provides consultant help to individuals and staffs.
3. keeps current on developments in education and in the fields of specialization; attends professional conferences.
4. conducts the piloting and implementation of new instructional materials and strategies.
5. serves as advisor-representative to various professional organizations.
6. interviews prospective teachers.
7. prepares demonstrations, programs, and reports on the work of the school for professional, parent, and community groups.
8. works directly with students in educational projects.
9. assists in the evaluation of teaching performance, instructional programs, and materials.
10. designs and develops goals and objectives for new curricula.
11. designs, develops, and conducts inservice activities.
12. works with principals, teachers, pupils, and parents in an effort to accomplish the improvement of instruction.
13. plans opportunities for continuing education for all certified personnel.

14. works to improve communication within the system and between schools and the public.
15. works toward a curricular and educational philosophy that strongly emphasizes the children's needs.
16. keeps the records and makes the reports required by law, by regulation of the state, and by the superintendent and school board.
17. provides consultative services in subject areas.
18. reviews and evaluates requests for changes in course offerings.
19. keeps abreast of research trends, innovations, and other aspects of the various subject areas.
20. disseminates information pertaining to research trends and innovations as well as reminders of sound teaching practices.
21. maintains a program of visitation at regular intervals at all schools.
22. attends meetings of administrative and supervisory personnel.
23. serves as a total resource person in the educational process.
24. screens requests from outside special-interest groups for student participation in community activities.
25. performs such other duties as assigned by the superintendent.

Supervisors are expected to do different things in different places, then, and to compound the confusion, many of these same things are often done by people who hold job titles other than supervisor. In recent years, many school systems have deliberately sought different job titles to designate individuals who undertake tasks historically assigned to the area of supervision. We now find numerous settings where people are called "coordinators," "resource personnel," "specialists," or even "directors." These titles have been modified over the years for many reasons, including the desire to find terms more descriptive of what individuals actually do, or to avoid the negative connotations conjured up by the "inspectors" and "managers" of previous supervisory eras. No matter how good the motivation, however, changing names can cause problems. A supervisor is not always a supervisor. In some school districts, moreover, formally designated supervisors undertake work duties that are not clearly supervisory in nature, while other individuals in the same district are given supervisory duties, but not the equivalent title.

This last statement underlines the difficulty many educators have in understanding and defining the field of educational supervision: The job simply doesn't exist in many settings. A great many people have not had any direct contact with a supervisor because many school systems are just too small to employ supervisory personnel; other systems have deliberately eliminated supervisors as "frills" whose traditional responsibilities can best be carried out by principals or other administrators. In these districts, the typical organizational arrangement might include a superintendent, an assistant superintendent or two, a business manager or treasurer, building principals, and teachers.

Possible Responses to the Controversy

Based on these observations, the immediate answer to the question "Is there such a thing as 'a' supervisor?" is no. But there *are* supervisors in education. We can clarify this issue in two ways. First, we can understand supervision not as an identifiable and stable role, but as an ongoing *process.* Second, we can analyze the generic tasks, duties, or responsibilities that are commonly associated with supervisory activities.

Describing supervision as a process rather than as a particular organizational role is a useful way to bring some clarity to a discussion of supervisory practice. If we consider individuals *regardless of their specific job titles* who engage in a *process of supervision,* we can free ourselves from worrying whether a supervisor in District A is the same as a supervisor in District B, or whether a curriculum coordinator is the same thing as a supervisor of curriculum. In addition, a process orientation to supervision reduces needless distinctions between such things as "generalist supervisors" and "specialist supervisors," or "school-based supervisors" and "central office supervisors." While distinctions such as these exist in various school systems, and some understanding of their similarities and differences is probably useful under some circumstances, a general understanding of the foundations of educational supervision is hardly enhanced by emphasizing subtle and often minute differences in supervisory practice. Rather, our knowledge base is substantially increased when we can find and focus on *similarities* among the activities of all who either formally or informally "supervise."

We can break down the distinctions that cloud our understanding of what supervision entails, then, by looking beyond the unique features of different supervisory roles and searching instead for the overlapping or similar duties undertaken by those who practice supervisory processes. The following list, frequently cited as a framework for describing generalized supervisory duties, was prepared by Ben Harris (1985) of the University of Texas at Austin. Performance in the nine distinct areas can be used to assess supervisory effectiveness. More importantly, the nine areas indicate the essential ingredients of effective supervisory practice, regardless of the supervisory context or the job title of any specific individual who engages in supervisory duties.

Supervisory Competency Areas

1. Developing curriculum.
2. Providing materials.
3. Providing staff for instruction.
4. Organizing for instruction.
5. Relating special public services.
6. Arranging for inservice education.

7. Developing public relations.
8. Providing facilities for instruction.
9. Evaluating instruction.

CONTROVERSY 2: IS THERE A DIFFERENCE BETWEEN ADMINISTRATION AND SUPERVISION?

One theme that recurs in virtually every discussion of educational supervision is the differences that exist, or do not exist, between those who are called school "administrators" and those who are called school "supervisors." A quick answer to the question "Is there a difference between supervisors and administrators" is yes; a distinction can be made between the two fields. We made the point in the previous section that immediate recognition normally follows when we talk about an administrative role such as that of the school principal. We also noted, in contrast, that confusion often reigns when we talk about supervision. A review of the precise nature of the differences between supervision and administration may prove helpful.

One important and traditional distinction made between supervisor and administrator is that administrators are typically referred to as "line officers" while supervisors are "staff members." Figure 3.1 is a *line-staff organizational chart* describing the governance structure and relationships in a typical school district.

The key distinction between those who serve in *line* positions and those in *staff* positions is that the former usually enjoy the formal, or statutory, authority to make decisions on behalf of the organization in which they are members. Staff members, by contrast, are responsible for responding to the directions provided by line officers and for implementing the decisions made by those in line positions. While this seems like a relatively simple distinction, it is not entirely accurate. Consider, for example, the fact that school principals are classified as administrators, or "line officers," which suggests that principals make decisions and are not required to respond to the direction of others. In fact, few modern school principals would view their jobs in these terms. A common view of the modern school principal is that he or she serves as a "middle manager," that the position lies somewhere between the imperatives expressed by the central administration and board of the school district and the wishes of teachers who understand that they must carry out those imperatives in their classrooms. In addition, teachers today rarely accept unreservedly the notion that they must respond "upward" to the dictates of formal authority figures in the organization. The classic distinctions between line versus staff, and supervision versus administration, then, are considerably blurred.

Despite this blurring of distinctions, administrators do have organiza-

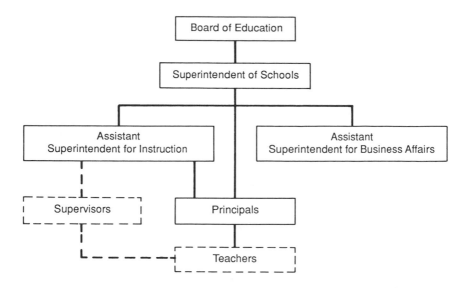

Figure 3.1. Typical line-staff organizational chart. (Solid lines indicate line positions.)

tional and often statutory responsibilities that supervisors do not. At least on paper, administrators have greater formal authority and control over the people who work in their organizations than do other individuals in the same organizations. Those "other individuals" include the supervisory staff. In the real world of schools, this distinction gets played out in a variety of ways. Teachers may be observed formally, for instance, by people designated both as administrators (the building principal, usually) and supervisors (a subject specialist from the central office). More often than not, however, if an unfavorable personnel decision must be made based on data gathered through classroom observations, the person *legally* responsible for making the decision and then communicating it to the teacher is an administrator. The supervisory staff may be asked to provide additional supporting documentation to assist the administrator in making his or her decision, but the authority resides at the administrative level.

The majority of encounters between supervisors and teachers, or administrators and teachers, are not as dramatic as a negative personnel review. There are numerous situations, however, where the differences between supervisors and administrators are reflected in their respective roles in working with teachers. In many school systems, supervisors are perceived as somewhat "closer" to teachers; in fact, they *are still* teachers in the minds of many people. Administrators, on the other hand, have moved to a world outside of teaching, and some imaginary barrier seems to separate them from classroom teachers. Clearly, these unfortunate views tend to reinforce the stereotypical divisions between administration and teachers and hinder the search for conditions that will contribute to schools becoming more productive and effective places.

Good school administrators must first have served as good teachers; effective principals must have been effective teachers (although effective teachers do not automatically become effective administrators). In any case, while the distance between administrators and teachers is certainly lamentable, suggesting that such separations do not exist would be a serious mistake. The persistence of this characteristic of school life needs to be recognized as a genuine part of the differences that exist between administration and supervision because it often drastically changes the nature of supervisory positions in school settings. In many ways, the educational supervisor is truly neither fish nor fowl. A supervisor is associated with teachers but no longer serves in the classroom. A supervisor is also given duties consistent with a formal leadership position but does not enjoy formal authority within the governance structure of the typical school system, unless the building administrator is described as a supervisor in a specified setting.

Historically, supervision has been concerned with the operation of the total school. In more recent times, however, school administrators have increasingly been involved in providing instructional leadership; school principals, superintendents, and other educational administrators are more and more involved in the "core technology" of schools—the curricular and instructional practices and teaching-learning processes. As a result of administrators' more active participation in what goes on in classrooms and the interaction between teachers and pupils, supervisors are less often seen as the people to whom schools normally (or rightfully) delegate responsibility for overseeing curriculum and instruction. If we view supervision as a process rather than as an isolated role, however, we can legitimately say not that a supervisor works with teachers to improve instruction, but that anyone who works with teachers and provides them with feedback concerning their classroom performance—including a principal—is engaging in supervisory behavior.

The final distinction made between supervision and administration is a bureaucratic and legalistic one related to the certification requirements imposed by various state education agencies. Many states treat supervisory certification as a first step toward becoming licensed as a school administrator. Requirements for supervisory certifications are often less demanding than those for an administrative certificate and require fewer courses and university credits. In some states this is beginning to change, and the role of the supervisor is being defined more or less apart from any other educational role. In Ohio, for example, those seeking administrative certification would be hard-pressed to also satisfy the equally demanding set of requirements recently established for aspiring supervisors (Ohio Department of Education, 1986). Some find this unfortunate and argue that many educators pursue several professional paths during their careers and should be able to seek multiple, simultaneous certificates. My view is that educators should indeed be able to follow different paths and pursue career opportunities. I would also suggest, however, that special skills are needed for specialized educational roles, and that more, not less, training may be needed to ensure competence in those areas.

Possible Responses to the Controversy

Differences do exist between educational administration and educational supervision that are truly felt in the real world of schools. These distinctions need not serve as dysfunctional barriers, however, to the ability of schools to operate effectively and sere the needs of learners. One observation in this regard seems particularly relevant at this point. Schools today are demanding people who are capable and talented, regardless of job titles. These capable and talented people will need to assume a variety of duties along the way. Thus, it is fair to say that school administrators will need to continue to cultivate additional skills and sensitivities related to effective supervisory behaviors and processes, and supervisors will need to be acutely aware of their managerial and administrative responsibilities.

CONTROVERSY 3: CAN SUPERVISORS EVER REALLY GET ANYTHING DONE?

To what extent do supervisors have the formal power and authority to see to it that anything is accomplished by the people who work in their schools or district? More will be said about this issue in Chapter 10, but a few comments concerning the nature of supervisory authority and power are offered here.

I would argue that supervisors can, in fact, "get things done." Certain obvious limitations, however, have traditionally been placed on people who serve in supervisory roles in schools. As I noted earlier in this chapter, supervisors are typically described as *staff,* and regardless of the fact that distinctions between "line" and "staff" are often not entirely clear, the prevailing expectation is that staff personnel are not able to give orders to others, or to make decisions to which others in the organization can be expected to respond. On a formal organizational chart, therefore, supervisors appear to be limited because they cannot require people to behave in a particular way. We should consider, however, whether it is realistic to suggest that *any* position found in a modern school system chart, either a line officer or staff member, truly possesses total control over the other members of the organization. Teachers' associations and unions have increasingly sought input into school system decision-making processes, and it seems increasingly unlikely that anyone—from superintendent to principal to instructional supervisor—can command total control over the members of that school system. Nevertheless, it remains true that statutory and other formal control mechanisms do indeed exist in all school districts, and these to a large extent dictate that certain individuals will be legally designated as "in charge." Typically and traditionally, those individuals are not supervisors but administrators.

There are other much more subtle ways in which educational supervisors are able to see that things get done. These methods rest in informal control and influence rather than in the control and power that derive from relationships depicted in a line-staff chart. The primary way in which educational supervisors exert influence results largely from a consistent demonstration of what others in the organization perceive to be expertise concerning a given curricular area. A reading supervisor's influence rarely derives from the fact that he or she holds a certain position in the school district's organizational chart or has an office at central headquarters. Instead, reading supervisors are respected and consulted because teachers believe that the supervisor *knows something about reading* that is relevant to the concerns of the teachers.

In addition to influence derived from their subject-area-related expertise, of course, supervisors also get things accomplished through the exercise of interpersonal influence. People tend to follow other people's direction if they find those other people appealing. Too much reliance on interpersonal and charismatic avenues of influencing others can be fraught with dangers. Building support entirely on personality styles and compatibility can lead to supervisory practices devoid of any substantive content. In schools, teachers look to colleagues who can provide answers and help in a *real* way to assist them in solving their *real* problems. At such times, likable people are simply in the way unless they can help solve someone's immediate problems.

Possible Responses to the Controversy

The question "Can a supervisor really ever get anything done?" has been answered to the extent that we believe a person in this role can be effective. However, such effectiveness requires skills that go far beyond traditional channels of formal control, power, or authority. Perhaps the ultimate answer to our question is found not in the analysis of influence patterns—based on expertise or personality—that are utilized, but instead on a concern essential to the basic assumption of proactive supervision. That assumption holds that a person will function at a much more effective level with a clear personalized understanding of what should be accomplished. If the goals of a supervisor are simply to enforce policy that has been formulated by other actors, and if there is no personal attachment or commitment to that policy, there is little likelihood that the supervisor will be able to convince those people with whom he or she works that the policy is worth following. On the other hand, tremendous power clearly rests in the sharing of other individuals' values and visions.

SUMMARY

In this chapter we have tried to advance our basic understanding of what supervision is all about through a review of some of the fundamental issues, or continuing controversies, related to the field. These controversies include the need to understand precisely who educational supervisors are, the distinctions that exist between supervision and administration, and, finally, the extent to which the nature of supervision actually allows you to achieve your goals and objectives.

In response to these issues, we proposed that supervision should be understood not as a job responsibility designated by a specific role and title, but rather as a *process* carried out by many different actors in an effective organization. In addition, we endorsed the need to seek areas of similarity between administration and supervision rather than dwell on differences that separate these two fields. Finally, consistent with the overall view expressed throughout the chapters of this text, we indicated that your effectiveness as a supervisor will be greatly enhanced if you have a strong internalized understanding of what your agenda for action will be. If you merely define your role as speaking for the organization, little will happen to benefit that organization. If, however, you take a proactive supervisory posture in deciding what goals and objectives of the organization are of greatest personal value, and if you communicate that value orientation openly, honestly, and often to the school staff, more effective organizational performance is likely to result.

SUGGESTED ACTIVITIES

1. Conduct a local analysis of supervisory jobs in your area. Interview one or more local school district personnel administrators to determine whether there are specific "supervisor" jobs. If jobs are not referred to as "supervision," how are they classified in different districts?
2. Interview both a person who has a clearly defined supervisory position and a school principal about the ways in which they might carry out some similar task, such as leading a curriculum evaluation project. Listen for differences in the ways in which these two individuals approach the same task. Are there any apparent differences between the strategies used by an administrator and a supervisor?
3. Ask a supervisor for examples of the ways in which she or he must engage in administrative behavior. Talk to a school administrator about supervisory duties.
4. Collect the organizational charts of three or more local school systems to determine the expressed differences between "line" and "staff" personnel.

REFERENCES

Harris, Ben M. (1985). *Supervisory behavior in education* (3rd ed.). Englewood Cliffs, NJ: Prentice-Hall.
Ohio Department of Education, Division of Certification. (1986). *Revised administrative certification standards.* Columbus, OH: The Department.

ADDITIONAL READINGS

Doll, Ronald C. (1983). *Supervision for staff development: Ideas and applications.* Boston: Allyn & Bacon.
Oliva, Peter F. (1984). *Supervision for today's schools* (2nd ed.). White Plains, NY: Longman.

PART II

Theory Into Practice

Throughout Part I we advanced the argument that the most practical way to understand educational supervision is as a set of process skills, rather than as a specific job or role. In Part II we will present and analyze a series of analytic "tools"—theories advanced by various perspectives in the social sciences—to help those of you engaged in supervisory activities. Only through this use of theory to guide action can supervisors function in a dynamic, proactive way.

CHAPTER 4

The Role of Theory in Improving Supervisory Practice

An important assumption throughout this text is that an understanding of theory in the social sciences represents a critical step toward enhancing our appreciation and understanding of effective supervisory practice; it is a way to gain critical new insights into "how things work" in organizations. One very practical consideration serves to support this assumption. When our perspec tives are rooted in theory, we also have access to a way of guiding our behaviors in everyday problems and situations. As a consequence, our actions will be based on something other than the same tired answers to the same tired questions. Developing a basic understanding of what theory is, and how it can be applied in school settings, will greatly contribute to your mastery of the process of proactive supervision.

DEFINITION OF THEORY

What is "theory?" To many, a standard and rather negative view of what theory is prevails in the field of education. My discussions with numerous school practitioners over the years suggest that educational theory is often viewed as a synonym for speculation or supposition, or as an attempt to represent some ideal that has little relevance to the real world. For many people actually working in the schools, theory is anything that does not possess an immediate, practical value.

There are many things that theory is not. It is not, for example, part of the philosophical branch of axiology, which deals with values—although you may develop a personal theory to guide your supervisory practice, as we discussed in Chapter 2—which rests on an analysis of your own values. In the strictest sense, mixing "theory" with "values" and "philosophy" represents an incorrect application of all these terms.

Theory is not simply the individualized application of one person's common sense, either. The problem we face whenever we talk about common sense, of course, is that what we label with this term is neither "common" nor "sensible" to everyone at the same time; common sense is, in fact, often a fiercely individualistic and personal view of reality. We need only think of the bit of "sense" commonly held in the Middle Ages that the earth was flat. Ultimately, such common-sense views have little practical use to any decision maker.

What is theory, then? Theory is an attempt to describe phenomena and interrelationships found in the real world in terms that reflect the true nature of the world. In its most fundamental form, theory is an attempt to collect elements of knowledge and truth from multiple sources—authority, tradition, intuition, common sense, observation, structured empirical research—to guide practice by informing decision makers of likely (if not always absolutely certain) consequences of their actions under certain conditions. The view of formal theory in the field of educational supervision, consistent with the view in the wider field of the social sciences, holds that theory is a type of generalization based on observable and verifiable reality. The assumptions of theory in the social sciences, then, have been borrowed extensively from the physical sciences.

For educational supervision in particular, the contemporary literature provides several useful definitions. Sergiovanni and Starratt (1983), for example, define theory as "a mode of thinking that leads to the generation of propositions amenable to testing either in the laboratory or in practice. It is a systematic, conceptual framework to be used in understanding present phenomena and in gaining insights into how to behave in the future, when faced with the same phenomena" (p. 121). Hoy and Miskel (1988) offered a similar, related definition of theory by observing that theory "is a set of interrelated concepts, assumptions, and generalizations that systematically describes and explains regularities in behavior in educational organizations" (p. 155). This second definition is particularly interesting because it suggests three important characteristics of social science theory: First, that theory is logically composed of concepts, assumptions, and generalizations; second, that the major function of theory is to describe, explain, and predict the nature of regularities in human behavior; and finally, that theory is heuristic—it stimulates and guides the further development of knowledge. Both definitions suggest that theory is *based* on present reality, but *usable* in building future understandings. These notions are consistent with and applicable to our view of proactive supervision.

It would be misleading to suggest that theories always appeal to us because of their clarity and precision as descriptions of present reality. They are, in fact, frequently full of terms and concepts difficult for us to grasp. Theories are, by their very nature, general and somewhat abstract. And more importantly, they are never absolutely "true" or "false." A theory must be open to some individual understanding and interpretation.

FUNCTIONS OF THEORY

Based on the definitions of theory we have cited, we can begin to identify specific outcomes to be accomplished through the application of theoretical perspectives to a field such as educational supervision.

Ultimately, the function of a theory in the social sciences is to provide generalizations and, eventually, explanations of the ways in which phenomena appear and are witnessed in "the real world." As a result, theory often serves as the basis for further empirical research, in which "theory-testing/theory-verification" is a stated goal. One function of theory has traditionally been to set up future research questions and to provide suggestions about what research results may be relative to a defined, specific issue. Consider, for example, the researcher who conducts a study based on an established theory of motivation, such as Maslow's view of need satisfaction, which holds that people will be motivated only as their lowest levels of need are met. If the researcher finds that people do seem to be motivated in this way, Maslow's view is supported. If people do not respond in the way predicted by the theory, further studies with different assumptions will be carried out.

A second widely accepted function of a theory is to provide an integrating, common feature in the further development of the knowledge base in a given field. Theory often leads to the generation of research; the findings of research lead to action; action leads to further theory refinement; and so on. Research emerges from a theory base, and this often stimulates the researcher to extend the existing knowledge base by building upon the assumptions and generalizations of an earlier theory and research base. The use of theory in this type of clarification and building process often leads to new, more precise issues worthy of serious investigation. Researchers might investigate, for example, how a certain theory is reflected in the ways teachers think about instruction. As research is conducted, the researcher will see an increasingly clear picture of how thinking takes place. As a result, the theory may be revised to reflect this research finding.

Finally, and perhaps most relevant to our presentation of supervision as a proactive process, is the fact that theory in the social sciences often guides action. Theory can help us make wise, reality-based decisions. Theory allows us to "make sense" out of the complex and often contradictory behavioral patterns that we so often see in the real world. While the first two functions of theory related primarily to the needs of most educational practitioners engaged in systematic research in schools, this last function is a cornerstone for effective supervisory practice, which reflects proactive, rather than reactive or crisis-oriented, behavior. The third function of theory captures the most straightforward of its uses, namely that it describes the nature of present conditions and events in a most accurate and economical fashion, and also predicts the likelihood of the same events and conditions occurring in a similar, predictable way in the future. A teacher aware of child-development theory that suggests that children learn best when they are personally ready to learn, for instance, may design a classroom environment where children with varying personal interests can find a variety of things to do.

STEPS IN THEORY DEVELOPMENT

Another way to clarify how theories are used to link present realities with future practice is to consider how they develop over time. Most theories appear to develop as the result of a movement through at least three identifiable, sequential steps: first, the discursive treatment of a topic; second, the development of a simple listing of characteristics; and third, the creation of a juxtaposed taxonomy of observed events. These first three steps are often followed by the building and sharing of theoretical models, also known as graphic depictions of theoretical statements. We will return to each of these steps in the next few pages to examine how they fit together, and how they may be used by the practitioner of supervision interested in the improvement of practice in schools.

1. Discursive Treatment of a Problem or Topic

This step, usually considered a starting point in the theory development cycle, basically consists of "brainstorming" or even "idle chit-chat" about some specific topic, issue, trend, or event. No attempt is made to offer any connection between and among random, disjointed observations.

As an example, consider the type of talk that can be heard in virtually every teachers' lounge in schools across the nation. Dozens, even hundreds, of random observations are made each day about how a particular group of students behaves, or the latest memo from the administration, or the policies recently formulated by the board of education at a public meeting. This kind of real world, random discussion might well serve as the beginning point for the theory-development cycle.

Let's imagine that a group of teachers makes some random observations about how the students in their classes tend to behave. Most teachers may comment that "the kids are pretty good here," while a few might note that some students "cause a lot problems" in the school. Names of individual students will probably emerge. Comments from other staff members range along a continuum stretching from "the kids here are angels" to "the kids are terrors." These comments come fast, without advance thinking; they are not offered in any specific order, but randomly represent what at least a subset of the teaching staff in a particular school believes about the nature of students in their care. They are "true" statements insofar as they represent the honest beliefs of people; they derive from each teacher's perceptions of the reality that he or she experiences on a daily basis. Theory in the social sciences often begins this way, even when the participants have no realization, and certainly no conscious desire in that direction, that they are laying the groundwork for the development of a theory in any formal sense.

2. Development of a Simplified Listing

Eventually, observations made in random fashion begin to be repeated with enough frequency that a list becomes apparent. Although this activity is the second step in a linear theory-building process, it is actually quite similar to and often simultaneous with the "discursive treatment" stage. Listings of phenomena begin to take shape almost immediately from random observations, and random observations nearly always lead immediately to the generation of lists.

As we suggested above, random observations about student behavior are virtually nonstop in most teachers' lounges throughout the year and across the nation. The same general observations occur with sufficient frequency to suggest that simplified listings of observed characteristics could easily be compiled. Unfortunately, the random observations of professional educators are not generally recorded in any systematic manner, and therefore a relatively small amount of formal theory is actually built upon the observations of classroom teachers. But theory building, on a very personal and informal level, is in fact going on continuously in schools. What rarely takes place is the type of codification and formalized listing described as the characteristic of this step in the formal theory-building cycle.

3. Formulating a Juxtaposed Taxonomy

At a certain point in the theory-building cycle, the random, limited observations of existing phenomena are placed in relationship to other features of the observed environment. In other words, discursive treatment is placed in context and a juxtaposed taxonomy created.

Returning to our teachers and their observations of student behavior, simple statements such as "The kids are terrors" are usually quickly followed by qualifying statements such as "when we get back to school after a long vacation period." Teachers frequently make use of context-based statements to guide their own professional behavior. Within a relatively short time, beginning teachers note that students tend to behave one way on Monday mornings, somewhat differently late in the afternoon on Wednesdays, and in a completely different fashion on Friday afternoons. And one year "in the trenches" is usually enough to show a teacher that students will react to directions differently before a long vacation break from how they act after that same break. This series of random observations of student behavior, then, when placed in the context of the school-year calendar, provides considerable guidance for the teacher planning instructional activities. Most instructors learn quickly that a major examination on the last afternoon before spring break will result in low grades and high frustration for students. For years, teachers have tended to search for "hands-on" activities that call for high physical involvement when they know students are preoccupied with thoughts of an upcoming week away from school.

A good theory must be able to describe the present with a high degree of accuracy; more importantly, it must be useful in terms of suggesting and predicting future events. The fact that students tend to be disengaged from classroom activities on days before vacations is in itself an interesting piece of descriptive information. However, this information is much more important in terms of what it offers to the classroom teacher for lesson planning at vacation times. The observation placed in context allows teachers to change their behavior to accommodate what they have learned. The real value in understanding theory is not simply that a theoretical perspective offers a novel way to describe real situations. Rather, the long-term value is that theory enables us to engage in proactive practice.

Model building. Although the steps just covered constitute the basic theory-building cycle, one additional activity is often included in this process, namely the building of a theoretical model. This may sound like a rather mysterious activity, but all we actually mean is that the interrelationships of variables or factors in a theoretical statement are depicted *graphically.* Although not an absolutely essential part of theory development, models are nonetheless an integral part of most conceptualizations that influence practice in the social sciences. We will include a number of these graphic depictions or theoretical models as we review theories in later chapters.

CHARACTERISTICS OF "GOOD" THEORY

A good, usable theory in the social sciences—that is, one which fulfills the assigned functions of describing present reality while also predicting the likelihood of events occurring in the future—should have at least some of the following identifiable characteristics.

1. A "good" theory must be based squarely on observed (and observable) events that are grounded in reality. Theories simply cannot be so

conceptually abstract or divorced from common reality that no one besides the individuals who formulate the theories can understand what is meant. Theories must communicate bits of reality to a relatively wide audience. Thus, "good" theories cannot be mere suppositions of a chosen few; they must be born of and tested in a reality that is shared by many at a time.

2. A "good" theory should explain things found in reality in a complete, yet succinct fashion. A statement that must use many qualifiers to explain exceptions to the rule is probably not a particularly "good" theory. A theory should say much in a few words, or in the case of a theoretical model, in as simple a graphic design as possible.

3. A "good" theory must be amendable to some type of systematic verification, validation, or testing process. It is not enough, for example, for a small group of teachers to note the behavior patterns of the students in a single elementary school. Someone else needs to be able to witness the same behaviors; a person, in a sense, must be able to walk in off the street and verify whether or not students, in fact, do behave as the teachers claim. More important, a good theory must "hold up" when it is transported to other settings. Is it true that students do not act seriously the day before a vacation? If this question can be answered similarly in a wide variety of different sites, then this theoretical assumption is likely to be a "good" one.

4. A "good" theory must have a future-time orientation, because it ultimately needs to be an accurate predictor of the way things will probably be. As we mention throughout this text, understanding and applying the theories of the social sciences to educational super-vision will be of little value unless this understanding somehow improves practice in the schools at some point in the future.

One way of thinking about what social science theory is, is to conclude that a "good" theory is like a pair of glasses worn to aid our vision. Theory should help us see the relationships between the goals of organizations and the abilities of the people who work in those organizations more clearly. We wear "glasses" to get a better look at things—the situations and events that might occur from time to time in the world of practice related to educational supervision. The corrective lenses of a good theory help us develop generalizable ways of responding and behavioral patterns that will serve both to guide actions and reactions, and, more importantly, to aid future planning and anticipation of events. The application of good theories does indeed permit more proactive, and less reactive, behavior. The ultimate importance of theory, and perhaps its stiffest test of "goodness," is that it provides consistent ways of looking at similar, but not wholly alike, events that are part of the world at work. Theory in this sense can be viewed as an important part of an educational leader's "bag of tricks."

RESTRICTIONS ON THE USE OF THEORY

Having said that, we need to share some important cautions about reliance on and usage of theory in the field of educational supervision. These cautions are in no way meant to detract from the value of theory as an ongoing guide to practice in supervision; rather, we list them only to suggest potential problem areas to those who might develop too great a reliance on theoretical formulations as guides to all behavior.

1. Although many elements of current supervisory practice date back to the origins of American public education in general, the field of educational supervision as currently practiced is still an emergent discipline. As a result, the events from which the initial observations and assumptions come are highly limited. There is no long established history, or "organizational memory," from which we can draw sufficient inferences for use in formal theory-building processes.
2. We need to recognize that biases are a constant threat to objectivity in the collection of sound observations. Idiosyncratic interpretation of reality is bound to enter the field of theory development at one point or another, and listings will remain the products of personal observation, wherein we can never be sure that the observers are totally free of prejudice.
3. Educational supervision is a complex and widely interpreted field. As a result, the totality of educational supervision can never be represented by one finite set of theoretical assumptions and models. In the chapters that follow, we will underscore this point by selecting for intensive review only a handful of the available theoretical perspectives that might prove useful to you in guiding your supervisory practices. There are, of course, a great variety of other perspectives, models, and theories that might also be useful to those who would serve as educational leaders; but no one theory can answer all our questions.

We have focused our discussion of theory up to this point almost exclusively on formal theoretical formulations in the social sciences. Before we move on, we should glance quickly at the applications of less formal, more personal theories to the enhancement of supervisory behavior.

DISTINCTIONS BETWEEN FORMAL THEORY
AND PERSONAL PHILOSOPHY

Much of what we have just said about the functions and characteristics of formal theory, along with the steps followed in the theory-building cycle, has relevance to the development of a personal philosophy as a way to guide and improve supervisory practice. While I have tended to suggest that theories are developed in more or less conscious fashion by those who wish to contribute to a general, widespread clarification of practice in the social sciences, theory also emerges in a considerably less visible and grandiose fashion. Most people periodically observe events in their personal "reality," form simple lists, and then place their observations in a context that enables them to behave in a more or less predictable way over time. We can cite again our example of the individual classroom teacher who, after some experience, knows that students tend to behave one way at certain times and differently at other times. The ability to accumulate such "theories" to guide personal practice is often pointed to as a characteristic that differentiates between "average" and "good" teachers. We can use the knowledge accumulated in one year to help us improve the next year—or we can simply repeat the same year, over and over. *Cumulative learning* is simply another way to describe what I refer to as the development of personal philosophies, theories, platforms, or guides to action.

Structurally, then, great similarities exist between the steps followed in formal theory building and individual or personal philosophy construction. Perhaps the greatest single difference is the extent to which we can generalize from the initial random observations. In the case of the formal theory building, the "discursive treatment" step might include random observations made by many different individuals in numerous settings over a long period of time; our own observations, on the other hand, are simply that—our own.

A potential danger exists in developing too rigid a stance toward a personalized theory. A fine line exists between taking a stance on a particular issue, based on highly personalized observations that are not necessarily shared by a wide segment of the general population, and closed-mindedness. Personal observations can become prejudices and biases. A teacher whose classes have included only a few Hispanic children might generalize based on observed behavior that Spanish-speaking students are (1) very ambitious, (2) very lazy, (3) very talkative, (4) very shy, (5) very bright, or (6) any one of thousands of other characteristics that might be assigned to *all* students based on the witnessed behavior of a very few in a highly limited setting. (Of course, merely increasing the number of observations does not guarantee absolutely that a theoretical formulation will be free of bias. During the earliest days of this nation, "theories" of witchcraft in New England were "proven" by the hundreds, perhaps thousands, of observations reported by reliable citizens of unacceptable behavior in the comings and goings of some of their neighbors.)

Formal theory, then, does not differ from personalized, informal theory solely in the extent to which observations are made by many people rather than one. Other distinctions need to be recognized. Formal theory, for instance, is open to ongoing testing and verification in an objective fashion. If those subscribing to the theories of witchcraft had been open to a dispassionate review of their assumptions (for requesting which, incidentally, the requester might have gotten burned at the stake), those theories might have had a much smaller audience. The theories used as the basis for much of our thinking in the social sciences are *formal;* they have been tested through empirical research and, as a consequence, have undergone periodic modifications. In addition, what are most often classified as important theories in educational supervision have been generalized across many different settings. A review of the Axiomatic Theory of Organizations by Gerald Hage in the next chapter, for example, demonstrates that it is as usable in schools as it might be in hospitals or private industry. To be sure, there is considerable value in developing individualized, personal, and informal theory, and it is a process that goes on with or without specific recognition of that fact in this book. However, there are limitations in allowing our behavior as leaders and supervisors to be guided too much by informal patterns. We also need knowledge of formal statements of theory.

SUMMARY

In this chapter we have explored the role of theory in the social sciences as a way to improve supervisory practice. As an introduction to this concept, we offered a number of definitions for theory and noted that theory is not, as often popularly described, solely abstraction or philosophy. Rather, theory attempts to reflect the nature of present reality based on observable phenomena. Steps in the theory-building cycle were described and related to the major functions and characteristics of "good" theory in the social sciences: the description and explanation of present events, and the prediction of the likely occurrence of future events and behavior. The chapter concluded with a review of some typical restrictions and limitations associated with the use of formal theory, and finally with a summary of the differences between formal and informal theory. We noted that both personal, informal theory development and formal theory building in the social sciences are important tools for use in educational supervision. However, formal theory makes use of widespread generalizations of observable phenomena and is normally subjected to some degree of objective testing and verification. As a result, some special features of formal theory make it particularly valuable to those who need to understand "the way things work" in organizations.

   Understanding of and reliance on theories is certainly not the only way for practitioners of educational supervision to function. There are many unfortunate examples of supervisors living solely in the world of theory who are very ineffective when faced with making decisions concerning "real world" issues. On the other hand, we firmly believe that some appreciation of theory is an important characteristic of successful followers of proactive supervision processes.

SUGGESTED ACTIVITIES

1. Analyze the way in which you or a colleague deal with parents, students who have discipline problems, or some other situation faced by school teachers, to determine the ways in which that approach is guided by the development of a personalized theory, in the ways described in this chapter.
2. Interview a supervisor or school administrator concerning the way in which he or she handled some sort of recent "critical incident." In your analysis, try to determine the steps that were followed by the person. Was there a similarity between his or her expressed behavior and the steps in the theory-building cycle described in this chapter?
3. Ask a number of people how they would define "theory." Determine from their responses the extent to which these individuals have a positive or negative view of theory.

REFERENCES

Hoy, Wayne K., & Miskel, Cecil G. (1988). *Educational administration: Theory, research, and practice* (2nd ed.). New York: Random House.
Sergiovanni, Thomas J., & Starratt, Robert J. (1983). *Supervision: Human perspectives* (3rd ed.). New York: McGraw-Hill.

ADDITIONAL READINGS

Halpin, Andrew. (Ed.). (1958). *Administrative theory in education.* Chicago: Midwest Administrative Center, University of Chicago.
Owens, Robert G. (1987). *Organizational behavior in education* (3rd ed.). Englewood Cliffs, NJ: Prentice-Hall.

CHAPTER 5

Organizational Analysis

In this chapter we will review the theory-based analysis of complex organizations and present two analytical approaches. The first we will call *formal analysis,* and the second *informal analysis.* Formal organizational analysis refers to the structure of organizations, including their stated and institutionally defined purposes and objectives. Informal organizational analysis deals with the characteristics of people who work in the institutions, along with the less visible and tangible features of organizations such as the psychosocial climate or "feel." The practitioner of effective and proactive supervisory processes needs to be aware of both the formal and the informal levels of analysis.

In the first part of this chapter, some theoretical perspectives that describe and predict behavior associated with formal organizations will be reviewed, including Gerald Hage's Axiomatic Theory of Organizations, Jacob Getzels's Social Systems, and the emerging conceptualization of Gareth Morgan's Organizational Metaphors. In the second part of the chapter, two perspectives in informal aspects of organizations, Matthew Miles' view of Organizational Health, and Organizational Climate as conceptualized primarily by Halpin and Croft, will be described. Throughout, we will indicate the ways in which these theoretical perspectives offer opportunities for the educational supervisor to improve his or her practice, and more importantly, the quality of life in schools.

FORMAL ANALYSIS: HAGE'S AXIOMATIC THEORY OF ORGANIZATIONS

One of the more enduring theoretical analyses of the formal characteristics of organizations is one proposed by the sociologist Gerald Hage (1965). While the term "axiomatic" (which means "so obvious as to be self-evident") may be open to some debate by reviewers, we include this framework for two reasons. First, the development and application of this theory follows directly the rational, linear theory-building cycle that we set forth in the previous chapter. Second, the theory offers some important insights into the operation of organizations to the extent that supervisory behavior can be greatly enhanced through an understanding of assumptions and properties found in the theory.

Historical Development

Hage's focus throughout his scholarly work as a sociologist has been to determine how societal institutions function. Hage began by simply looking at a wide array of organizations—hospitals and nursing homes, private companies, and educational institutions, among others. By reviewing the characteristic components in diverse locations, Hage and his colleagues were able to note conceptually similar features that existed in all organizations, regardless of types. Thus, the processes of discursive treatment of a topic (random observations) and the development of a simplified listing of phenomena were completed as nearly simultaneous activities. In this earliest phase of the historical development of Hage's Axiomatic Theory, then, the first descriptive function of a theory was completed.

Structural and Outcome Variables

Hage's examination of complex organizations yielded a primary, simple finding: All organizations, regardless of their type and purpose, may be conceived of as having two basic characteristics, structure (or the way in which they are put together), and outcomes (the purposes for the organization.) Further analysis indicated that all organizations have at least four common structural components: centralization, complexity, formalization, and stratification. These may be defined as follows:

Centralization: A measure of the proportion of jobs in an organization that participate in decision-making processes. An organization where only a few people tend to make all or most decisions is highly centralized, whereas an organization where there is widespread and broad-based involvement in decisions is low in centralization, or decentralized.

Complexity: The number of occupational roles and specialties, and the level of training required by people in an organization to fulfill the roles and specialties needed. Organizations with many complicated jobs where people must receive a lot of advanced training to do those jobs are high in complexity.

Formalization: The proportion of jobs that are codified, along with the range of individual variation and interpretation that is allowed in the performance of jobs. An organization where people are expected to comply with the features of a very specific job description is high in formalization. If there are opportunities for many employees to do many different tasks without regard to official responsibilities, an organization is low in formalization.

Stratification: The differences that exist in income levels and prestige found within an organization. When there are gaps between employees in terms of salary levels and other forms of organizational reward, there is high stratification.

A few additional comments need to be made concerning these structural variables. First, some kinds of organizations are typically relatively high or low in terms of each factor. For example, a large modern hospital is normally very high in complexity, given the tremendous amount of specialization now found in the field of medicine. Moreover, hospitals are also institutions with high stratification: Cardiac surgeons make more money and have greater prestige and visibility than do general surgeons, emergency room physicians, or radiologists; physicians stand far apart from (and above) nurses, orderlies, or any of the scores of other jobs found in most hospitals. By contrast, consider the characteristics of another type of organization, the mom-and-pop grocery store. Here, decision making is highly decentralized, there is little complexity, and stratification does not exist. We should be aware, however, that there can be gradations in each of these structural components in the *same types* of organizations. Not all hospitals are the same: Some are more stratified than others.

This second observation has particular relevance to discussions of schools. While schools might, in general, fall somewhere around the middle of a continuum of all organizations, some schools are obviously different from others in terms of centralization, complexity, formalization, and stratification. Some schools feature opportunities for greater participation by teachers in schoolwide decision making. Other schools have greater job specialization and, perhaps as a result, more levels to increase discrepancies in terms of prestige. In fact, the nature of the size and grade levels served by a school also has a good deal to do with the relative degrees of any of Hage's structural elements that might be present. High schools, particularly ones with a strong departmental structure and many specialists on the staff (nurse, guidance counselors, librarians, and so forth) are much higher in their degree of complexity than are the majority of elementary schools. On the other hand, some elementary schools serving many students across a range of several grades will be more complex than elementary schools enrolling pupils in only two or three grades, or elementary "one-room" schools. In addition, the degree of formalization and stratification will vary in schools where there are many specialized roles, as contrasted with a setting where there is but one administrator and, perhaps, no more than 10 classroom teachers.

Organizations may also be understood through their outcome characteristics. Hage described four: production, efficiency, job satisfaction, and adaptiveness.

> *Production:* In most organizations, production is defined simply as the number of things that are produced during a given period of time. High production results from a lot of things created or built, and low production occurs when few items may be measured or counted.
>
> *Efficiency:* This outcome variable is a measure of the cost associated with the production of the items produced. High efficiency is the result of situations where the ratio of cost-per-item or unit is low. Low efficiency, quite obviously, is the reverse: An individual item costs a great deal to produce. Incidentally, "cost" is defined here as the amount of any resource—money, time, labor, and so forth—that is expended.
>
> *Job satisfaction:* Originally, Hage defined job satisfaction as the rate of turnover of employees. This definition has proved inadequate for most present institutions where people tend to stay on their jobs whether they like them or not. Sergiovanni and Starratt (1983) more recently defined satisfaction as the extent to which an organization deliberately focuses on the fulfillment of human needs as a formal, stated objective. As a result, organizations where there is a continuous, deliberate focus on the needs and interests of employees are considered high in satisfaction.
>
> *Adaptiveness:* Also frequently described as "innovativeness," adaptiveness refers to the number of new program initiatives started within an organization during a given period of time. A manufacturing company would be considered high in adaptiveness if it introduced many new products in a calendar year. By contrast, a company that tended to "stand pat" and stay with the same merchandise year in and year out would be low in adaptiveness, or innovativeness.

As was true of structural variables, the types of organizations may also be generally relatively high or relatively low in these four outcome variables. Social welfare agencies, for example, might be expected to stress open concern for enhancing the nature of human relationships and be described as "high" in job satisfaction, whereas other organizations (perhaps a stock brokerage) might have less marked interest in the improvement of warmth and job satisfaction. A research and development institute might place great emphasis on the construct of adaptiveness because the company was created primarily to develop an abundance of new ideas and products. A very "old line" and stable producer of one identifiable product line such as high-quality writing instruments might rarely, if ever, be inclined to bring out something as "new and different" as a ballpoint pen. Variations occur, however, even among organizations with similar titles and interests.

Similarly, individual schools differ significantly in terms of the outcome variables. One school may have a reputation for very high standardized test scores (an indicator of "productivity"), while a neighboring school has a history of much lower scores. One system may produce X number of National Merit Scholars at a per-pupil expenditure rate of $3,800, while another district boasts of even more scholars, and it spends only $3,500 per student—a difference in efficiency. Such analyses based on the outcome of efficiency are particularly popular, of course, whenever a school district tax initiative appears on a local community ballot.

Mechanistic versus Dynamic Organizations

After Hage had analyzed organizations in terms of structure and outcome, he had essentially finished that stage of the theory-development cycle that we referred to earlier as the simplified listing. In the next stage of theory formulation, Hage related two prototypic organizational patterns that could be described in terms of the structural and outcome variables. These two organizational types are defined as *Dynamic* and *Mechanistic.* Table 5.1 indicates the relative degree of structural and outcome variables possessed by each type.

Neither the Mechanistic nor the Dynamic organization should necessarily be viewed as better or worse than the other; these two designations serve only to describe two polar opposite organizations. Table 5.2 compares two opposite organizational structures by Wynn and Guditus (1984). If we ask "Should a school tend to be a Dynamic or a Mechanistic organization?" two answers are possible. First, individual schools are already best understood as Dynamic because they emphasize widespread involvement in decision making (low Centralization), little reliance on formal job descriptions (low Formalization), few distinctions among staff members in terms of prestige or income differences (low Stratification), but many special technical skills demonstrated by teachers and other staff (high Complexity). Other schools typify the Mechanistic model because they have the opposite structural characteristics.

Second, "perfection" for schools, as for any organization, depends largely on the goals of that particular school. Different structural characteristics yield different outcomes. If a school's goals include stability (low Adaptiveness),

TABLE 5.1. "DYNAMIC" VERSUS "MECHANISTIC" ORGANIZATIONS, AS DESCRIBED ACCORDING TO THE RELATIVE AMOUNT OF FOUR STRUCTURAL VARIABLES AND FOUR OUTCOME VARIABLES.

Dynamic Organizations	Mechanistic Organizations
Structural Variables	Structural Variables
High Complexity	Low Complexity
Low Centralization	High Centralization
Low Formalization	High Formalization
Low Stratification	High Stratification
Outcome Variables	Outcome Variables
High Adaptiveness	Low Adaptiveness
Low Productivity	High Productivity
Low Efficiency	High Efficiency
High Job Satisfaction	Low Job Satisfaction

SOURCE: Reprinted from *An axiomatic theory of organization,* By Gerald Hage, published in Administrative Science Quarterly, 10, 3 (December 1965) by permission of Administrative Science Quarterly.

TABLE 5.2. COMPARISON OF TWO MODELS OF ORGANIZATIONS ("DYNAMIC" VERSUS "MECHANISTIC") IN TERMS OF 10 SELECTED CRITERIA.

	Mechanistic (Bureaucratic)	Dynamic (Professional)
Decision Making	Centralized	Widely participative
Work	Individual jobs are self-contained and isolated	People function in face-to-face groups collaboratively
Control	Through hierarchical structure	Through interaction of involved persons
Tasks	Specialized and differentiated with precise specifications of jurisdictions	Continuously enlarged through consensus in context of total organization
Authority	Determined by hierarchical status	Shared and determined by consensus
Relationships	Unilateral management action based on passive conformance	Emphasis on mutual dependence and cooperation based on trust and confidence
Mood	Competition and rivalry	Cooperation
Nature of Organization	Rigid	Flexible
Commitment	To superiors	To the task and "ethos of progress"
Climate	Closed	Open

SOURCE: From Wynn, Richard, & Guditus, Charles W. (1984). Team Management: Leadership by Consensus Copyright © 1984 by the Merrill Publishing Company, Columbus, OH. Reprinted by permission.

high achievement test scores (a possible example of high Productivity) without spending too much money (high Efficiency), and without much concern for the needs of staff (low Job Satisfaction), the appropriate model would be the Mechanistic organization. Other goals might suggest that the Dynamic model was more appropriate.

Illustrations of Actual Applications

The ultimate educational value of any theoretical formulation such as Hage's Axiomatic Theory of Organizations is that it can help us make decisions that improve the quality of what takes place in schools. Knowledge of the Axiomatic Propositions listed below represents little more than an empty academic exercise unless that knowledge serves to direct our supervisory behavior so that we can more effectively guide school or district personnel to achieve their goals. Let us look now at how an understanding of this particular theory might guide us toward a more proactive approach to supervisory practice.

Propositions of the Axiomatic Theory of Organizations
1. The higher the centralization, the higher the production.
2. The higher the formalization, the higher the efficiency.
3. The higher the centralization, the higher the formalization.
4. The higher the stratification, the lower the job satisfaction.
5. The higher the stratification, the higher the production.
6. The higher the stratification, the lower the adaptiveness.
7. The higher the complexity, the lower the centralization.

Suppose that an educational supervisor is assigned the task of working with a particular school where there has been a long history of low staff morale, and where little attention has been paid to the human dimension of organization. In Hage's terms, the school would be described as low in the outcome variable of job satisfaction. If the supervisor's goals include increasing this variable so that teachers and staff feel their personal needs are being addressed, the Axiomatic Theory might suggest a number of avenues for change, all in the *structural* characteristics of the school. Job satisfaction can be increased by raising the level of complexity in the organization, or by lowering centralization, formalization, and stratification. While any one of these changes is likely to have a positive effect on the job satisfaction variable, the most readily modified structural characteristic of a school is probably the extent to which people believe that they are involved in organizational decision making. Thus, the proactive supervisor interested in increasing satisfaction among school employees might increase opportunities for teachers and staff to participate in making important and relevant decisions. Many successful educational leaders make this kind of structural shift to achieve different outcomes almost intuitively. Effective supervisors need not make use of Hage's technical, theoretical language to act in this way. The essential understanding of the principle that organizational job satisfaction tends to be higher when people are involved in making relevant decisions is all we really need.

If Hage's theory is valid, however, modification of one structural component might cause undesirable side effects in terms of outcomes. Remember, for example, that the productivity and efficiency levels of organizations are generally lower in those organizations where centralization is lower. The net effect of involving people in a school's decision-making processes might indeed be a staff that is happier, but one that does not "produce" as much or as efficiently as a staff in a school where one person makes all the decisions.

The real practical value of a theoretical framework such as Hage's, then, is not that it tells us what we are supposed to do in all cases. No theory is meant to serve as a cookbook. To the contrary, understanding a given theory should provide us with an awareness of the possible outcomes of a set of actions that we might follow. In the case we just examined, no one can say whether it is better to have a "satisfied staff' or a "productive and efficient staff." Such a choice must be made by the leader in a way that is consistent with goals, objectives, vision, values, and individual philosophy.

FORMAL ANALYSIS: GETZELS'S SOCIAL SYSTEMS

Jacob Getzels, a psychologist on the University of Chicago's faculty in the 1950's, developed a second formal theoretical model that supervisors may find useful in understanding what takes place in formal organizations.

Historical Development

Getzels's initial work was carried out largely in the years immediately following World War II and involved the analysis of such diverse settings as the military, hospitals, universities, private businesses, and public schools. Getzels isolated essential properties of all these different organizations and was able to conclude that, regardless of the organizations' stated purposes, all such units possess two common essential dimensions, one that describes the structure of the organization as a societal institution, and the other that provides a review of the people who work within the institution. The value of observing these two dimensions interacting with one another is that, when analyzed as interactive characteristics, they provide a description of much of the human behavior found in organizations.

The Structural Dimension and Its Component Elements

The dimension of social systems that deals with the structure of organizations is referred to in Getzels's theory as the *nomothetic, normative,* or *sociological* dimension. The component elements of this dimension are the *institution, roles,* and *expectations* (Getzels and Guba, 1957)

Society has created many different institutions, each of which is theoretically designed to carry out some societally identified and required function. Because society requires that there be ways of helping sick people, hospitals (or other forms of health care organizations) have been created. Schools exist largely because society has indicated that there shall be organizations that educate people. Police agencies have been created to deal with the need to protect people and their property.

When institutions are thus formed, the roles within them are also created and institutionally defined. "Roles represent dynamic aspects of positions, offices, or statuses within the institution" (Lipham, 1974, p. 66). Schools have a number of standard roles: student, teacher, administrative personnel, supervisory staff. In fact, institutions and roles form an intense interrelationship: Institutions would not exist without the presence of certain roles (e.g., schools would not exist without students), and roles are meaningless without institutions (e.g., a teacher would be lost, to some extent, without a school).

The third component element of the nomothetic dimension of Getzels's social systems model is the expectation that exists for the performance of any particular institutionally defined role. Teachers, students, and others serve in roles within the school, which is a social institution, and each of these roles evokes certain specific types of behavior. Teachers act in certain ways (with some limited variation allowed); students do other things to play out their institutional responsibilities, and so forth.

The "People" Dimension and Its Component Elements

The second dimension of Getzels's social systems model is concerned with the nature of the people who serve within organizations. This aspect is called the *idiographic, personal,* or *psychological* dimension and is also composed of three elements: the *individuals* (which correspond to the institution in the nomothetic dimension) who belong to organizations, each of whom has a unique *personality* that, in turn, is defined largely in terms of particular *needs.* The two dimensions of the social systems model are represented by the model depicted in Figure 5.1.

The pictorial representation of Getzels' model illustrates a number of concepts that are useful to the educational supervisor. The congruence

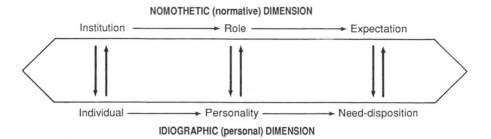

NOMOTHETIC (normative) DIMENSION

Institution ⟶ Role ⟶ Expectation

Individual ⟶ Personality ⟶ Need-disposition

IDIOGRAPHIC (personal) DIMENSION

Figure 5.1. Model of the social systems model of Getzels showing the two component dimensions and their elements. (Reprinted from J.W. Getzels and E.G. Guba, 1957. Social Behavior and the Administrative Process. *School Review, 65,* 429 by permission of the University of Chicago Press. Copyright © 1957 by the University of Chicago Press.)

demonstrated between the individual component elements of the two dimensions in the model suggest a neat, parallel alignment of individual personalities and institutionally defined roles. As the model suggests, this type of clear overlap is a strong indication of organizational effectiveness, because people who work in the organization are doing what they want, and their jobs are fulfilling their needs. Unfortunately, in many organizations and at many times, the definition of a role is far from consistent with the personality and needs of the individual who fills it. At such times conflict occurs, and the extent to which this conflict is serious is a critical indicator of whether or not a particular organization will achieve the kind of balance between institutional demands and human needs that leads to effectiveness.

Illustrations of Actual Applications.

Understanding Getzels's central ideas allows the educational supervisor to be more effective, particularly in the context of our definition of supervision: Supervision is the process of overseeing the ability of people to meet the goals of the organization in which they work. Throughout this work, we have suggested that the supervisor has a legitimate stake in maximizing the match between people and organization; as suggested by Getzels's model, we assume that people who are involved with and interested in their jobs will do those jobs better, and that the organization will benefit through increased productivity and effectiveness.

Examples are plentiful in most school settings of the mismatches between institutional roles and individual personalities. Teachers are frequently assigned duties such as "cafeteria patrol," which are at best tolerated and at worst seen as totally opposed to their view of professional responsibility. Many teachers define their role as working constantly with highly motivated students, whereas in fact the role of the teacher in most schools today requires working with some kids who do not even want to come to school, let alone learn. Frequently a lack of congruence exists between assigned roles and individual personalities. The value of a theoretical model such as the social systems paradigm is not that it tells the supervisor that conflicts will occur from time to time, but that it allows us to predict such conflicts in certain cases, sometimes conflicts so severe as to make the operation of the school or district a likely failure. Once again, the model of organizations as social systems has the potential of increasing more proactive behavior on the part of the practitioner of educational supervision.

MORGAN'S ORGANIZATIONAL METAPHORS

The final theoretical perspective we will consider concerning the formal characteristics of complex organizations is that of Gareth Morgan (1986). Morgan attempts to provide managers, supervisors, and other leaders with ways to learn how to "read" what is going on in the organizations in which they work. He suggests that metaphors provide a useful way of understanding the subtle differences among the purposes, practices, policies, and underlying philosophies of organizations:

> It is easy to see how this kind of thinking has relevance for understanding organization and management. For organizations are complex and paradoxical phenomena that can be understood in many ways. Many of our taken-for-granted organizations are metaphorical. . . . For example, we frequently talk about organizations *as if* they were machines designed to achieve predetermined goals and objectives, and which should operate smoothly and efficiently. And as a result of this kind of thinking we often attempt to organize and manage them in a mechanistic way, forcing their human qualities into a background role. (Morgan, 1986, p. 13)

Listing of Major Metaphors

Morgan suggests eight predominant metaphors that describe organizations:

1. "Organizations as machines." This metaphor derives from the era of scientific management and suggests that organizations resemble machines because of the prevailing expectations for reliable, durable, and predictable behavior. People who work in such organizations are seen as expendable and wholly interchangeable components. The usefulness of this metaphor is that it suggests we can design organizations to maximize predictability, especially in devising problem-solving strategies, but its major shortcoming is that creative approaches to problem solving are destroyed, and the people who

work in such settings participate in a dehumanized environment that provides little support for individual creativity.

2. "Organizations as organisms." This metaphor suggests that organizations have needs, interests, and life cycles, just as living organisms (including human beings) do, and that we can better understand the workings of organizations by considering them in terms of features like cellular structure. The usefulness of this metaphor is that we become increasingly aware of such things as the "social ecology" in which organizatons exist; this metaphor emphasizes our need to appreciate the dynamic nature of the relationships between organizations and their environments. This image of the organization as a living, breathing organism dissolves, however, as we realize the level of abstraction necessary to create it.

3. "Organizations as brains." This metaphor emphasizes the organization's capacity to be guided by conscious rationality while still safeguarding such characteristics as flexibility and creative action. Its usefulness lies in its suggestion that organizations are capable of learning and of self-organization—of creating, for instance, a series of appropriate responses to problems and "storing" that creation for future use. The major shortcoming of this metaphor is that, in its emphasis on rationality, it may prevent us from recognizing the important reality that much of what occurs, especially in the struggle for power and control of organizations, is in fact irrational.

4. "Organizations as cultures." This metaphor suggests that we can best understand organizations by examining them in the context of culture. Understanding value components is thus a critical factor in organizational analysis; we cannot understand how Toyota operates, for example, without understanding how Japan operates. This perspective places a premium on subtle behaviors, but it is limited in that understanding a culture, finally, is impossible. Cultures are fluid, their values, beliefs, and traditions constantly changing; we are prevented, then, from ever entirely understanding the working of an organization.

5. "Organizations as political systems." This metaphor suggests that we can best understand organizations by recognizing that they represent ongoing attempts to gain control over finite resources. The analyst must discover the nature of special interests, conflict, power, and authority because it is *these* processes, and not more rational or logical ones, that finally lead to organizational action. This is a particularly realistic view of what takes place in organizations, but its danger is that too much emphasis placed on political agendas may increase the amount of political activity within an organization. Hidden agendas can become operating practice, and honesty and openness abandoned.

6. "Organizations as psychic prisons." This metaphor suggests that

organizations frequently construct views of reality that cause their members to be trapped, because they lose contact with larger, more accurate visions of reality. Organizations often create their own assumptions about what is and is not possible for members to attain, and these assumptions limit the extent to which members feel free to explore new avenues of behavior. Examples of this kind of "group think" occur regularly in politics, as for instance in the Bay of Pigs invasion or the Watergate or Iran-Contra scandals, where those "on the inside" were convinced by the assumptions of the group that their behaviors were appropriate, even though those same behaviors seemed entirely inappropriate to virtually all outside observers. This metaphor's strength is that it encourages critical analysis of what the organization considers "real"; its weakness is that it suggests that members of organizations are often "trapped" when in fact they have consciously selected the view of reality that underlies their actions. We then must ask, who controls "reality"?

7. "Organizations as emblems of flux and transformation." This metaphor suggests that organizations constantly change and must be understood as symbols of a larger, unending evolutionary process. Traditionally, change has been viewed as a process that organizations must endure; this metaphor suggest that organizations are *proactive* and create their own constant change. The weakness of this view is that organizations, like people, in fact frequently change in *reaction* rather than proaction; people do not always create their own visions of change.

8. "Organizations as instruments of domination." This metaphor suggests that organizations can best be understood in terms of elites that use organizations to promote selfish interests though the manipulation of others. It serves as the basis for a radical critique of organizations. The constant danger in this metaphor, however, is that it can move us toward cynicism by suggesting that conspiracies of elite, controlling classes abound, and that the control of lower social classes is the sole focus of organizations. In short, a naive belief inheres in this metaphor that organizations (and the people who control them) are entirely rational in both purpose and action.

Practical Application of Morgan's Metaphors

Morgan's Metaphors of Organizations represent another tool that supervisors may use to increase their personal insights into how organizations function. As Morgan notes throughout his work, the metaphors provide a "road map" that leaders may use to "read and understand" strengths and weaknesses in various organizations. For those in supervisory roles that require working with many different organizations (i.e., different school buildings, districts, or multiple educational agencies such as state education departments, universities, and so forth), this ability to sense the nature of *differences* among those organizations can be critical to successful relations. You will no doubt find some metaphors more desirable than others. Those in control of organizations make the same choices; they often view their organizations as one (or a mixture) of Morgan's eight models. The reality of a description comes largely from the leader's perceptions of its characteristics. Whether the supervisor likes it or not, therefore, some organizations must be understood as "political systems" or even as "instruments of domination." You may find this awareness useful in understanding why things happen as they do in different settings.

You may also find Morgan's framework useful in assessing your own personal assumptions regarding the nature of organizations and building an individual philosophy and action plan. When we pause to consider our basic views concerning the "goodness" or "badness" of organizations, "rationality versus irrationality," "openness or closedness," or any of the other issues that are raised in the various metaphors, we become involved in an important reflective process that may lead to increasing clarification of our beliefs and identification of nonnegotiable values.

Finally, as Morgan has noted, an additional value in examining competing metaphorical descriptions of organizations is that it encourages each of us to confront the paradoxes that exist in the world around us and to think in new and more expansive ways about them. We can "imaginize" or attempt to see the world in completely untested ways, and our creativity may lead to the formulation of new metaphors. Only through this type of thinking can more creative solutions to existing problems be found, a process entirely consistent with our view of proactive supervision.

INFORMAL ANALYSIS: MILES'S ORGANIZATIONAL HEALTH

The theoretical perspectives of Hage, Getzels, and Morgan differ considerably from one another. However, they are similar in the sense that they all represent descriptions of the *formal* characteristics of organizations with emphasis on structure and predictable interrelationships rather than sensations or feelings. In the following sections we will look at the contributions of Matthew Miles, Andrew Halpin, and Donald Croft, all of whom examined the *informal* features of organizations.

Matthew Miles is not the only theorist to suggest that organizations can be seen as "healthy" or "unhealthy." Chris Argyris (1965) used this same construct and has suggested that, in order to be effective and healthy, an organization must accomplish the following basic, core activities:

1. Achieve its goals;
2. Maintain itself internally;
3. Adapt to its environment

Miles (1965) built on these characteristics and defined a healthy organization as one that "not only survives in its environment, but continues to cope adequately over the long haul, and continuously develops and extends its surviving and coping activities. Short-run operations on any particular day may be effective or ineffective, but continued survival, adequate coping, and growth are taking place" (p. 162). The analogy exists, then, with healthy human beings who are able to respond positively to whatever barriers occur in their pursuit of long and prosperous lives. Healthy people are not always without illness; rather, they are able to avoid prolonged stages of being incapacitated. The immune system remains intact because of overall good health.

By contrast, the unhealthy person has numerous, recurring encounters with illnesses, some of which are relatively minor, some life-threatening. The long-term prognosis for such individuals is poor; they will probably enjoy shorter life spans than other, healthier people. Robert Owens (1986) described "unhealthy" organizations in much the same way:

> The unhealthy organization . . . is steadily ineffective. It may cope with its environment effectively on a short-term basis with a "crash program," a concentrated drive to meet a particularly threatening situation, or other "administration-by-crimes" techniques, but in the long run the unhealthy organization becomes less and less able to cope with its environment. Rather than gaining in its ability to cope with a situation, it declines in this capacity over time and it tends to become dysfunctional. (p. 218)

The unhealthy organization is one with a continually ineffective "immune system." The unhealthy organization uses "crisis orientation" just as the ineffective supervisor uses "reactive leadership."

Miles identifies 10 dimensions that serve to indicate the relative health of an organization:

1. *Goal focus:* the extent to which people in an organization understand and accept the goals of the organization. In a healthy organization, these goals are further defined as being *appropriate, achievable,* and well-accepted by organizational members.
2. *Communication adequacy:* the ease and facility of communication that takes place within the organization as well as between the organization and its external environment. In healthy organizations, the flow of information is not constrained from one level to another, and shared information is accurate.
3. *Optional power equalization:* the balance among organizational members that ensures that no one party can coerce and corrupt other members. Healthy organizations demonstrate a relatively low degree of informal influence-seeking behavior by their members.

4. *Human resource utilization:* the effective use of organizational personnel, to the end that they feel as if they are growing, developing, and being satisfied in their jobs. In healthy organizations, there is evidence that members are working as hard as they believe they can and, more importantly, are experiencing personal and professional pride in this effort.

5. *Cohesiveness:* the extent to which members like their organization and want to remain a part of it. Healthy organizations are those in which all members make a firm commitment to invest personal energy toward the goal of increasing the strength of the total organization.

6. *Morale:* feelings of well-being and satisfaction expressed and demonstrated by organizational members. People express happiness at being part of healthy organizations.

7. *Innovativeness:* the tendency of an organization to grow, develop, and become "better" over time, as demonstrated by a general willingness to try new programs and procedures. Healthy organizations are those that indicate openness to new ideas that may be tried as a way to stimulate continued growth toward meeting external environment changes.

8. *Autonomy:* the tendency of an organization to determine its own standards and behaviors in harmony with external demands but without acquiescing to those demands. Healthy organizations show a consistent independence from other organizations, but without rebellion or other potentially destructive behaviors.

9. *Adaption:* the ability to an organization to anticipate changes in environmental demands and engage in self-corrective behaviors that indicate an ability to adapt to those demands. Healthy organizations provide evidence of ongoing sensitivity to changes in environmental pressures, and they make change accordingly with great regularity.

10. *Problem-solving adequacy:* the maintenance of strategies for sensing problems, along with techniques for regularly dealing with organizational crises in a rational fashion. When a healthy organization has problems (as all organizations do, from time to time) it has established ways of dealing with these issues.

Implications of the Theory for Supervisors

The concept of organizational health has some useful applications in the world of educational supervision. We can conclude from the above review, for example, that there is probably no organization that is high in all areas at all times. In other words, there probably has never been and never will be a completely healthy organization. Schools will never be perfect, just as no human being will be without periodic bouts with illness. The value of a conceptual frame of reference such as the one proposed by Miles is that it permits the proactive supervisor to serve as *diagnostician* by reviewing the nature of some critical features of schooling. Are people communicating openly? Is there obvious involvement and commitment being demonstrated by teachers to the stated goals of the school? Is there a spirit present suggesting that people want to try new approaches to instruction? If the answer to these questions is yes, the supervisor has a fundamentally healthy organization. If most questions yield a no response, there is a lot of work to do.

INFORMAL ANALYSIS: ORGANIZATIONAL CLIMATE

A frequently discussed characteristic of organizations in recent years is "climate," or the psychosocial "feel" of an organization, and one of the earliest and most familiar attempts to gain a handle on this characteristic is the work of Andrew Halpin and Donald Croft (1963).

Halpin and Croft based their work on the fairly simple notion that schools and other organizations have unique personalities just as do human beings. The two researchers developed an instrument, the Organizational Climate Description Questionnaire (OCDQ) (Halpin, 1967), to measure the relative absence or presence of eight factors determined to have an impact on the informal "feel," or climate, of a school. These factors, or dimensions, were grouped into two major categories, one descriptive of teachers' behavior and the second of principals' behavior. The individual dimensions related to teachers are disengagement (tendency to be uninvolved in school activities); hindrance (sense of being burdened by too much inconsequential work); esprit (morale); and intimacy (friendly social relations). The behaviors of principals include aloofness (formal and impersonal actions); production emphasis (preference for tight monitoring of staff performance); thrust (effort to "move the organization"); and consideration (tendency to treat staff in a warm and humane fashion). The climate of a particular school is defined by the extent to which each of these eight dimensions is measured (through the interpretation of the OCDQ administered to teachers and principals) as "high," "medium," or "low."

Halpin and Croft suggest six different profiles of organizational climate:

1. *Open climate:* an energetic organization that is moving toward its goals while its staff members are satisfied in their personal social needs.
2. *Autonomous climate:* an organization in which leadership emerges primarily from the group and the formal leader exerts little control over the staff members.

3. *Controlled climate:* an environment that is impersonal and highly task-oriented.
4. *Familiar climate:* a highly personal, but undercontrolled environment in which personal needs are satisfied, but little attention is paid to task accomplishment.
5. *Paternal climate:* an organization in which the formal leader tries consistently to constrain leadership emerging from the group; the leader tries to do it all alone.
6. *Closed climate:* an organization that demonstrates considerable apathy by all members.

These six climates reflect the degree to which the organization is high or low in the eight dimensions reviewed above (See Table 5.3)

Applications of the Theory to Supervision

Halpin and Croft's organizational climate concept is not meant to be used as a tool for judging the quality or lack of quality of a particular school. A "Closed climate" is not necessarily and automatically less desirable than an "Autonomous" or "Open climate," even if some climate profiles may seem more appealing to us than others. Rather, the true value of the organizational climate conceptualization rests in the useful perspective it provides for analyzing the organization and understanding how to introduce new concepts to school groups and the ways in which the people who work in a school may be compelled to engage in more goal-related behavior. For example, if you determine that a particular school reflects the "Paternal climate" (where the principal tries to do it all) you will probably need either to seek ways to help the principal delegate some activities, or be satisfied with a limited set of goals and objectives. By contrast, in an "Autonomous climate" you would be well-advised to work directly with individual staff members interested in engaging in particular types of work.

SUMMARY

In this chapter we provided several useful theoretical models for educational supervisors who would like to become more *proactive* through the use of organizational analysis. Organizational analysis, as we noted early in this section, is but one of a number of *theory-based perspectives* that supervisors may find useful.

The first part of the chapter reviewed three theories that describe and analyze the *formal* nature of organizations. The first, Hage's Axiomatic Theory of Organizations, suggests that complex organizations are best understand as *dynamic* or *mechanistic,* depending on the relative amounts of eight different variables, four related to organizational structure and four to outcomes. The

TABLE 5.3. PROFILES OF SIX DIFFERENT ORGANIZATIONAL CLIMATES, DESCRIBED IN TERMS OF THE RELATIVE ABSENCE OR PRESENCE OF EIGHT TYPES OF ORGANIZATIONAL BEHAVIORS.

Climate:	Disengagement	Hindrance	Esprit	Intimacy	Aloofness	Production Emphasis	Thrust	Consideration
Open	low	low	high	medium	low	low	high	high
Autonomous	low	low	high	high	high	low	medium	medium
Controlled	low	high	medium	low	high	high	medium	low
Familiar	high	low	medium	high	low	low	medium	high
Paternal	high	medium	low	low	low	high	medium	high
Closed	high	high	low	medium	high	high	low	low

SOURCE: Andrew W. Halpin and Donald B. Croft (1963, March). *The Organizational Climate of Schools*, Administrator's Notebook, 11, 1–2. *Reprinted by permission of the publisher.*

major relevance of this theory for supervisors is its indication that, while changes in structure and outcome may be a part of daily organizational life, such modifications have a great likelihood of altering much of the rest of an organization.

The second theory, Getzels's concept of social systems, suggests that organizations must be understood in terms of a constant, dynamic interaction that takes place between two dimensions, nomothetic (institutional) and idiographic (personal). A congruence between institution and individual, role and personality, and expectations and needs is strong indication of overall organizational effectiveness. Getzels's concept encourages supervisors to look at practices in their schools or districts to determine if a sufficient "goodness of fit" exists between the system and the people who work in it. An absolutely perfect match can never be achieved, but an awareness of serious discrepancies can help supervisors head off major, dysfunctional conflict.

Gareth Morgan's eight different organizational metaphors are designed to help us gain a more complete understanding of the ways in which institutions function. The metaphors are also useful in that they provide some important insights into the assumptions held by others concerning organizational behavior and purpose.

We also reviewed theories of organizational analysis based on *informal* perspectives. The first, Matthew Miles's description of organizational health, focuses on the relative presence of 10 different dimensions including goal focus, communication adequacy, resource utilization, and so forth. We noted that no school is likely ever to possess equally high amounts of each of these characteristics. However, an appreciation of the 10 dimensions can help the proactive supervisor who seeks to engage in ongoing diagnosis of the schools and districts with which he or she normally works.

The second concept reviewed is organizational climate, as first defined by Andrew Halpin and Donald Croft, who suggest that schools have identifiable climates analogous to the personalities of individual human beings. These climates, which range from "open" to "closed," are the products of behaviors demonstrated by two key forces in any school, the teachers and the principal. Again, the overall value of this perspective is that it offers the supervisor one more tool in understanding the complex behaviors and relationships that impact on the effectiveness of schools.

All these perspectives, quite different on the surface, have a few things in common. The first and perhaps most obvious commonality is that all may be used by supervisors to understand succinctly an enormous amount of subtle and complex information about organizational behavior: Formal theory can describe "a lot in a few words." Secondly, all the models avoid the tendency to try to provide complete answers. Each attempts to analyze organizations, but none provides recipes for behavior or action. Finally, none of these models is an absolute unto itself. I present them as but a few examples of frameworks that supervisors might consult as they engage in *proactive* and *analytic*—and therefore *effective*—supervision.

SUGGESTED ACTIVITIES

1. Make use of the constructs in Hage's theory of organizations and prepare a questionnaire to be distributed to the staff of a school to determine their perceptions of the strength of the various structural variables. Distribute the questionnaire in two or three schools.* Are there differences in terms of structure? What about differences in terms of outcomes?

2. Obtain a copy of the Halpin and Croft OCDQ instrument for measuring school climate, or any other similar scale that is used to measure this quality of schools. Administer it in two or more schools to see if there are obvious differences.

3. Using Morgan's organizational metaphors as a guide, interview four or five teachers from your school to see if they reach any consensus regarding the type of organization apparently represented by your school.

REFERENCES

Argyris, Chris. (1965). *Integrating the individual and the organization.* New York: Wiley.

Getzels, Jacob W. (1952). A psycho-sociological framework for the study of educational administration. *Harvard Educational Review, 22,* 235–246.

Getzels, Jacob W., & Guba, Egon G. (1957). Social behavior and the administrative process. *The School Review, 65,* 423–441.

Hage, Gerald. (1965). An axiomatic theory of organizations. *Administrative Science Quarterly, 10*(3), 289–320.

Halpin, Andrew W. (1967). *Theory and research in administration.* New York: Macmillan.

Halpin, Andrew W., & Croft, Donald B. (1963). The organizational climate of schools. *Administrator's Notebook, 11,* 1–2.

Lipham, James M. (1974). *The principalship: Foundations and functions.* New York: Harper & Row.

Miles, Matthew B. (1965). Planned change and organizational health: Figure and ground. *Change processes in the public schools.* Eugene, OR: University of Oregon Center for the Advanced Study of Educational Administration.

Morgan, Gareth. (1986). *Images of organization.* Beverly Hills, CA: Sage.

Owens, Robert. (1987). *Organizational behavior in education* (3rd Ed.). Englewood Cliffs, NJ: Prentice-Hall.

Sergiovanni, Thomas J., & Starratt, Robert J. (1983). *Supervision: Human perspectives* (3rd ed.). New York: McGraw-Hill.

Wynn, Richard, & Guditus, Charles, W. (1984). *Team management: Leadership by consensus.* Columbus, OH: Merrill.

---

* In this or any other activity involving research at one or more schools, make sure you obtain permission from the necessary people before beginning and follow all required procedures.

CHAPTER 6

Leadership

Many would argue that leadership is synonymous with supervision in school settings. The literature is filled with frequently confusing suggestions, as we shall see in Chapter 9, that educational administration is a maintenance of the organizational status quo, whereas supervision involves the bringing about of organizational change. The unfortunate implication is often that supervisors are the "good guys" who "wear the white hats," while administrators block innovation and creativity and are generally anti-progressive. I do not subscribe to this simplistic notion. Rather, *effective proactive supervision is compatible with effective administration.* Good supervisors need highly refined administrative skills, and good school administrators, as noted in Chapter 3, must have excellent supervisory abilities. Leadership, however, is a commodity required of *both* supervisors and administrators. In fact, leadership is a characteristic increasingly required of *all* professional educators—teachers, administrators, and supervisors.

In this chapter, I will attempt to develop a broad view of leadership by first seeking a definition that applies in a variety of contexts and then reviewing theoretical views from both descriptive and normative perspectives. The chapter concludes with an examination of the concept of instructional leadership, an emerging issue that concerns the responsibilities of all practitioners of proactive educational supervision, and with some general comments about the analysis of leadership.

ALTERNATIVE DEFINITIONS

When we talk about how an organization works, we almost invariably talk about leadership. The presence or absence of this characteristic has a strong and direct impact on the effectiveness of an organization. Nevertheless, organizational analysts continually struggle to find a basic definition for the concept of leadership. In this section we will review several alternative definitions in an attempt to determine some basic features that we need to recognize in analyzing leadership in schools.

Gary Yukl pulled together a number of different definitions of leadership in his work on *Leadership in Organizations* (1981):

1. Leadership is "the behavior of an individual when he is directing the activities of a group toward a shared goal" (Hemphill and Coons, 1957, p. 7).
2. Leadership is "interpersonal influence, exercised in a situation, and directed, through the communication process, toward the attainment of a specified goal or goals" (Tannenbaum, Weshler, and Massarik, 1961, p. 24).
3. Leadership is the "initiation and maintenance of structure in expectation and interaction" (Stogdill, 1974, p. 41).
4. Leadership is "an interaction between persons in which one presents information of a sort and in such a manner that the other becomes convinced that his outcome (benefits/cost ratio) will be improved if he behaves in the manner suggested or desired" (Jacobs, 1970, p. 232).
5. Leadership is "a particular type of power relationship characterized by a group member's perceptions that another group member has the right to prescribe behavior patterns for the former regarding his activity as a group member" (Janada, 1960, p. 358).
6. Leadership is "an influence process whereby O's actions change P's behavior and P views the influence attempt as being legitimate and the change as consistent with P's goals" (Kochan, Schmidt, and DeCotiis, 1975, p. 285).
7. Leadership is "the influential increment over and above mechanical compliance with the routine directives of the organization" (Katz and Kahn, 1978, p. 528).

Although these seven definitions represent a wide range of ideas about organizational leadership, they do display some common themes. First, all suggest that the central feature of leadership is an interpersonal relationship where one individual controls, or at least influences, the behavior of another person. Second, most of the definitions suggest that leader behavior implies some sort of change, that leaders promote movement in the organization or in the behaviors of people in the organization.

James Lipham and James Hoeh (1974) provide another definition of leadership that is appealing largely because of its emphasis on the responsibility of a key actor to promote and sustain positive and needed change. For Lipham, leadership is ". . . that behavior of an individual which initiates a new structure in interaction within a social system; it initiates changes in the goals, objectives, configurations, procedures, inputs, processes, and ultimately the outputs of social systems" (p. 196).

Recent research on leadership has emphasized a simple observation: Leaders must have followers. The result of this emphasis has been the analysis of a set of behaviors often described in the literature as "followership." I will not dwell on this concept at this point, but it will be relevant later in the chapter when we talk about the characteristics of effective instructional leaders who "empower" their followers.

Regardless of the definition we choose, we must recognize that leadership is a critical issue both in schools and other organizations. Warren Bennis and Burt Nanus (1985), in their study of leadership behavior in a variety of settings, noted that this issue has particular relevance today for at least three reasons:

1. Organizations are suffering from a "commitment gap": People do not believe in what their organizations stand for because leaders have not developed a sense of belief in their followers.
2. The level of complexity in modern society is higher than it has ever been before. Predictability and stability are characteristics that are virtually absent from most organizations today.
3. Organizational credibility is disappearing. Generally accepted authority figures are being questioned and challenged more often today because so many leaders have disappointed their followers in recent years.

As a result of these observations, Bennis and Nanus suggest that leadership is no longer a simple academic term to be understood by social scientists, but a very real, everyday concept that has meaning for everyone. The proactive educational supervisor has a special interest in learning more about leadership and must develop a genuine and very personal definition of this concept.

DESCRIPTIVE VERSUS NORMATIVE VIEWS

There are two fundamentally different ways in which leadership has been analyzed in recent years. The first of these is *descriptive,* where leadership is defined as a particular set of identifiable, observable behaviors, actions, traits, or characteristics. No effort is made to suggest the correct or appropriate ways in which leaders may achieve or carry out these features. Descriptive views present "what is," not "what ought to be."

The second way of analyzing leadership is *normative,* where an agenda is provided that is intended to shape future behavior and practice. Normative views suggest "what ought to be," or at least how things are likely to appear, given certain changes taking place in the environment. A normative analysis of leadership behavior might define those activities that should be followed for an individual to appear as a certain type of leader, under certain conditions.

Both normative and descriptive perspectives offer insights into leadership helpful to the effective educational supervisor. In the context of our discussion about the development of formal theories in the social sciences in Chapter 4, however, we should note that descriptive theories include only the first two steps in the theory-development cycle (discursive treatment of a topic and simplified listing). Normative theories correspond to the third step in the process, the statement of a juxtaposed taxonomy, because of their emphasis on predictive power. As we noted in Chapter 4, both description and prediction are necessary if the explanatory values of a true theory are to be found.

Before moving into a review of either descriptive or normative theories, we should consider the ways in which leadership has been conceptually developed from an historical frame of reference.

HISTORICAL DEVELOPMENT OF LEADERSHIP

The analysis of leadership in organizations has proceeded through at least four major stages: the "great person"; traitist; situational or sociological; and behavioral.

"Great Person" Approaches

The "great person" perspective is a psychologically based approach that suggests that leadership is determined primarily by the personality of an individual. If we wish to understand what characteristics comprise leadership, then we should look to how a particular individual, or "great person," demonstrated leadership in the past.

One of the most famous practitioners of this theory of leadership was General George Patton, who often determined how to deal with a problem by reviewing what famous historical characters had done under similar circumstances. An avid student of military history, Patton often charted a path for the American army during World War II based on the strategies of Caesar, Hannibal, or other great military leaders. The "great person" approach to leadership analysis is seen more frequently than we might at first assume. Young children, for instance, have long been advised to read the biographies and autobiographies of famous people in order to learn the ways in which such people lived their lives. If you learn about Thomas Edison, Martin Luther King, Helen Keller, or some other famous "great person," the implication is that you would also grow up to be famous, inventive, brave, wise, or whatever.

While this approach to understanding leadership is temptingly simple, it has severe drawbacks that limit its usefulness as a guide to the development of leadership skills. For one thing, we can never find a single "great person" as role model, because the exact circumstances of two lives will never be precisely the same. Reading about the life of Abraham Lincoln does not enable us to follow in his footsteps, because so much of Lincoln's career and behavior was shaped by the conditions in early 19th-century Illinois.

A second limitation of the "great person" view is that the "person" has historically been defined in male terms. The net effect of this sexism has been that women who aspire to leadership roles have been forced, usually in rather subtle ways, to find male role models; they have been trained to "act like a man." Ultimately, this ignores natural differences between ways in which men and women might function most effectively in leadership positions, a major problem identified by Charol Shakeshaft (1987) in her analysis of gender differences in school administration.

Finally, "great person" approaches to leadership limit the creative behavior of present leaders. Instead of asking "What would Caesar have done under these circumstances?" the modern leader might more profitably explore new ways of facing a problem. By relying exclusively on the past behaviors of others for guidance, people in leadership roles will rarely bring about the changes so often needed in dynamic organizations.

Traitist Approaches

The "great person" approach suggests that we study individual leaders; a related view suggests that to understand how leaders behave, we should examine several individuals to determine common characteristics or *traits*. The student of leadership, for example, might note that leaders of successful corporations were generally tall, went to Ivy League universities, and drove big cars. We might then conclude that the way to get to the top of a major company would be to enroll at Yale, buy a Cadillac, and, if possible, grow a few inches (or at least wear elevator shoes)!

Once again, the traitist approach to the study of leadership is appealingly simple and straightforward. It suggests that an educational supervisor who wants to be perceived as an effective leader might constructively spend time finding out which of his or her predecessors were viewed as effective, and then identifying traits found in all those individuals so that they might be copied. While the realization that "dressing for success" does sometimes produce an executive and thus may make trait analyses seem like reasonable strategies, there are some obvious drawbacks.

For one thing, traits analyzed in this approach are frequently characteristics over which we have little control, as in the example above. A follower cannot, of course, suddenly become tall. Additionally, there is a danger in generalizing widely from limited examples. The lives of Abraham Lincoln and Lyndon Johnson might reinforce the notion that physical height has a relationship to leadership ability, but how then do we explain the abilities of Napoleon in both the military and the political spheres?

Finally, traitist leadership approaches are restrictive because of the several biases that past leadership reflects. If we were to select school principals or superintendents on the basis of traits common to past holders of these positions, we would limit our search to white, married males who had previously been coaches. The fact that the majority of present school administrators possess several of these same traits is probably testimony to the popularity of the traitist perspective. Popularity, however, is no excuse for the maintenance of a delimiting practice.

Situational Approaches

In sharp contrast to the "great person" and traitist approaches that emphasize psychological characteristics in the study of leadership, the *situational* or *sociological* approach maintains that leadership is determined less by the characteristics of individuals than by the requirements of the group or the setting in which the individual works. According to this view, acts of leadership are the direct result of situations that arise in groups or organizations that call for those acts. Thus, an individual's exercise of leadership is brought about by the demands of the group with which that individual must interact. Hemphill (1949) conducted a comprehensive sociological study of the impact of leaders according to differences among groups. He found such variables as viscidity (the feeling of cohesion in a group), hedonic tone (the degree of satisfaction of group members), size of the groups, homogeneity of group members, and intimacy among the group to correlate significantly with leadership effectiveness. Inevitably, however, researchers realized that if the study of leadership focused purely on such situationally specific issues as how particular groups react to particular individuals, then the study of leadership, per se, would end.

A good example of situational leadership analysis is found in the actions of the World War I hero, Sergeant Alvin York. York would probably never have been recognized in history and would have remained a poor Tennessee farmer if the war had not happened when it did so that he could enlist in the army and then be in the right place at precisely the right time to capture more German prisoners of war than any other soldier. The clear limitation on this theory that situation alone creates leadership is that it ignores almost completely the individual's characteristics as a leader. Alvin York would not have been a military hero without World War I, but his leadership potential might have been realized in some other field. We have no way of knowing.

Behavioral Approaches

The most recent approach to the analysis of leadership examines the *behavior* of the leader and balances elements of both the psychological ("great person" and traitist) and the situational approaches. This perspective, reflected in Lipham's definition cited earlier, recognizes that a leader's behavior is the result of a complex blend of both personal characteristics and the situation in which the leader must act. The basic assumptions of this belief, which currently dominates the field of leadership analysis, are these:

1. People behave according to specific behavioral styles. This occurs because people differ in how they perceive a situation, work at the accomplishment of tasks, interact with others, and make decisions.
2. People behave differently depending on the contextual circumstances. Consequently, it can be said that behavior changes.
3. There is no single "right way" for people to behave, but most people have a primary operating style that is most common and comfortable for them.
4. What is comfortable and "right" for one person might feel uncomfortable and "wrong" to another.
5. An organization functions best when it capitalizes on the strengths of each individual, encouraging the recognition and celebration of differences.

The predominant perspective of leadership today, then, holds that each person has a basic style that needs to be understood and appreciated. Such styles are determined by a wide array of individual psychological characteristics in interaction with features of the environment. This behavioral approach underlies most popular *descriptive* and *normative* theories of leadership.

Additional Issues

No matter what approach we use to analyze leadership, we must also consider certain basic issues including locus, frequency, potency, and scope of leadership. The *locus* of leadership is the social system in which leadership occurs—be it classroom, school, school district, or entire community. The *frequency* of leadership, or how often a leader engages in certain behaviors, is also important. On the one hand, leaders may attempt too many acts of leadership too often without actually implementing, evaluating, or achieving effective outcomes. On the other hand, some people in leadership positions may rarely engage in any active leadership attempts at all. There is no consensus as to what constitutes the optimal balance between "too frequent" and "not often enough." *Potency* refers to "the extent to which an initiated change by a leader represents significant departure from that which exists, i.e., the magnitude of an initiated change" (Lipham and Hoeh, 1974, p. 186). Finally, *scope* or range of leadership is significant. Leadership may be functionally diverse or functionally specific; some leaders have undefined and virtually unlimited responsibilities and obligations, whereas for others, the obligations, breadth, and depth of the leadership role are limited and functions circumscribed.

ALTERNATIVE DESCRIPTIVE MODELS

Three descriptive leadership models that have significantly influenced current research and are based on behavioral terms are those developed by Halpin and Winer (1957), Bowers and Seashore (1966), and House (1973).

Halpin and Winer

According to these two researchers, a leader's behavior is composed of two basic dimensions, *initiating structure* and *consideration.* These two concepts reflect Getzels's nomothetic and idiographic dimensions (see Chapter 5). Andrew Halpin (1957) defines them in the following ways:

1. *Initiating Structure:* Behavior that delineates the relationship between the leader and members of the work group, and endeavors to establish well-defined patterns of organization, channels of communication, and methods of procedure.
2. *Consideration:* Behavior that indicates friendship, mutual trust, respect, and warmth in the relationship between the leader and the staff.

Bowers and Seashore

These researchers suggest that leadership behavior consists of goal emphasis, work facilitation, support, and interaction facilitation. These four dimensions are defined as follows:

1. *Goal Emphasis:* Behavior that stimulates enthusiasm for meeting the group's goals or achieving excellent performance.
2. *Work Facilitation:* Behavior that helps goal attainment by scheduling, planning, and coordinating.
3. *Support:* Behavior that enhances someone else's feelings of personal worth and importance.
4. *Interaction Facilitation:* Behavior that encourages members of the group to develop close, mutually satisfying relationships.

House

Robert House used three terms derived largely from the work of Halpin and Winer for describing leadership behavior: instrumental, supportive, and participative behavior. They are defined as follows:

1. *Instrumental Leadership:* Behavior that delineates the relationship between the leader and members of the work group and attempts clearly to define patterns of the organization without autocratic or punitive control.
2. *Supportive Leadership:* Behavior that indicates friendship and warmth toward the work group by the leader.
3. *Participative Leadership:* Behavior that allows subordinates to influence decisions by asking for suggestions and including the subordinates in the decision-making process.

Table 6.1 suggests some obvious similarities among these three theoretical perspectives in the ways that leadership behavior in organizations is described. Subtle distinctions can also be found in the individual component dimensions suggested in each model, but the overlap is significant.

Each of these theoretical models of leadership can help us understand some of the basic characteristics of leadership behavior. All are descriptive in nature, however, and therefore somewhat limited because they only present ways of stating what can be observed concerning leadership. Of greater value to the practicing educational supervisor or administrator are normative perspectives of leadership behavior, three of which we consider in the following section.

ALTERNATIVE NORMATIVE MODELS

The three analyses presented below extend the basic descriptions of leadership behavior so that they may be used to predict more or less desirable ways in which people "ought" to behave. These three views are the Managerial Grid® of Blake and Mouton (Figure 6.1), Reddin's 3-D Theory of Leadership, and the Behavior Matrix developed by the Northwest Regional Laboratory for Educational Development.

Managerial Grid

As is true of most conceptualizations of leadership, the Managerial Grid model of Robert Blake and Jane Mouton (1964) suggests that leadership consists of two behavioral dimensions: a concern for people, or interpersonal relationships; and a concern for tasks, production, or things. Blake and Mouton's Managerial Grid, depicted in Figure 6.1, particularly resembles Halpin and Winer's two-dimensional leadership theory.

92

TABLE 6.1. THREE DESCRIPTIVE THEORIES OF LEADERSHIP SHOWING THE
COMPARABILITY OF THEIR COMPONENT DIMENSIONS.

Halpin and Winer	Bowers and Seashore	House
1. Initiating Structure	1. Goal Emphasis	1. Instrumental
2. Consideration	2. Work Facilitation	2. Supportive
	3. Support	3. Participative
	4. Interaction Facilitation	

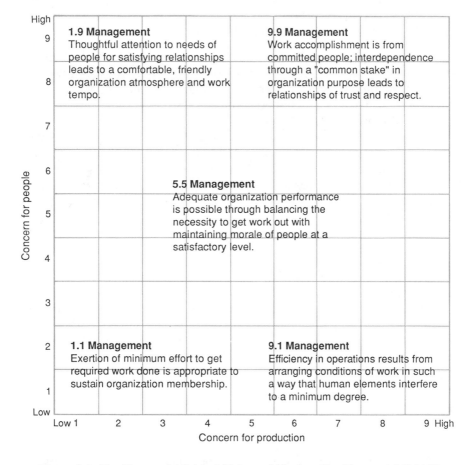

Figure 6.1. The Managerial Grid of Blake and Mouton. *The Managerial Grid III: The Key to Leadership Excellence,* by Robert R. Blake and Jane Srygley Mouton. Houston: Gulf Publishing Company, Copyright © 1985, page 12. Reproduced by permision.

The Managerial Grid allows us to analyze leadership behavior in terms of both concern for people and concern for product, on a continuum of 1 (low) to 9 (high). According to Robert Owens (1987), Blake and Mouton make clear that 9, 9 (high in both concerns) is the leadership behavior pattern likely to be most effective in most organizations to achieve the best results.

> "Results" means the effectiveness of the organization in (1) achieving its goals and (2) maintaining a high level of morale. Goal achievement might be measured by such indicators (in schools) as test scores, rate of dropouts, percent of graduates going on to further education, employee-management relations, community support for bond issues, and feedback from employees on the performance of graduates. Morale may be indicated by such things as absenteeism, number of grievances, employee-management relations, and cohesiveness of the group. (Owens, 1987, p. 134)

The Managerial Grid model does not simply provide more terms to describe leadership behaviors; rather, its implications about the relative effectiveness of certain behaviors provide useful directions for any individual seeking to perform as an effective educational leader. A grid rating of 1, 1, for instance, would hardly be an appropriate pattern of behavior for a supervisor or administrator called upon to provide direction to a school staff. A 9, 9 rating, on the other hand—where equivalent emphasis is placed both on the needs of teachers, students, and staff, and on school outcomes—would be optimal. Variations on this most desirable level are likely, of course; a supervisor who is a proponent of the human relations ("Warm Fuzzies") philosophy would probably come closer to a 9, 1 behavior rating (high concern for people, low concern for production), while a supervisor who believes in scientific management ("Superstition") might achieve something closer to a 1, 9 (low concern for people but high concern for production).

The Managerial Grid is widely used in both public and private management circles not only as a diagnostic, descriptive device to help individuals understand their behavior, but also as a way to appreciate places where one set of behaviors may be more or less appropriate than others.

Reddin's 3-D Theory of Leadership

The normative 3-D Theory of Leadership developed by W. J. Reddin (1970) goes a step beyond the Managerial Grid, yet builds on the same basic logic (concern for people versus concern for tasks). The major distinction between Reddin's view and the Managerial Grid is that, at its most basic level, Reddin's model does not suggest that any one single combination of behaviors is necessarily better than any other combination. Figure 6.2 demonstrates Reddin's basic model, which simply provides descriptive classification in four quadrants: *Separated* (low in concern for people and task), *Related* (high in concern for people, low in task orientation), *Dedicated* (low in concern for people, high in task orientation), *Integrated* (high in concern for people and

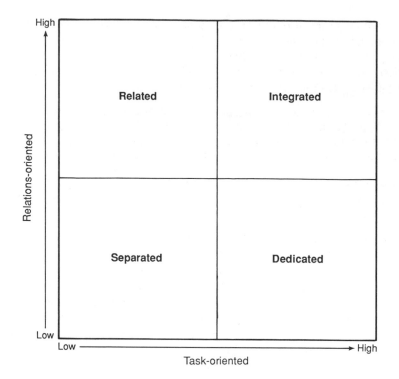

Figure 6.2. Basic model of Reddin's 3-D Theory of Leadership.

task). The critical point to remember is that, at this basic stage, Reddin's quadrants are purely descriptive; none is better or worse than any other.

Reddin's theory becomes normative, however, when it goes on to suggest that the basic four behaviors are more or less appropriate *depending upon the unique characteristics of the situation* that exists in the leader's organization. As the model in Figure 6.3 suggests, for example, the leader who demonstrates an "Integrated" style might appear to be inappropriately compromising in some circumstances; in other situations, the "high in concern for both people and task" style might be perceived as truly "Executive." The "Separated" leader (low in concern for people and tasks), viewed as disconnected and a "Deserter" in some situations, might be an effective and organizationally needed "Bureaucrat" in other cases. Sergiovanni and Starratt (1983) summarize the overall value of Reddin's 3-D Theory of Leadership in the following way:

> Af first glance the theory seems complex and the labels chosen by Reddin confusing and on occasion inappropriate. But the language system is worth deciphering, for the concepts and ideas basic to the theory are powerful and important. A key to this theory is the notion that the *same style* expressed in different situations may be effective or ineffective. (p. 183)

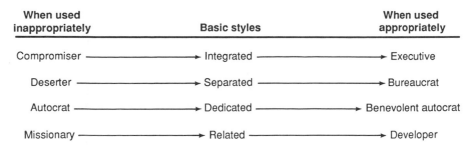

When used inappropriately	Basic styles	When used appropriately
Compromiser	Integrated	Executive
Deserter	Separated	Bureaucrat
Autocrat	Dedicated	Benevolent autocrat
Missionary	Related	Developer

Figure 6.3. Effective and ineffective expressions of leadership style according to Reddin's 3-D Theory of Leadership.

The basic problem with Reddin's theory is that "appropriate" and "inappropriate" situations are not clearly defined. Nevertheless, Reddin's view of effective leadership behavior as a dynamic and situational, rather than static, phenomenon is important.

Behavior Matrix

The final normative view of leadership behavior that we will consider is the Leadership Behavioral Matrix developed by researchers at the Northwest Regional Laboratory for Educational Development in Portland, Oregon, which again suggests that two dimensions comprise leadership behavior. The major difference between this perspective and the ones we have reviewed above is that the Northwest Laboratory Matrix suggests that a person is *either* task-oriented *or* people-oriented, and *either* introverted or extroverted in terms of how he or she works with others. Figure 6.4 depicts the basic Leadership Matrix model, which classifies the behavior of an individual according to four distinct styles

1. *Promoters* (Extroverted and people-oriented, these individuals get involved with others in active, rapidly changing situations. They are typically outgoing and friendly and can get things going, but may settle for less than the best results. Promoters are highly competitive.)
2. *Supporters* (Introverted, people-oriented types who value interpersonal relations, these individuals try to minimize conflict and promote the happiness of others.)
3. *Analyzers* (Introverted, task-oriented people who are problem solvers and like to have all the data before making a decision. Thus, some people get frustrated with their slow decision making.)
4. *Controllers* (Extroverted and task-oriented individuals who love to run things and have jobs done in their own way. These people will make sure the task is completed on time and to their satisfaction.)

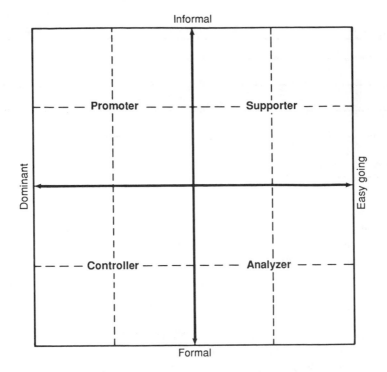

Figure 6.4. Leadership Behavioral Matrix. (Northwest Regional Educational Laboratory. Portland, Oregon. Reprinted by permission of the publisher.)

The critical observation in this description of leadership behaviors is that no one style is better than the others; there are no "right" or "wrong" styles. Individuals in each of the four quadrants of the Behavior Matrix have strengths and weaknesses that may be called upon in different situations to create more effective organizational outcome.

The Leadership Behavior Matrix is particularly useful in analyzing potential conflicts, which are most apt to occur along the diagonals of the quadrants depicted in Figure 6.4. Thus, the most powerful conflicts tend to take place between promoters and analyzers, and between controllers and supporters. Consider, for example, the possibility of conflict between a patient, thoughtful analyzer who wants more and more facts before acting, and the more impulsive promoter. Moreover, the action-oriented controller will no doubt have a difficult time dealing with the more laid-back supporter. Conflicts are clearly going to take place in schools where all of these various behavioral styles are represented, and they will be increasingly visible and powerful as people become more wedded to the predominant behavioral characteristics of a particular quadrant. More extreme promoters will probably have even more direct problems in dealing with more extreme analyzers.

The Behavior Matrix, like Blake and Mouton's Managerial Grid and Reddin's 3-D Theory of Leadership, is a behaviorally based, normative model of leadership analysis. All three, properly understood, can provide direction and guidance for effective supervisory leadership practices.

In the next section of this chapter we will consider the ways in which behavioral views of leadership have been applied to school settings by looking at the concept of instructional leadership.

EMERGING ISSUE: INSTRUCTIONAL LEADERSHIP

In recent years discussions of leadership in the context of educational organizations have built upon the behavioral theories of leadership that we have reviewed here. Increasingly, educators have recognized the importance of supervisory and administrative personnel as key determinants of the overall effectiveness of schools (Austin, 1979; Brookover and Lezotte, 1980; Lipham, 1981) and have made repeated attempts to isolate and define a particular type of leadership behavior unique to schools. The label generally attached to that behavior is "instructional leadership."

Despite the amount of discussion about, as well as support for, the concept of instructional leadership, little has been done to define that concept operationally. Few studies have been undertaken to determine the specific behaviors of supervisors or administrators who serve as instructional leaders. Early efforts tended to define leadership behavior in very narrow terms. As a result, most early descriptions focused only on the ways in which school principals became directly involved with instructional activities, and the perception grew that only those principals who spent nearly all of their time either teaching classes or observing teachers were legitimately serving as instructional leaders. This narrow view has more recently been rejected for at least two reasons. First, we now recognize that individuals other than principals (e.g., supervisors, superintendents, or department chairs) might indeed engage in instructional leadership behaviors. Second, we have increasingly realized that instructional leadership can take forms that go well beyond direct intervention in classroom activities. The definition of instructional leadership suggested by Liu (1984) is useful in describing this concept:

> Instructional leadership consists of direct or indirect behaviors that significantly affect teacher instruction and, as a result, student learning. (p. 33)

Liu divides the tasks of instructional behavior leadership into two categories—direct and indirect. In very broad terms, we might classify direct leadership activities as staff development and teacher supervision and evaluation, and indirect leadership as instructional facilitation, resource acquisition and building maintenance, and student problem resolution. Examples of specific behaviors related to each of these broad categories are shown in the following list.

Factor I: Staff Development

Work with a committee to plan and implement the staff development program.

Survey staff members to determine topics and activities for a year-long staff development plan.

Provide inservice training for the support staff on how their roles relate to the instructional program.

Factor II: Resource Acquisition and Building Maintenance

Maintain the building in order to provide a pleasant working condition for students and staff.

Acquire adequate resources for teaching.

Allocate resources on the basis of identified needs according to a priority ranking.

Factor III: Instructional Facilitation

Establish priorities so that, by the amount of time devoted to it, instruction is always first.

Work according to the belief that all students can learn and achieve at high levels.

Support teachers who are implementing new ideas.

Factor IV: Teacher Supervision and Evaluation

Involve staff members and people from the community in setting clear goals and objectives for instruction.

Work according to the belief that all teachers can teach and teach well.

Have conferences with individual teachers to review their instructional plans.

Factor V: Student Problem Resolution

Assist teachers in dealing with discipline problems.

Enforce school attendance policies to reduce tardiness and absentee rates.

Interact directly with students to discuss their problems about school.

Using these classifications and descriptions of instructional leadership behaviors, Liu studied two groups of high school principals, one "effective" and another "not effective." He found that the effective group engaged in instructional leadership behaviors more often than the other group, and that those behaviors reflected both direct and indirect instructional leadership. As a result, we now recognize that the analysis of instructional leadership behavior is considerably more complex than first thought, and that supervisors and administrators who strive to exhibit instructional leadership must be prepared to engage in a wide range of activities that support the instructional priorities of the school. We suspect, then, that instructional leadership is as much a product of a personalized educational philosophy as it is of any particular activities that a person follows.

One of the most comprehensive recent efforts to gain a better understanding of what behaviors comprise instructional leadership was carried out by the Association for Supervision and Curriculum Development (ASCD), which looked at the work of numerous principals (elementary, middle, junior, and senior high school levels) who had been identified as instructional leaders. Five behavioral patterns were identified in those individuals who were viewed as effective leaders:

1. *They provide a sense of vision to their schools:* They demonstrate the ability to articulate what a school is supposed to do, particularly in terms of what it should do to benefit children. Effective instructional leaders leave little doubt that the purpose of the school is to find ways in which children may learn successfully. This vision, or mission, guides all other actions.

2. *They engage in participative management:* They encourage a better organizational climate in the school by allowing teachers and staff to participate meaningfully in real decision making, and not merely in an effort to "play at" getting people to be involved when decisions are already made. The staff senses greater ownership in the priorities and programs that are available to help children.

3. *They provide support for instruction:* Instructional leaders are so committed to maintaining quality instruction as their primary organizational focus that when decisions must be made concerning priorities, instruction always comes first. These individuals make it clear to all around them that energy will be expended to assure that resources are available to enable the instructional program of the school to proceed unabated.

4. *Instructional leaders monitor instruction:* They know what is going on in the classrooms of their schools. This monitoring may take several forms, from direct in-class intensive observation to merely walking around the building and talking with students. The critical issue, regardless of the particular procedures followed, is that instructional leaders are aware of the quality of instruction being carried out in their schools.

5. *They are resourceful:* Instructional leaders rarely allow circumstances in their organizations to get in the way of their vision for

quality educational programs. As a result, they tend not to allow the lack of resources, or apparently prohibitive school or district policies, or any other factors from interfering with their goals for their schools.

Instructional leaders carry out these five behavior patterns very differently. Thus, people with different personalities and philosophies, values, and attitudes can be equally effective as educational leaders. In addition, entirely different schools can serve as settings for instructional leadership of the type identified through the ASCD work.

Effective school leaders share many behavioral patterns, predictably, with leaders in other organizations. Bennis and Nanus (1985), in a study of a wide variety of effective organizations, discovered five strategies followed by successful leaders:

1. *Strategy I: Attention through vision:* Leaders create a focus in an organization, or an agenda that demonstrates an unparalleled concern for outcomes, products, and results.
2. *Strategy II: Meaning through communication:* Effective communication is inseparable from effective leadership.
3. *Strategy III: Trust through positioning:* Leaders must be trusted in order to be effective; we trust people who are predictable, and whose positions are known. Leaders who are trusted make themselves known and make their positions clear.
4. *Strategy IV: The deployment of self through positive self-regard:* Leaders have positive self-images, self-regard that is not self-centered, and they know their worth. In general, they are confident without being cocky.
5. *Strategy V: The deployment of self through the "Wallenda Factor":* Before his death, the famous aerialist Karl Wallenda was said to have become more preoccupied with not failing than with succeeding. Leaders are able consistently to focus their energies on success rather than on simply avoiding failure.

Other researchers have created other lists of successful leadership behaviors parallel to these efforts by Bennis and Nanus, ASCD, and Liu. Such lists typically feature considerable overlap with what we have reviewed here. What is highly significant about all of these efforts is that they represent attempts to move the study of leadership to levels of analysis not found in most past treatments. For educational supervisors, this is good news. It offers the possibility that specific, effective leadership behaviors may now be identified in greater numbers than they were in the past. While such efforts should never be viewed as gospel to be followed for leadership, or panaceas to cure the absence of direction often found in schools, they do provide practitioners with a rough road map to follow in the search for more effective educational programs.

GENERAL COMMENTS ABOUT LEADERSHIP

While I have tried to present an ordered view of the nature of leadership as it has been analyzed in school settings, I have only scratched the surface of a very complex topic. The search for precise understanding of what contributes to effective organizational leadership has been at the center of virtually every analysis of organizations ever conducted. People always have been and will continue to be absolutely fascinated with determining "Who leads?" and "How do they do it?" People will always try to put into some kind of order the notions that they have about leadership.

Researchers have only gotten a very brief glimpse into what takes place in leadership to this point. Many facets of this critical topic have not yet been explored. For example, researchers have tended to look almost exclusively at leadership behavior as demonstrated by those who have formal leadership titles in schools and other organizations. The roles of principals, supervisors, and superintendents have been examined, to the virtual exclusion of the study of others who clearly are leaders, but do not have titles. As anyone who has ever worked in or around schools will easily recognize, leadership is *not* the exclusive property of the administrators, and anyone who assumes that it is could be making a terrible error in judgment. A second area where more research is needed is the phenomenon of "followership," and the nature of the dynamic relationships that occur between leaders and others in their organizations. The concept of "transformative leadership" (energy directed toward enabling others to sustain needed change), first described by James McGregor Burns (1978) and expanded into an emphasis on empowerment by Bennis and Nanus (1985), appears to hold promise for increasing our understanding of how leaders interact with others. Leaders must have followers, and interest must be directed toward that fact.

Finally, any discussion of leadership typically includes some views that Bennis and Nanus call the "myths of leadership." We will conclude this analysis of leadership as a formal theory domain in the social sciences by listing these myths and noting why they should not be viewed as limitations.

> *Myth 1. Leadership is a rare skill.* (In fact, virtually everyone has some leadership potential, and opportunities are great for many people to assume formal and informal leadership roles in a variety of settings.)
>
> *Myth 2. Leaders are born, not made.* (As we noted when we looked at the "great person" approaches to leadership, the major capacities and competencies of leadership can indeed be learned if there is a basic

desire to learn them. Acquiring the knowledge and skills for effective leadership is not necessarily easy, but most people have the fundamental capacity to become powerful leaders.)

Myth 3. Leaders are charismatic. (Most leaders are quite human, and they rarely possess any magic talents that are unavailable to the rest of us. In fact, some evidence indicates that what we call charisma is the *result* of leadership, not the reverse. Good leaders often gain respect and admiration from their followers because of the ways in which they demonstrate leadership qualities.)

Myth 4. Leadership exists only at the top of an organization. (As we noted in the ASCD review of instructional leadership behaviors, successful leaders actively strive to increase opportunities for staff members to take leadership roles in schools through conscious efforts at participative management schemes. Leaders are not threatened by allowing others to have some control over the organization.)

Myth 5. The leader controls, directs, prods, and manipulates. (Leadership is not the exercise of absolute power, but rather the empowerment of others to make use of their full potential. As a result, any effort at control for its own sake might not be an activity of leadership at all, but rather an effort to dominate. Ultimately, organizations that are faced with this type of strangling behavior will either cast out the leader or simply die as organizations.)

SUMMARY

In this chapter we have reviewed a second theory base typically associated with the analysis of educational supervision, that of leadership. Leadership is often referred to as the single most important area to be developed by anyone interested in pursuing a school supervisory or administrative role. Supervisors can be neither proactive nor effective without considering some of the basic issues of leadership theory presented in this chapter.

We looked first at a variety of definitions of leadership found in the literature and settled on Lipham's view because of its emphasis on leadership as a *behavioral* process that focuses on change and on the development of *interaction* patterns with other actors in the leader's environment. We reviewed the basic differences between *descriptive* and *normative* conceptualizations of leadership—a rather subtle shift in recent years from efforts to describe *what* leadership is to attempts to tell people *how* to behave as leaders.

In the next section we considered four historical frameworks for the analysis of leadership, including the *"great person", traitist, situational* or *sociological,* and the current *behavioral* approaches. We noted the major limitations for each of the first three approaches and suggested why most present efforts to explain leadership make use of the behavioral perspective, which emphasizes the relationships that exist between individual characteristics and the context in which people work.

Next we considered several popular theories of leadership analysis: the *descriptive* theories of Halpin, Bowers and Seashore, and House; and *normative* perspectives represented by the Managerial Grid of Blake and Mouton, Reddin's 3-D Theory of Leadership, and the Behavioral Matrix developed by the Northwest Regional Laboratory for Educational Development. We reviewed the increasingly popular concept of instructional leadership and the strong parallel between educational leadership of this kind and the behavior of effective leaders in other types of organizations.

The chapter concluded with some general comments and observations on the nature of the complex phenomenon of leadership in schools.

SUGGESTED ACTIVITIES

1. Interview a group of teachers to determine their perceptions of what leadership should be. Compare the definitions that are presented with the alternative perspectives of leadership that are discussed in this chapter.
2. Using the listing of "leadership myths" that were described by Bennis and Nanus, compose a rating scale that may be used to collect data concerning perceptions of whether people agree or disagree with each of the stated "myths."
3. Talk with people who are not in professional education to determine their perceptions of what "leadership" is. Again, compare their statements with the "great person," traitist, situational, and behavioral perspectives.
4. Interview at least five practicing school administrators or supervisors to determine their personal definitions of "instructional leadership." How successful do these individuals feel about actually engaging in behaviors that are part of their definitions? What prohibits people from serving as instructional leaders? What contributes to their ability to serve in this capacity?

REFERENCES

Austin, G. R. (1979, October). Exemplary schools and the search for effectiveness. *Educational Leadership, 35*(1), 10–14.

Bennis, Warren, & Nanus, Burt. (1985). *Leaders: The strategies for taking charge.* New York: Harper & Row.

Blake, Robert R., & Mouton, Jane S. (1964). *The managerial grid.* Houston, TX: Scientific Methods.

Bowers, D. G., & Seashore, S. E. (1966). Predicting organizational effectiveness with a four-factor theory of leadership. *Administrative Science Quarterly, 11*(2), 238–263.

Brookover, W. B., & Lezotte, L. (1980). *Changes in school characteristics coincident with changes in student achievement*. East Lansing: Michigan State University, College of Urban Development.

Burns, James MacGregor. (1978). *Leadership*. New York: Harper & Row.

Halpin, Andrew W. (1957). A paradigm for research on administrative behavior. In R. F. Campbell & Russell T. Gregg (Eds.), *Administrative behavior in education*. Chicago: University of Chicago, Midwest Administrative Center.

Halpin, Andrew W., & Winer, J. A. (1957). A factorial study of the Leadership Behavior Description Questionnaire. In R. M. Stogdill & A. E. Coons (Eds.), *Leader behavior: Its description and measurement* (Research Monograph Series No. 88). Columbus: The Ohio State University, Bureau of Business Research.

Hemphill, John K. (1949). *Situational factors in leadership*. Columbus: The Ohio State University Press.

Hemphill, John K., & Coons, A. E. (1957). Development of the leader behavior description questionnaire. In R. M. Stogdill & A. E. Coons (Eds.) *Leader behavior: Its description and measurement*. (Research Monograph Series No. 88). Columbus: The Ohio State University, Bureau of Business Research.

House, Robert J. (1973). A path-goal theory of leader effectiveness. In W. E. Scott, Jr., & L. L. Cummings (Eds.), *Readings in organizational behavior and human performance*. Homewood, IL: Irwin.

Jacobs, T. O. (1970). *Leadership and exchange in formal organizations*. Alexandria, VA: Human Resources Research Corporation.

Janada, K. F. (1960). Toward the explication of the concept of leadership in terms of the concept of power. *Human Relations, 13,* 345–363.

Katz, D., & Kahn, R. L. (1978). *The social psychology of organizations* (2nd ed.). New York: Wiley.

Kochan, T. A., Schmidt, S. S., & DeCotiis, T. A. (1975). Superior-subordinate relations: Leadership and headship. *Human Relations, 28,* 279–294.

Lipham, J. M., & Hoeh, J. A. (1974). *The principalship: Foundations and functions*. New York: Harper & Row.

Lipham, James M. (1981). *Effective principal, effective school*. Reston, VA: National Association of Secondary School Principals.

Liu, Ching-Jen. (1984). An Identification of Principals' Instructional Leadership in Effective High Schools. Unpublished Ed.D. Dissertation, University of Cincinnati.

Owens, Robert. (1987). *Organizational behavior in education* (3rd ed.). Englewood Cliffs, NJ: Prentice-Hall.

Reddin, W. J. (1970). *Managerial effectiveness*. New York: McGraw-Hill

Sergiovanni, Thomas J., & Starratt, Robert. (1983). *Supervision: Human perspectives* (3rd ed.). New York: McGraw-Hill.

Shakeshaft, Charol. (1987). *Women in educational administration*. Beverly Hills, CA: Sage.

Stogdill, Ralph M. (1974). *Handbook of leadership: A survey of theory and research*. New York: Free Press.

Tannenbaum, R., Weschler, I. R., & Massarik, F. (1961). *Leadership and organization*. New York: McGraw-Hill.

Yukl, Gary A. (1981). *Leadership in organizations*. Englewood Cliffs, NJ: Prentice-Hall.

CHAPTER 7

Motivation

Regardless of how individual practitioners of supervision look at their work (i.e., as "inspectors," or disciples of human relations, for example), and regardless of whether they subscribe to the assumptions and practices of the proactive supervisory process, a key supervisory responsibility is inevitably the fostering of employee *motivation*. In this chapter we will consider a number of alternative theoretical views of organizational motivation. As we have done in previous chapters, we will first provide a definition of motivation and an overview of differing conceptual perspectives of motivation. The chapter concludes with a brief discussion of the relationship among the personal philosophy of education developed by an individual to guide professional supervisory behavior, the implementation of proactive supervisory processes, and employee motivation.

DEFINITION OF MOTIVATION

Motivation is one of the most important and challenging supervisory responsibilities undertaken in schools or any other organization. Unlike the concepts we explored in earlier chapters, however, motivation can be defined in a relatively simple and satisfactory way. Lovell and Wiles (1983) defined motivation as "the level of effort an individual is willing to expend toward the achievement of a certain goal" (p. 50). In attempting to motivate other people, we essentially must look for answers to the following three questions, which have been faced by managers, supervisors, and administrators in many different types of organizations throughout recent history:

105

1. What makes some people work hard, while other people hardly work at all (or, at least, work as little as possible)?
2. How can certain people—educational supervisors, for example— positively influence the performance of the people who work for them?
3. Why do some people leave organizations, show up late for work, refuse to be committed, or generally "tune out" of their job responsibilities, while other people tend to get to work early, stay late, and engage in all types of behavior indicative of a strong commitment to their labor and "go the extra mile"?

Each of these questions is a legitimate aspect of the overall issue of how to increase human motivation. Clearly, there are no "perfect" answers to all, or perhaps even to any of these three questions. There is no way to ensure commitment by *all* employees *all* the time. Neither is there a way to guarantee that any single employee will remain highly motivated and committed at all times. The search goes on, however, for the most appropriate motivational techniques. Several theoretical perspectives have been offered over time to aid in this search.

ALTERNATIVE CONCEPTUALIZATIONS OF MOTIVATION

Recent studies of motivation have looked at this important supervisory issue from at least four alternative conceptualizations. The basic assumptions and features of each of these conceptualizations will be reviewed in the following sections.

Need-Satisfaction Theories of Motivation

If any one perspective can legitimately be called predominant, *need theory* probably comes the closest. The theorists most closely associated with this perspective are Abraham Maslow and Frederick Herzberg, each of whom has developed a slightly different scheme for analyzing motivation in organizations.

Maslow's Theory of a Hierarchy of Needs. The basic assumptions underlying Abraham Maslow's *Motivation and Personality* (1970) are familiar to many of us. One primary belief is that people are motivated by their individual needs to address certain natural concerns. These concerns, in turn, can be rank-ordered hierarchically in terms of potency.

We need to recognize two important premises in order to understand

Maslow's perspective more completely: First, human beings are best defined and understood as "wanting creatures" who are motivated by a consistent desire to satisfy certain needs; and second, individuals pursue needs in a linear, sequential progression according to the following levels of intensity and potency:

1. *Physiological needs* (most basic human needs such as hunger, thirst, and shelter).
2. *Safety needs* (the desire to find a safe and secure physical environment).
3. *Belongingness needs* (an individual's desire to be accepted by his or her peers).
4. *Esteem needs* (the desire to have a positive self-image and to receive recognition from others).
5. *Self-actualization needs* (the concern for the development of full individual potential).

Figure 7.1 represents the hierarchical relationship of these needs.

The key concept in Maslow's model is that the needs indicated in the pyramid must be achieved in a hierarchical fashion. Individuals will not be motivated toward a higher level of concern and performance until lower needs are satisfied. If they are not, tension, rather than a positive sense of motivation, is created within individuals. There is little sense in trying to motivate people by focusing on esteem (professional recognition) while they are hungry or apprehensive about being accepted by peers.

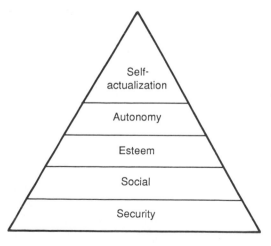

Figure 7.1. Pyramid depicting the hierarchical nature of human needs according to Maslow.

Herzberg's Need-Satisfaction Theory of Motivation. The research done by the psychologist Frederick Herzberg is based largely on the same assumption about needs-satisfaction promoted by Maslow. In some ways, in fact, Herzberg's motivation theory (Herzberg, 1966) represents a natural refinement of Maslow's basic hierarchical framework.

Two major premises or assumptions serve as the basis of Herzberg's theory:

1. "Hygiene factors" are those job-related elements that can reduce satisfaction. These factors cannot, in themselves, motivate a worker; they can only *prevent dissatisfaction.* Hygiene factors are generally defined as those tangible elements such as wages, fringe benefits, and working conditions (see the list below). When an employee's pay is low, for instance, he or she will probably be dissatisfied; raising the pay, however, will not necessarily raise satisfaction (and therefore motivation) proportionately.

2. "Motivators" are factors whose presence in a worker's life leads to satisfaction, but whose absence does not necessarily lead to dissatisfaction. Among these are achievement, recognition, responsibility, and advancement.

Hygiene Factors
1. Work environment (organizational climate and physical conditions)
2. Type of supervision
3. Salary and fringe benefits
4. Job security
5. Attitudes and policies of the administration
6. Status

Motivators
1. Achievement
2. Advancement
3. Characteristics of the work itself
4. Growth (personal and professional)
5. Responsibility
6. Recognition

If Herzberg's theory is correct, then, it implies that such things as salary increases and improvement of fringe benefits must not be ignored, but that increasing pay or the quality of insurance plans will not *in itself* motivate employees to excel in their work.

Critique of Need-Satisfaction Theories. Three basic criticisms have tended to follow the work of both Maslow and Herzberg and their views of human motivation. First, critics suggest that both Maslow and Herzberg suffer from problems of definition that result in poor predictive power for their theories. A classic question, asked particularly of Maslow, is, "What is 'self-actualization'?" If we cannot define the term, how can we determine if a person has attained this level? How can we even direct our behavior toward attaining it? It is relatively simple to appreciate the attainment of lower-level goals such as those associated with physiological and safety needs. Higher-order needs such as esteem and self-actualization, on the other hand, are unclearly defined.

Second, the work of both Maslow and Herzberg is criticized as insufficiently dynamic. Inherent in both views is the assumption that individuals *wait* for needs to arise in their lives before they respond; they do not actively seek ways to increase their effectiveness. These views, then, suggest that needs manipulate people, rather than that people control needs.

Third, critics find in Herzberg's theory no clear-cut distinctions between hygiene factors and motivators. Factors classified as motivators in one organization may be referred to as hygiene factors in another organization, or even by other people who work in the same organization.

Implications of Need Theories for the Supervisor. Practicing educational supervisors can find at least two major values in the concepts defined by needs-satisfaction theories. One is the implication that supervisors, administrators, and others engaging in educational leadership should be responsible and held accountable for creating a climate in their schools or districts conducive to the ongoing process of personal growth and self-fulfillment by employees.

A second value is that a supervisor's knowledge of what might satisfy or dissatisfy teachers and other staff members can be an important tool to improve their effectiveness. One major supervisory responsibility is to increase employee motivation; the danger, however, is that the power to motivate might become manipulative.

EQUITY THEORIES OF MOTIVATION

Equity theories suggest that the most important factor in employee motivation is the extent to which workers perceive a sense of equity in the work environment. Simply stated; if workers believe they are being treated fairly, they will be more satisfied and work harder toward achieving personal and organizational goals.

Implications of Equity Theories for the Supervisor

If the assumptions on which equity theories are based are correct, then supervisors must determine ways to ensure that their employees believe they are being treated fairly on the job. Employee *perceptions* of a given situation are important, because "fairness" cannot be entirely based on any objective reality. The supervisor's duty, then, is to make sure people perceive the treatment they are receiving as equitable; to do this requires that the supervisor first determine what people perceive as fair.

Equity theories tend to place considerable emphasis on the use of monetary and other tangible rewards because it is easier to distribute equitable dollars in recognition of valued performance than it is to distribute equitable recognition or esteem. For the supervisor, then, equity theories suggest the need to seek tangible or visible rewards for employees.

One issue that we need to understand in our discussion of equity theories is the difference between "equitable" and "equal." *Equality* implies the need to provide every employee with exactly the same rewards; everyone is treated the same. *Equity* is the concept of finding the fair or right amount of reward for each individual according to need. An equitable workplace is not one in which every employee receives the same things. I emphasize this because supervisors frequently attempt to provide equity in the workplace through equal treatment, and this is not what equity theories advocate.

REINFORCEMENT THEORIES
OF MOTIVATION

When we talk about motivation through reinforcement, we immediately think of the contributions of B.F. Skinner. Skinner's basic assumptions are quite simple. *Reinforcement theory* assumes that human behavior can be engineered, shaped, or altered by manipulating the reward structures for various forms of behavior. This manipulation is called *positive reinforcement.*

In this approach, performance standards are first clearly set, and improvement results from the application of frequent positive feedback linked to the attainment of stated performance objectives.

Implications of Reinforcement Theory
for the Supervisor

Reinforcement theory probably makes greater demands on supervisors than any other popular approach to motivation. The supervisor is largely responsible for manipulating and altering a number of features of the work environment. For example, supervisors must clearly set standards and inform their employees as to which behaviors are desirable in reaching those standards and which are not. The supervisor or administrator who based practice on reinforcement theories would probably spend a considerable amount of time at the beginning of the school year defining rules and procedures and explaining the consequences of violating those rules. Breaking from policy would bring a swift reprimand, and adherence to policy would be rewarded openly.

In addition, reinforcement theory assumes that performance can be improved by providing continuous feedback to employees concerning the nature and quality of their work toward the established goals and standards. In a school setting, then, this suggests that the supervisor would engage in a good deal of monitoring behavior to evaluate teacher performance as a way to start the feedback process. The rewards or consequences offered for good performance must be proportionate to the behaviors exhibited by the employees. In other words, the supervisor must live by the motto, "When people do good jobs, tell them so."

Reinforcement theories of motivation stand in direct contradiction to equity theories. According to reinforcement theories, supervisors should work to ensure that all employees are *not* rewarded equally. Instead, they should always be rewarded differently according to their levels of performance. Again, supervisors should be aware of the possibility that their behavior might be overly manipulative or exploitive of the teaching staff.

EXPECTANCY THEORIES OF MOTIVATION

According to expectancy theories of motivation, when people value something, they will be motivated to engage in actions based on the strength of that valuing. Porter and Lawler (1966) have been most closely associated with this view of organizational motivation, and they offered the following observations concerning the nature of expectancy theories:

1. Behavior is determined by a combination of forces in the individuals and forces in the environment.
2. People make decisions about their own behavior in organizations.
3. Different people have different needs, desires, and goals.
4. People make decisions among alternative plans of behavior based on their own perceptions, or expectancies, of the degree to which a given behavior is likely to lead to some desired outcome.

Implications of Expectancy Theories for Supervisors

Because employee behavior ultimately derives from forces in the person *and* in the environment, a supervisor who subscribes to expectancy theories of motivation must first know the organizational and personal outcomes that each employee tends to value most. The supervisor would therefore need to spend time talking with staff to determine what outcomes have the greatest value. Without such knowledge, the supervisor would be unable to seek a motivational focus. In addition to determining the staff's desired outcomes, the supervisor needs to assess what behaviors and outcomes he or she desires from the staff. To do this the supervisor needs to have a well-articulated personal educational philosophy or platform to provide guidance and plan of action.

Expectancy theories of motivation also imply that supervisors must make certain that the goals, behaviors, and outcomes they desire are actually attainable, and that the desired outcomes are linked directly to desired levels of performance.

The supervisor adhering to this theoretical framework would need to determine the exact reward structure most likely to ensure that employees will continue to make progress toward the attainment of organizational goals and objectives. The supervisor first needs to analyze the nature of the total work environment to locate any potentially conflicting expectancies. Does one part of the organization value one type of employee behavior while another department suggests rewards for an entirely different behavior? If such conflicts exist, the supervisor might need to make some adjustments to reduce the number of mixed messages being transmitted to staff.

The supervisor would also need to make certain that, where possible, the changes in organizational outcomes are large enough to motivate and change the behavior of employees. Trivial changes and rewards will automatically result in trivial changes in levels of employee performance. This will, in turn, result in trivial outcomes for the organization.

Reliance on expectancy theories for motivating employees also suggests some modifications in organizational policies and procedures. For example, pay and reward systems might generally need to be redesigned, and considerably more effort put into rewarding people for organizationally desirable performances. Consequently, extremely precise employee appraisal and evaluation systems would be needed to guide the distribution of employee rewards.

Expectancy theory requires careful reexamination of tasks, jobs, job descriptions, and the roles of employees within the organization. Supervisors must understand the importance of formal and informal employee group structures, because such structures are important determinants of ultimate employee performance.

The final implication for supervisors who "buy into" the concept of expectancy theory is that they must pay considerable attention to individual employee needs, concerns, and interests. Such sensitivity to individual issues is not found in many organizations, but it needs to be developed and maintained if expectancy theories are to be employed with any consistency.

INDIVIDUAL PROFESSIONAL PHILOSOPHY AND APPROACHES TO MOTIVATION

In the previous section we reviewed four alternative theories about how people are motivated in organizations. Ideally, we could settle on one "best" way to encourage greater commitment to organizational goals and objectives in all situations, but no such satisfyingly simple solution exists. The motivational strategies you select as an educational supervisor will depend largely on your own individual educational philosophy. In particular, how you view the role of teachers and others who work in schools will determine to a large extent how you try to motivate them. If, for example, you believe that teachers are fundamentally nothing more than employees of the school district, and that they need much close direction to control their behavior, then your approach to motivation might well be based on reinforcement theory, which suggests that people can be "conditioned" to operate in a desired manner. If, on the other hand, you view teachers as a highly skilled group of professionals, then you might well approach motivation through needs-satisfaction theory. In particular, Herzberg's views might appeal to you.

Your personal educational platform also comes into play in determining to what extent you support McGregor's Theory X and Theory Y, described earlier. Do you, for example, begin with the assumption that people are basically lazy? If so, your attempts at motivating them would differ significantly from those you would make if you believed that most people really do wish to work hard.

Finally, we need to point out that no one ever truly motivates another person. There is no causal relationship between your selection of a motivation theory and an outcome of greater staff commitment. Ultimately, whether or not a person works harder rests in that person's own choice. More important in a supervisor's motivational effectiveness is not the specific tactic used but the extent to which the staff believes in the supervisor, and the consistency of the supervisor's performance. In order to achieve the kind of consistency that employees admire, educational supervisors must operate from a foundation of principle and belief about education; again, the development of a personal educational philosophy is a vital ingredient in performance effectiveness.

SUMMARY

In this chapter we reviewed a number of theories concerning motivation of employees in organizations. We noted that motivation is yet another example of how important theory can be in effective supervisory practice, but we also pointed out that motivation is a critically important supervisory responsibility. We stressed that motivation is ultimately the responsibility of those who are to be motivated, but that a knowledge of alternative theoretical perspectives can serve as a critically useful tool for effective supervisors.

We offered four theoretical approaches to motivation in this chapter: the currently popular *needs-satisfaction* theories of Maslow and Herzberg; *equity* theories, which suggest that fairness in the workplace is the most important motivational factor; *reinforcement* theories as developed by B.F. Skinner and others; and *expectancy* theories, which suggest that employees respond favorably to conditions that they value. We concluded with a review of the relationship between motivational strategies and the educational supervisor's individual educational philosophy.

SUGGESTED ACTIVITIES

1. List the things that someone could do to make you want to work harder than you already do. To what extent are these motivational factors compatible with any of the theories that were reviewed in this chapter? Are you likely to respond to the satisfaction of needs? Your sense of fairness and equity? Also, list the things that make you feel as if you do not want to do something. Is there a pattern present in the same way as for the motivating factors?
2. Interview three or four teachers in a school and determine the same kinds of motivational factors that we reviewed in the exercise above.
3. Watch several television commercials for a number of different products. Try to classify the approaches that are used in an effort to motivate you to buy the advertised products.
4. "Motivation" is used very ambiguously in daily discussions. Whenever you hear a reference to this concept, think about whether the person using the term is really referring to the concepts described in this chapter. If the term is being used precisely, classify the strategy for motivation that is being suggested, according to the theoretical models described in this chapter.
5. Observe a teacher's class and keep a record of the motivational strategies that are used with students during a one-hour period.

REFERENCES

Herzberg, F. (1966). *Work and the nature of man.* Cleveland: World Publishing.
Lovell, John, & Wiles, Kimberly (1983). *Supervision for better schools,* (3rd ed.). Englewood Cliffs, NJ: Prentice-Hall.
Maslow, A. H. (1970). *Motivation and personality* (2nd ed.). New York: Harper & Row.
Porter, L. W., & Lawler, E. (1966). *Managerial attitudes and performance.* Homewood, IL: Irwin.

ADDITIONAL READING

Vroom, V. (1964). *Work and motivation.* London: Wiley.

PART III

The Realities of Supervision: Communication, Change, Power, and Conflict

In Part III we will discuss specific, ongoing concerns of effective proactive supervisors. In contrast with the previous sections, emphasis here is on general characteristics of each topic, rather than theoretical aspects.

CHAPTER 8

Communication

The issue of organizational communication is relevant to an analysis of proactive supervisory processes for at least two reasons. First, the supervisor who would like to lead rather than simply react to crises would profit greatly from understanding and ultimately joining into the patterns of communication that are being followed by those who work in the organization. Particularly important is the ability to comprehend both those areas where barriers to effective communication are present and how those barriers might be removed. Effective supervisors will gain considerably from insight into the patterns of communication employed by their school staff.

DEFINITION OF COMMUNICATION

For our purposes we will define communication simply as the effort on the part of an individual or group to transmit information to another person or group. This transmission process, which is often extremely difficult to implement in a satisfying and effective manner with any degree of regularity or clarity, is nonetheless simple to describe and to depict graphically, as in Figure 8.1.

As Figure 8.1 indicates, communication involves two major actors, a sender (or speaker) (S), and a receiver (R). The contact between these two ends of the communication process is established by forwarding a message (M) across some recognized channel. As we will see in our subsequent discussion of the types of communication that exist in organizations, our basic diagram can be modified to reflect, for example, two-way commu-

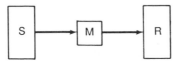

Figure 8.1. Illustration of the basic act of communication, or the transmission of a message (M) from a sender (S) to a receiver (R).

nication. In addition, our description of available modes of communication will reveal that there are normally a variety of channels available to senders of messages.

FUNCTIONS OF COMMUNICATION

Research indicates that there are at least three major functions assigned to the process of communication in organizations.

First, communication can help people within organizations clarify their understanding of the organization's goals, objectives, procedures, and rules. One of the basic assumptions of any organization is that it represents a unified collection of "something" that is different from other such collections. What constitutes the reality of an organization, therefore, is often little more than a compilation of stated objectives, goals, rules, policies, and procedures. Normally, organizations are also described in terms of their products. In fact, we might argue that the intended *outcomes* of an organization provide its unique identify. An automobile manufacturer, for example, is branded as a company that makes cars because that is precisely what its stated goal is. However, designating a certain intended outcome is sufficient only in providing an initial identity to an organization. More is needed to maintain that identity over time; we suggest that this sort of maintenance is carried on through ongoing intraorganizational communication patterns. The workers in an auto company *know* that their organization is a producer of cars because that fact is consistently communicated to them. It may seem like a trivial point to think that assembly-line workers putting together Fords know that Ford makes cars because the company tells them so. On the other hand, consider the hundreds of small companies that have merged with many other similar companies, only to be swallowed up by huge multinational corporations. Individual employees may easily lose sight of the focus of a company when they work for a conglomerate. The way in which the identity of a company is established and certainly retained in many cases today is through a process of ongoing communication.

A second function of organizational communication is that it can serve as an essential feedback mechanism. Effective communication processes can provide information for an organization engaging in needed corrective actions. To illustrate this point, let us return to the case of the multinational corporation serving as a holding company for many smaller organizations. If communication is consistently open and candid within the corporation, and if a strong value is placed on dialogue and two-way communication involving corporate executives, mid-level managers, and employees, any blurring of the organization's identity in the minds of its members will quickly become apparent. More important, if communication channels are open and available, anytime that the "message" of the company begins to be lost in the minds of its clients or customers, that fact will be returned to corporate decision makers, who can modify those practices that caused the confusion. In 1987, a number of large corporations, including Hertz rental cars and United Air Lines, joined under a new corporate banner, Allegis. In the days immediately following this merger, the Allegis name and logo were employed quite prominently in advertising and promotional literature. At the same time, marketing analysts for the newly formed corporation found that consumers were expressing resentment and apprehension about the demise of "well-known companies." Were they now to fly "the Friendly Skies of Allegis"? As this negative reaction became understood more clearly, the corporation moved not to change the initial merger, but rather to downplay the new corporate name, which meant nothing in the marketplace. Soon, the Allegis logo was reduced to a small stamp on the written material of component companies, and Hertz returned to top billing as "Number One." This phenomenon is not entirely dissimilar to what goes on in schools when they have been swallowed up in other mergers of districts going through consolidations.

We could provide many similar examples of the importance of effective communication in organizational feedback and enhancement. Cancelled television shows have been brought back to life because of viewer complaints; politicians have been ousted from office as a consequence of petition drives. The key notion here is that open channels of communication, while potentially frightening to decision makers because they may provide unhappy news, are essentially features for growing and productive enterprises.

The third major function of effective communication is that, as noted before, it is the "glue" that holds together organizations. We often hear that a school or other institution has suffered a "breakdown in communication," or that "people aren't communicating with one another." By contrast, when a school is particularly effective, we rarely notice anything related to the communication patterns at all. The need for open and consistent communication in effective organizations is so great that we normally assume that people in such organizations *are* communicating. Only when this facet of life is disrupted is its importance fully understood. The last and probably most crucial function of communication is to prevent total organizational breakdown.

Communication processes serve three important functions. They help to clarify organizational goals, objectives, procedures, and rules; they provide avenues for organizational effectiveness through consistent feedback; and such processes, if absent, lead to the likely destruction of an organization. Based on these functions, the practitioner of proactive supervision needs to look constantly at the importance of communication.

Types of Communication

In a review of the characteristics of communication patterns and their implications for school administrators, Russell Spillman (1975) noted that there are essentially three types of communication processes that take place in any organization. The supervisor needs to be aware of the strengths and limitations of each type because all will be required at one point or another in the life of a school. The three types of communication are one-way communication, one-way communication with feedback, and two-way communication.

One-way communication. Here, the speaker, or communicator, sends a message through some channel or mode directly to a receiver (see Figure 8.2). Although there are likely to be effects from the message, one-way communication strongly implies that the speaker is not concerned with the effect, and that there is no provision made for the relay of the effect from the receiver back to the speaker.

One-way communication must occur in all organizations from time to time. Someone must occasionally "tell" others some information, regardless of what those others might wish. Nevertheless, there are problems associated with one-way communication, and the source of these is generally the quality of the initial transmission of the message at the sender's level. The nature of "what" is to be communicated must be absolutely clear; once the speaker sends the message to the receiver, there is no way to clarify any misconceptions that may occur. One-way communication might be compared to a person firing a rifle shot into the air—not a dangerous practice in itself, but potentially fatal because no one can be absolutely certain as to where the bullet will eventually land.

Examples of one-way communication are plentiful in schools: Public-

Figure 8.2. Representation of the concept of one-way communication. Information proceeds directly from the sender (S) to the receiver (R) and concludes at that point.

address announcements, memos in teachers' mailboxes, PTA newsletters, and so on. One-way communication is not "bad" in itself; it is a highly efficient way for schools to share information because it is economical in terms of both time consumed in preparing the initial message and money spent in preparation. People in schools often need bits of information presented to them, and one-way communication is highly appropriate in such cases. Problems may arise, however, if there is a virtually total reliance on this limited type of communication. Other methods are needed.

One-way communication with feedback. This is essentially the same process as one-way communication, but using a method that allows feedback from receiver to sender—perhaps face-to-face contact, or some other strategy that permits regular feedback so that the sender's message may be modified (see Figure 8.3).

One-way communication with feedback is the activity that takes place constantly in the classroom. When teachers use formal lecture techniques to instruct the students in their classes, there is no formal dialogue with students. This is essentially one-way communication. But in most cases, even when students are not deliberately asked to participate, an effective teacher will remain sensitive to subtle clues suggesting the extent to which students understand the content of the lecture. A puzzled look on some students' faces will typically nudge the teacher to restate the phrase just presented in the lecture. In communication terms, then, the receiver conveys a message—in this case a very subtle one—to the initial sender that, in turn, transforms the nature of the message. Good teachers make use of this process constantly.

Utilizing this type of communication to the exclusion of others can, however, have negative consequences. If the sender relies on subtle feedback almost exclusively as a way to receive messages from the receiver, the sender is still in control of the act of communication. True learning involves dialogue. On the other hand, as we saw earlier, one-way communication even without feedback is entirely legitimate in some circumstances. If the content and nature of the message being transmitted is such that no adjustment is needed or wanted, feedback is not truly appropriate. We should note,

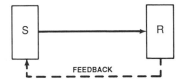

Figure 8.3. Diagram showing the concept of one-way communication with feedback. The sender (S) transmits information directly to the receiver (R) and no direct response is expected. However, feedback is provided from the receiver to the sender, although the sender may do nothing with this feedback.

however, that soliciting feedback when you have no intention of modifying the original message is much worse than not providing for feedback in the first place.

Two-way communication. This communication type is characterized by the presence of two or more communicators or speakers, each of whom sends messages, and each of whom also receives messages. Diagrammatically, we can see that what takes place in two-way communication is a continuous shifting of the individual's role from sender to receiver to sender, and so forth (see Figure 8.4).

True open dialogue where all parties talk and share ideas with one another is the essence of two-way communication. The most important feature here is that, although one party may *initiate* the communication activity, no one *controls* the dialogue, and each message is transferred on an equal basis from sender to receiver. True parity is achieved between the senders and the receivers.

Two-way communication occurs in school settings where there is true open dialogue and shared decision making. Team-teaching situations, or administrative councils where all staff members have input into school policies and procedures, often exemplify this process. It may also be seen in individual classrooms where open student-teacher discussion and dialogue take place. Communication processes will break down and be ineffective, however, if two-way communication is "played at" rather than truly embraced as a valued activity. In many instances, open, two-way communication is publicly espoused as an ideal, but one or more parties in the process in fact fail to listen openly and hear accurately the messages sent

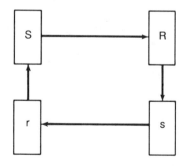

Figure 8.4. Diagram of complete two-way communication process. Initial message is transmitted from the sender (S) to the receiver (R). At that point, the receiver becomes a sender (s) and transmits either a new message or a modification of the original message to the initial sender, who now plays the role of receiver (r). The process of communication may end at this point, or it may continue through the same loop again, or with additional senders and receivers added.

by others. Such token openness probably does considerably more harm than good.

Two-way communication, of course, is not *always* the best way to achieve a specific goal. When nonnegotiable information must be shared with a school staff (e.g., the district's policy statement regarding students' involvement in field trips), two-way communication is probably not appropriate. The *formulation* of the policy may indeed have involved considerable open dialogue. Once formulated, however, that policy needs to be announced in a straightforward manner. The key, we believe, is not using two-way communication in all circumstances but rather knowing *how* to use this process at the appropriate time to enhance overall communications in the organization.

FORMS OF COMMUNICATION

Three means or modes of communication are present in most organizations. These may be listed as *verbal* (or spoken) communication, *written* communication, and *nonverbal* communication.

Verbal Communication

The most prevalent form of *intended* communication in organizations, *verbal communication* is used in a deliberate way to send messages between speakers and receivers. This involves certain advantages and disadvantages.

Spillman (1975) noted that verbal communication is spontaneous and reflects the immediate needs of a speaker. We need no advance preparation to articulate an idea verbally, although verbalizations can also be planned well in advance. The first advantage of verbal communication, then, is that a need can be made known "on the spot." Second, verbal communication takes little additional effort by its speakers and receivers, and other than the time that may be expended in the actual process of talking, it uses no greater organizational resources. Finally, verbal communication is momentary. Words shared in haste are, fortunately, soon forgotten; permanent scars are less likely when no record exists of what has been communicated.

Obviously, these same advantages can also become disadvantages. For example, the fact that verbal communication leaves no permanent record can be an advantage *unless* what was said is worth remembering. Temporary statements are soon forgotten. Moreover, verbal communication is easily misunderstood by receivers, who might believe they heard one message when something else was actually being said. A final disadvantage is that closure of the verbal communicative act may be difficult, if not impossible, to achieve. There is no exclamation point, question mark, or final period to signal the close of a verbalization.

Written Communication

Written communication is a staple of organizations. In schools, all manners of written forms, notes, and memos are used routinely and extensively.

One of written communication's most powerful advantages is that it provides a permanent record. Minutes of meetings and letters can be filed and referred to at a later time. In addition, written documents serve to accurately preserve information that may be crucial to the operation of the organization. Policies, procedures, and other guidelines that need to be followed to ensure efficient operation are logically kept in a written format so that all members of an organization have a constant reference point to clarify activities. Another advantage is that written methods are a good way to transmit complicated information or hard-to-remember facts and concepts. Imagine providing oral directions for assembling a detailed electronic gadget. Quite a few Christmases would have been ruined if bicycles had not been assembled the night before by parents following *printed* instructions!

A major disadvantage of written communication is its impersonality. Think of a time when a memo was slipped into your mailbox, rather than a message being transmitted through face-to-face confrontation. Written communication can also be relatively slow and expensive to prepare, and the speaker or sender can never be entirely assured that the message has been received, understood, and acted upon. There is no guarantee that a memo will be read.

Nonverbal Communication

Too often we assume that spoken or written words are the only means we have of communicating. These means are clearly the most widely used in organizations, but increasingly we are realizing the importance of the process of *nonverbal communication.*

Nonverbal communication is the subtle expression of attitudes, emotions, and even the physical state of the sender or speaker (Spillman, 1975) through voluntary and involuntary gestures. A wince, a smile, a glance off into space, or a toe tapping are all examples of powerful, nonverbal signals of what we are feeling or thinking. Nonverbal communication also greatly modifies the words that we utter; it either affirms or denies what is being said. Throughout the history of schooling, for example, students have been masterful in determining if teachers "mean business" by watching *the way* in which things are said.

Skill at understanding nonverbal cues is a significant benefit to the supervisor who would engage in proactive practice. A major advantage of the ability to sense and analyze accurately nonverbal messages is that this means of communication is almost constantly present in what is taking place in a school. Students give cues nonverbally and so do teachers. On the other hand, while nonverbal messages are constantly present, they are extremely difficult to control, because neither speaker nor receiver can always see what others are doing to send messages. Speakers may actually be hidden from view when they speak or write. Nonverbal messages can and often do contradict what we say in verbal or written form. As a result, receivers tend to use nonverbal cues to judge the accuracy and honesty of verbal statements. If a difference exists between nonverbal and verbal cues, people tend to trust more completely the nonverbal behavior; the old maxim "Actions speak louder than words" is very true.

Nonverbal messages are not controllable in the same way that written or verbal forms are. We cannot talk about disadvantages and advantages as if speakers had a real choice whether or not to express nonverbal cues. However, we must not take lightly the following effects of nonverbal behavior:

1. Nonverbal messages establish the status and honesty of the speaker in the mind of the receiver. Receivers tend to judge quickly if speakers are egotistical and self-serving, or sensitive and caring. Nonverbal behavior also serves to disclose the presence of hidden agendas that may be held by speakers.
2. Nonverbal communication indicates what others think of us; significant messages about senders' feelings and attitudes toward receivers are conveyed through nonverbal behaviors. It is not unusual, for instance, for a person to "hear" that someone has trust in him or her, but to see that the person is actually suspicious or even hostile because the speaker makes no eye contact, drums the fingers when talking, and so forth.
3. Nonverbal cues are frequently utilized to check the reliability of what is being said. In other words, nonverbal indicators tend to either reinforce or minimize verbal messages. "Is what I am hearing really what is being said?" may be determined by watching for clues other than the actual words that are being said.

All three of the communication approaches we have reviewed here are found in all organizations, and the effective supervisor cannot "hide" behind one type to the exclusion of others. Instead, the supervisor must be able to discern the advantages and disadvantages, as well as the likely consequences to the organization, of consciously making use of one means of communication or another.

POTENTIAL BARRIERS TO COMMUNICATION

Proactive supervision involves a constant effort to reduce the potential barriers to effective communication, which might be categorized in three large groupings: barriers related to the person, barriers based on the role of the speaker, and barriers found in the role of the receiver (Spillman, 1975).

Personal Barriers

The sources of personal barriers, or barriers derived from the speaker, may be classified as *egocentric* limitations, *personality* limitations, or *self-concept* limitations.

Egocentric barriers can never be totally overcome. All individuals are somewhat restricted in their ability to communicate absolutely and completely, because each person must judge the world from a unique and highly idiosyncratic perspective. Personality limitations grow out of individual characteristics; some people have difficulty as speakers, for instance, simply because they are shy or timid. Finally, our own self-concepts can serve to prevent us from being completely open, honest, and effective in instigating communication.

Barriers Based on the Role of the Speaker

Roles are normally defined as socially ascribed statuses within organizations. Roles also take on certain characteristics that are apart from the specific individuals who fulfill the roles, and these characteristics can become serious barriers to the degree of open communication possible in an organization. The role of the supervisor or administrator is sometimes symbolically more powerful, for example, than the person who fulfills that role might wish it to be. Thus, the designation of someone in a role might very well in itself constitute a barrier to communication. We could point, for example, to what happens when a person who has been a teacher for several years is suddenly named to the principalship of the same school. The individual may begin to lose contact with former colleagues simply because he or she is now an administrator.

Receiver Barriers

Sometimes the effectiveness of the communicative act is affected negatively by the receiver, not the speaker. There are a number of ways in which this occurs.

For one thing, receivers sometimes simply lack interest in the message being sent; they see no relevance in it. Part of this might derive from the fact that the receiver is not sophisticated enough to appreciate the message, or lacks the necessary background or knowledge base to understand it. Also, receivers often have biases that serve to filter out what they really do not want to hear and that, in fact, sometimes prevent the communication process from beginning in the first place. Barriers such as differences in age, sex, social position, or cultural heritage often serve to screen out the real meanings needed for effective communication. The so-called generation gap of the 1960s and the battle cry that "You can't trust anyone over 30" effectively prevented dialogue between different groups, for instance, during that turbulent decade.

Finally, communication may be hindered by specific situational circumstances that screen out a message as it proceeds from speaker to receiver— too much noise, not enough time, additional external distractions, and so forth. Think of the last time you tried to concentrate on a lecture given in a classroom that was either too hot or too cold, for example. In fact, many people question whether much real communication can take place at all in our modern world because it is so cluttered with what appear to be an overwhelming number of such situational barriers.

SKILLS TO IMPROVE COMMUNICATION

Regardless of the constraints that exist to carrying out effective communication, people *can* talk to one another. However, understanding and enhancing the communication process is also largely dependent upon the development of a set of specific skills to increase its accuracy. Richard Gorton (1986) has suggested some useful strategies for this important effort.

1. *Paraphrasing.* Restate the main ideas of others in order to clarify those ideas. ("In other words, what you're saying is. . . .")
2. *Perception Checking.* Check to see that your perception of what has been said is accurate. ("If I understand you correctly, you're saying. . . .")
3. *Relating Things to Personal Feelings.* Communication can break down because receivers have a negative reaction to statements; what we say offends, often unintentionally. Confront such negative feelings openly when they occur. ("When you say that, I feel like. . . .")
4. *Use Objective Descriptions.* The use of highly subjective terms that imply personal value statements hurts open communication. Describe behaviors with objective terms, when possible, so that people are less likely to say, "It's not *what* you're saying that I reject, but rather *how* you're saying it."
5. *Feedback.* Give and accept in return constructive and honest feedback to keep communication channels open between and among all parties.

SUMMARY

A major responsibility of the educational supervisor must be to keep communication going in both the school and the district. We assumed implicitly at the beginning of this chapter that organizations generally will not be effective if people do not know what is going on. Further, the effective leader (supervisor, administrator, or anyone else who impacts positively on the organization) is highly committed to open communication. As Bennis and Nanus (1985) noted, leaders communicate at all times, and the more effective the communication, the more effective the leadership.

In this chapter we began by noting some basic definitions and concepts of the communication act. Next we reviewed types and modes of communication and noted that, depending on circumstances and setting, different modes may be more appropriate than others, even when we generally feel more negative toward some approaches. For example, written memos (one-way communication) might not seem highly desirable, but there are times when this strategy is in fact the most appropriate. The important issue is that a variety of techniques must be used to keep communication channels open.

The chapter concluded with a review of typical constraints and barriers to effective communication and of skills that the supervisor may develop in an effort to reduce the barriers when they occur.

SUGGESTED ACTIVITIES

1. Observe the class of a colleague and keep track of the amount of time spent in each of the major types of communication that are described in this chapter. After class, ask the teacher to estimate the percentage of time that he or she spent using both one-way communication and two-way communication, then compare your findings with the teacher's estimate.
2. Carry out the same analysis as above, but follow a practicing school administrator or supervisor for a part of a school day instead of watching a teacher. Again, share your findings with the administrator's self-perceptions.
3. Conduct a survey to determine why people believe there are barriers to effective communication. Next, question people about the ways in which they believe communication is enhanced. Put together a brief overview of your findings in a way that may be presented to a teaching staff during an inservice day. Make sure that you ask people for some suggestions regarding the possible improvement of communication in their school.

REFERENCES

Bennis, Warren, & Nanus, Burt. (1985). *Leaders: Strategies for taking charge.* New York: Harper & Row.

Gorton, Richard. (1986). *School leadership and administration: Important concepts, case studies, and simulations* (3rd ed.). Dubuque, IA: Brown.

Spillman, Russell. (1975, Summer). The nature of communication. *The Administrator, 5*(4), 4–9.

CHAPTER 9

Change Processes

As the late James Lipham (1965) pointed out in what has become a classic statement about leadership, the fundamental essence of leadership must always be conceived of as the process of bringing about needed change. Implicit within any leadership role, whether director of a private corporation or educational supervisor, is a responsibility to foster the type of change that will stimulate continuous growth and development in an organization. Administration or management, on the other hand, deals with maintaining the status quo in an organization. This distinction confronts us directly with a classic, continually perplexing problem that school supervisors must face. As we noted in Chapter 3, supervisors who wish to be effective in that role must generally engage in administrative duties and behaviors on occasion. As a result, the supervisor who is charged with the responsibility of providing leadership or organizational change, in Lipham's terms, must also take care to guard the status quo when that is the most appropriate route for a school to follow. Is effective educational supervision an impossibility, then? Or at best a case of trying to walk an exceedingly narrow line between the competing demands of "changing" and "maintaining"? *No change* can mean organizational stagnation; *change for the sake of change* can result in organizational dysfunction. Being effective in this paradox of leadership and administration is like Goldilocks trying to find the perfect bowl of porridge: We need to be careful not to select something either "too hot" or "too cold"; it must be "just right." The supervisor has to know just the right times to push for change, and also when to hold the line.

In this chapter we explore organizational change processes as they relate to the practice of proactive educational supervision. We will review a number of conceptualizations of change that have appeared frequently in the literature and then some of the most typical and consistent barriers to promoting needed change in organizations. While change is a necessary condition for the improvement of organizations, it is in no way an easy condition either to promote or sustain. As a result, this chapter concludes with a consideration of some of the strategies that may be followed to reduce the typical constraints that inhibit needed organizational change.

ALTERNATIVE CONCEPTUAL MODELS OF CHANGE

Douglas Paul (1977) categorized the major existing descriptions of organizational change in four broad theoretical models: problem solving, social interaction, research-development-diffusion (RD&D), and linkage. In the sections that follow, we will look at a brief description of the underlying assumptions and most salient characteristics of each of the four principal models of change.

Problem-Solving Model

This model suggests that change is a logical effort to provide solutions to problematic states perceived by an organization. The basic view on this model is that, if something is wrong, change must occur. The role of the supervisor is to first determine as much as possible concerning the precise nature of the problems faced in an organization, then suggest modifications in policy and practice that might serve to solve the identified problems.

A rich tradition of support for this conceptualization of change can be found in the work of, among others, Bennis, Benne, and Chin (1969), Lippitt, Watson, and Westley (1958), and Fullan (1973). A major assumption underlying this view of change is that organizational problems, even when complex and threatening, can be identified with sufficient clarity to enable rational solutions to be formulated and applied. This has led to the development of analytical schemes that suggest that organizational dilemmas may be tracked along a predictable continuum, to the extent that the leader can know when to initiate change in the same way that a physician might have a clear idea of when to introduce a new treatment to an ill patient. The Concerns-Based Adoption Model (CBAM) for staff development, devised by Gene Hall and Susan Loucks (1976) at the University of Texas Research and Development Center on Teacher Education, is an effective application of this change process. Although we will look at this model in greater detail in Chapter 17, we want to note here that it serves as an excellent example of a practice founded on the problem-solving approach to change. The CBAM suggests that organizations demonstrate clearly identifiable *Levels of Use* of certain activities, and members of organizations experience certain key *Levels of Concern* regarding the activities being introduced into their world. Because these two factors are rational, the supervisor (or any other leader) can consciously effect matches between Level of Use and Level of Concern, thereby resolving organizational problems and increasing the satisfaction and sense of efficacy felt by the people within the organizations.

Lippitt (1969) identified six basic elements of the problem-solving model of change, including (1) identifying the problem, (2) diagnosing the problem, (3) retrieving related knowledge and discussing its implications for overcoming the problem, (4) forming alternatives to action, (5) testing the feasibility of alternatives, and (6) adopting and implementing the selected alternative. These steps call attention once again to the most obvious characteristic of this model: It makes use of linear and rational thinking as the foundation for change.

Another outcome of the problem-solving perspective is a belief that networking among different organizations is a commendable practice. If we believe that organizational problems are basically rational, then we may assume that many schools, districts, or other organizations face roughly the same problems from time to time. Potentially creative solutions to these recurring problems can come from many systems working together, rather than facing each problem in isolation.

Perhaps the greatest drawback to the problem-solving approach to analyzing organizational change is found in this same absolute faith in the rationality of organizations. The approach firmly suggests that solutions can be identified for all problems, and that change can be controlled so as to reduce the negative impact of the problems. The model tends to ignore the fact that solving organizational problems does not always involve selecting the clearly "best" response, but rather involves finding a path that is less imperfect than any others available.

Social Interaction

Change often occurs in organizations solely because people in those organizations talk to other people who convince them to try something a little different. This is the basic assumption found in *social interaction,* a model for change analysis that has its roots in the field of agriculture. Ryan and Gross (1943), Rogers (1962), and Rogers and Shoemaker (1971) were among the early proponents of this view, which was first recognized as the process followed by farmers who shared information concerning the development of new hybrid corn seeds. (The process is sometimes called the "agricultural model of change," and change agents are spoken of in the same terms used to describe county extension agents in farming communities.) Paul (1977) noted three important characteristics of this model, which distinguish it from other conceptualizations of change:

1. It strongly emphasizes communication channels and messages to be utilized for diffusing innovations;
2. It recognizes interpersonal influence patterns leading to the adoption of innovations as legitimate features of organizational life;
3. It focuses on stimuli for adoption of innovative practices that originate outside of the adopting system.

In addition, the social interaction model implies strongly that potential users of an innovation will subject both the innovation and the innovator to a good deal of scrutiny before accepting it, and that this scrutiny will be based to a large extent on the ways in which the potential users of the innovation within the adopting organization "feel" about the possible change.

This explains, at least in part, why the social interaction model is also occasionally referred to as the "organization development" (OD) model of change. The model places a great deal of emphasis not only on the nature of interaction that occurs between the user organization and the external environment that initially introduces the innovation, but perhaps more importantly on the nature of the population within the adopting organization. Schmuck and Miles (1971), for example, argue in *Organizational Development in Schools* that the user-group population is never a passive body. Instead, innovations are always institutionalized in a school or any other setting because of the workings of the social interaction network within the school. As a result, the supervisor whose notion of change was founded on a belief in social interaction would probably invest considerable time and energy in working with a school staff to increase internal receptivity to desired innovations.

The application of the social interaction model as a way to stimulate change in an organization normally follows a rather consistent pattern. First, people hear about a new and innovative practice, normally through face-to-face contact with direct users of the innovation or others assumed to have direct information concerning the practice. Next, proponents of the new process engage in a period of attempted persuasion, the goal being to mold opinion of potential users in a positive and supportive way about the benefits of the new product or practice. Third, potential users make a conscious decision either to use or not to use the suggested innovation. Finally, if the new practice is adopted, efforts are made to determine whether or not the decision was a good one.

A number of theorists in the field of change, including Havelock (1969) and McLaughlin (1976) have raised serious questions regarding the extent to which the social interaction model may be applied realistically to educational settings. The greatest objection is that innovations in schools, unlike new breeds of corn, are generally intangible and therefore difficult to assess and evaluate.

Although this observation may seem to limit the use of the social interaction model as an approach to planned change in schools, the model nevertheless deserves our attention, particularly in its emphasis on personal contact and interpersonal relations. The educational supervisor needs to recognize the power associated with personal relationships formed between people who work within school systems and others outside those systems whose ideas or products may have great value to what goes on in schools. Encouraging visits to other schools, attending meetings of professional associations, and inviting outside consultants and guests to visit schools serve to increase social interaction between the school and its external environment, which, in turn, might provide opportunities for introducing new and more effective educational practices from outside. A supervisor mindful of the need to cultivate patterns of positive interaction within the school would probably encourage faculty retreats, staff discussions, schoolwide decision-making processes, and many other approaches to enhancing the quality of interaction inside the school as well.

Research-Development-Diffusion Model

Clark and Guba (1975) and House (1974) are most directly associated with what has become known as the research-development-diffusion model (RD&D) of change. The fundamental assumption here is that processes of change based on structured research are begun in order to produce new ideas, practices, or products, which are then disseminated to possible users through a conscientious effort toward diffusion. Havelock (1973) noted that five basic assumptions underlie the RD&D model of change:

1. Both the development and the application of an innovation are assumed to take place in an orderly sequence that includes research, development, and packaging prior to a mass distribution procedure.
2. The management of this sequence requires extensive planning over a long time period.
3. A division and a coordination of labor are necessary among elements in the RD&D system.
4. A rational consumer is assumed, one who will adopt an innovation on the basis of a mass dissemination program.
5. High initial development costs are balanced by the long-term benefits that come from an efficient, high-quality innovation that can be used by a mass audience.

In practice, what normally happens is that new users of an innovative practice are assisted by the initial researchers and developers to make certain that the innovation is successfully installed. This approach to understanding change has been particularly influential in educational settings in national educational policy in recent years. During the mid-1960s the federal government initiated an effort designed to increase the amount of research-validated information available to local school practitioners interested in improving practice. One of the tangible results of this initiative was the creation of a network of federally funded research and development centers at major universities across the country, at which faculty served as basic researchers, and another network of regional educational laboratories supported jointly by federal funds and by the sale of contract services to state and local education agencies. Although subtle differences existed between the centers and laboratories regarding the ways in which they would function and be governed, they were both commissioned to support a strategy for bringing about change in schools that was research-based, rational, and generally in line with the model suggested by Robert Owens (1986), which is shown in Figure 9.1.

The RD&D model of change, not surprisingly, holds a considerable attraction for the academic community, which so often assumes that change without data validated through research in the social sciences is not worth the effort. University faculty tend to place great stock in the linear concepts of research, development, and diffusion because the findings of basic research serve as the starting point for all future progress. Unfortunately, this stance, highly satisfying to many researchers, does not always fit with the reality of school systems, where practitioners need immediate responses to their concerns and have little time for what they see as the time-consuming work of basic research. Proactive supervisors are likely to be caught in some conflict over this issue. On the one hand, they will want to seek validated information to serve as the basis of their work with schools, thus promoting more thoughtful and less crisis-oriented behaviors. On the other hand, crises *do* arise, and practitioners seek answers even before the last bit of data is collected, the final statistical analysis completed, or the peer-review panel accepts a piece of research for publication.

No matter what its limitations, the RD&D model of change must still be recognized as a potentially powerful conceptualization of how organizations adopt innovative practices. Over time, this model has been modified considerably by proponents like Havelock (1972), who suggested that, in the initiation of organizational change, there should be a rational sequence in the evaluation and application of an innovation; research, development, and packaging of a program change should occur before dissemination of the program change; there should be planning on a massive scale; there should be a rational division of labor and coordination of jobs; and that proponents of the innovation should be willing to accept high initial development costs prior to any dissemination activity.

This brief overview of the research-development-diffusion mode of change suggests some clear potential strengths and weaknesses concerning the possible use of this conceptual framework for installing organizational change. We need also to recognize at least one more assumption inherent in

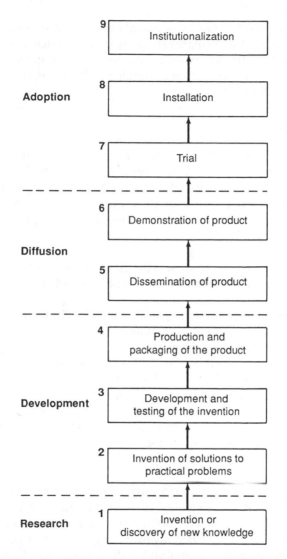

Figure 9.1. Robert Owens's concept of the Research, Development, Diffusion, and Adoption Model of Change. (Robert Owens (1984). *Organizational Behavior in Education,* 3rd Edition, p. 211. Reprinted by permission of Prentice-Hall Inc., Englewood Cliffs, NJ.)

the RD&D model, regardless of whether it serves as a plus or a minus: Tremendous emphasis is placed on the adopting organization's ability to implement an innovative practice in line with the stated expectations for "proper" use of a research-based model. As Paul (1977) noted, "the . . . model places responsibility for accurate replication of R&D products in the user organization." As a result, the supervisor who approaches change from this perspective must be knowledgeable about the research and development carried out to support a particular innovation. In practice, many innovations are not "allowed" to be disseminated to a new setting unless someone from that setting has received substantial training in the proper presentation and use of the innovation.

Linkage Model

Bhola (1965) and Havelock (1973) are most often associated with the final model of organizational change that we review, namely the linkage model, which is the most recent view of how change may occur in organizations. Linkage borrows some characteristics from each of the other models reviewed, and it assumes that change proceeds through four distinct levels (Lipham & Hoeh, 1974):

1. In a fashion similar to what takes place in the problem-solving model, new knowledge relevant to an identified problem is searched for and retrieved;
2. Educational researchers (as in the RD&D model) carry on the research, development, and diffusion of research findings to a particular school where a problem exists;
3. Attention is focused on the relationship and communication systems among the researcher, developer, practitioner, and consumer, as is true of the social interaction model;
4. The linkage process model is enacted. In this phase, each organizational participant is helped to see what other members of the organization are doing in their respective parts of the process of changing.

It is the fourth step of the model where linkage relationships are formed and supported to serve as a catalyst to innovation being accepted within the user organization. This is also the point in the model that calls for the greatest leadership skill and supervisory involvement. Someone must facilitate the linkage processes required for staff within the school, as well as for those who provide information about the innovation from agencies external to the school. The supervisor is a likely candidate for that role of facilitator, or what the literature often describes as a "linker" or "linkage change agent."

The linkage model synthesizes some of the best features of the other three models we reviewed, and, as a result, it has considerable value for use by supervisors in school settings. It does have some limitations, however, not the least of which is that it makes tremendous demands on the abilities of individual supervisors, who must be directly attuned to the activities taking place within the school in order to determine needs for changes, and must also understand the nature of intraorganizational communication that may serve to support desired changes. Supervisors must also be aware of opportunities afforded for change and improvement from agencies in the external environment. Finally, supervisors must possess the communication and interpersonal skills required of anyone who consistently attempts to bridge different groups. In short, the linkage model of organizational change is a powerful one, but it makes heavy and perhaps unrealistic demands on supervisors.

Each model of change reviewed here offers a unique view of how innovation is introduced into a system. There are some common characteristics of organizational change, however, on which all models agree. Gene Hall (1987) recently suggested the following summary of what is known about the phenomenon of change:

1. Change is a process, not an event.
2. Change is accomplished by individuals.
3. Change is a highly personalized experience.
4. Change involves developmental growth.
5. Change is best understood in operational terms.
6. The focus of facilitation should be on individuals, innovations, and the context.

Each of these observations also implies important responsibilities to the supervisor, who must become actively involved in fostering change and not be content merely to sit on the sidelines and wait for things to happen.

BARRIERS TO ORGANIZATIONAL CHANGE

One overriding concern about change must be addressed by the practitioner of supervision as a proactive process. Because of a number of existing barriers, change is difficult to initiate, implement, and maintain in an organization such as a school.

John Lovell and Kimball Wiles (1983) recognized the importance of the educational supervisor's role in stimulating change and identified the following typical barriers to organizational change in schools. For each barrier, we have suggested a way in which this issue is often played out in schools.

1. *Lack of commitment to system goals:* If the teachers or other staff members of a school do not either understand or accept the school's goals, they will not endorse a change to ensure that those goals are being met. This often occurs in settings where the administrative team assumes total control over the establishment of goals. Teachers typically will do little to support an agenda mandated by others, particularly if substantive change is required.

2. *Inadequate feedback:* Teachers frequently lack concrete information and evaluative feedback concerning their performance. We will consider this problem in greater depth in Chapter 14, but it has implications for change processes as well. Teachers' feelings of being left to drift lead to tension, anxiety, and the type of low morale that causes people to withdraw into their roles and avoid any risks required for change.

3. *Inadequate knowledge about the conditions of teaching and learning:* Change implies that some ideal way of behaving is fixed in people's minds as a goal. A high percentage of classroom teachers and others in schools, while serving quite successfully, are nevertheless lacking in the kind of knowledge base that would suggest desirable goals for improved performance and change.

4. *Attitudes toward or values about the proposed change:* If people start out with negative views about an innovation, that attitude will be hard to change. When the concept of team teaching was introduced as an innovation to teachers a number of years ago, it did not take root in many settings because teachers started with negative assumptions even before the practice was formally introduced.

5. *Satisfaction with status quo:* Teachers demonstrate the same reluctance to change their behaviors that others do. The old saying "If it ain't broke, don't fix it" applies equally to educators, who are not always convinced of the need to change the way they have done things in the past. This phenomenon is likely to be strongest in schools where there is a highly stable and mature teaching staff.

6. *Inadequate skill development:* If people lack the skills needed to carry out a new program, they will resist change. A teacher who has little ability to work with groups of gifted students, for example, will resist being required to do just that as part of a new thinking-skills program.

7. *Strong vested interests in the status quo:* People may believe that they will lose something for which they have worked if changes are made in the system around them. Consider, for example, a case where a teacher foresees losing leadership status as chair of a subject department in a junior high school under a new organizational pattern for a middle school that proposes to dissolve departments.

8. *Lack of organizational support:* People will resist supporting a change if they believe that the larger system will not reward or endorse the change. Teachers often express resentment toward engaging in practices that they believe the central office will not wholeheartedly endorse.

9. *Closedness rather than openness in the system:* Teachers who work in schools in what Halpin calls an "open" organizational climate will

be more likely to accept change. "Closed"-climate schools offer fewer opportunities for social interaction that might, in turn, spark greater interest in and support for change.

10. *Lack of compatibility between the change proposal and other dimensions of the organization:* When a change is introduced to one grade level team of teachers, for example, other teams may be affected by the change. If the reports from the first team are not positive, resistance will follow. On the other hand, when a small group gets "turned on" by an idea, others may follow readily.

11. *Threat to individuals:* The issue here is simple yet powerful: People fear new situations. Even a seemingly minor innovation introduced into school practices represents a new situation, and some resistance can be anticipated on that basis alone.

12. *Inadequate knowledge about restraints and possibilities in a situation:* People sometimes avoid participating in a change process because they assume that some unknown conditions will necessarily prohibit the change from being successfully implemented.

13. *Static organizational role structure:* Organizations do not always enjoy the kind of leadership that supports needed change. The majority of a teaching staff may push for some type of curricular or program change, but the principal may prohibit the change from taking place.

14. *Inadequate expertise for solving problems:* Change often brings with it certain problems related to transition. For the most part, people lack expertise in working with ambiguity and other problems that often accompany organizational change. In schools, teachers are generally well-prepared to serve in their assigned instructional roles, but they have had little or no preparation in handling the acceptance of innovation.

15. *Threat to officials in the organization:* The implementation of change in an organization implies significant modifications in existing power structures. Traditional leadership roles and the agendas held by those who inhabit these roles may need complete revision. Such modification, or even the possibility of such change, often carries with it great threats to those who have been "in charge" in the past. This potential "changing of the guard" causes the old guard to dig in its heels and resist. In schools, we often see resistance when principals or other administrators who have held their leadership positions for a long time are suddenly confronted with a change that they believe will erode their control of the schools. Teacher union activities in recent years have caused a considerable amount of negative reaction among some administrators, who believed that teachers wanted to change things "too fast and too much." Recent

suggestions by educational reformers that the role of the principal as now defined is obsolete are, of course, not winning many administrative supporters.

16. *Inadequate rewards for change efforts:* People are often aware of the need for some type of organizational change and have the competence to bring the change about, but they do nothing simply because they decide that the rewards of the change effort will not be sufficient. Teachers might be asked to adopt a new language arts curriculum, for example, but decide that the costs for doing so, in terms of extra meetings, lack of additional pay, and so forth, far outweigh possible rewards.

These identified barriers to organizational change are useful to us in more accurately understanding the nature of organizational behavior. Simply stated, people generally have a tendency to remain constant in their behaviors. Change requires effort; it is easier not to move. Fortunately, people sometimes do engage in innovative practices. To encourage them in that process, proactive supervisors may find recent research on the phases of change useful.

PHASES OF CHANGE

To this point, we have looked at organizational change as if it were a singular event, introduced in sum into the lives of people in an organization. In reality, however, change usually occurs slowly and in clearly defined, deliberate steps. Understanding the nature of these steps may prove helpful to the educational supervisor interested in reducing some of the typical barriers identified above.

Many conceptual frameworks have been developed to analyze the sequential patterns through which change occurs. Rogers (1962) suggests that planned change and innovation efforts proceed through five identifiable and discrete steps: awareness, interest, evaluation, trial, and adoption. Hage and Aiken (1970) modified this view to suggest that four steps—evaluation, initiation, implementation, and routinization—were in fact present in the introduction of innovation. Zaltman, Duncan and Holbek (1973) proposed two major stages and five substages of change, as the following list shows.

I. Initiation Stage
  1. *Knowledge-awareness substage* (Potential adopters of an innovation must be aware that the innovation exists and that there is an opportunity to utilize it in the organization.
  2. *Formation of attitudes toward the innovation substage* (Organizational members form attitudes toward the innovation. Once the initial search

has taken place, the attitudes taken by organizational members are important.)
   3. *Decision substage* (The information concerning the potential innovation is evaluated.)
II. Implementation Stage
   1. *Initial implementation substage* (The organization makes the first attempt to utilize a particular innovation.)
   2. *Continued-sustained implementation substage* (If the implementation has been successful because organizational members understand it and have information about implementation, the innovation will continue to be important.)

Table 9.1 compares the stages of change in these three conceptual frameworks. In addition, there has been some effort to examine the links between a given substage and the typical barriers to innovation through each of those substages.

At the "knowledge-awareness" substage, for example, Havelock (1969) noted not only the strong tendency that organizations show toward trying to maintain stability, but also the constant personal threat that change suggests to organization members; people wonder, "What is this going to do to *me*?" Barriers at the "attitude-formation" and "decision" substages often stem from organizational tendencies to modify the nature of messages so that the meaning of those messages might be ignored. Because they feel unprepared, organizations often do whatever they can to subvert any effort toward change.

When an innovation reaches the "initial implementation" substage, it intersects with organizational disequilibrium at its highest point; members find it hard to know what they have really gotten themselves into. In other words, people at this point may not be absolutely clear as to the precise reasons why they ever began the change process in the first place. Finally, the

TABLE 9.1. COMPARISONS OF THE VARIOUS STAGES OF CHANGE AS DEFINED AND CONCEPTUALIZED IN THREE DIFFERENT THEORETICAL MODELS.

Rogers (1962)	Hage and Aiken (1970)	Zaltman, Duncan, and Holbek (1973)
Awareness		I. Initiation Stage
		1. Knowledge-Awareness
	1. Evaluation	2. Formation of attitudes
Interest		toward the innovation
Evaluation		3. Decision
Trial	2. Initiation	II. Implementation Stage
		1. Initial implementation
Adoption	3. Implementation	
	4. Routinization	2. Continued-sustained implementation

greatest barrier to change at the "continued-sustained implementation" substage is undoubtedly the fact that people often lose interest quickly in any innovation.

OVERCOMING THE BARRIERS

Despite the most effective of supervisory efforts, change is difficult to initiate, implement, and maintain in any organization for a multitude of reasons. There are many different barriers to change in general, as well as particular inhibitors that are characteristic of each identifiable stage in the process of adopting innovations. Although it is unlikely that all barriers can be totally overcome, Watson (1966) identified 12 different ways in which people in leadership roles might be able to minimize the resistance to change found in their organizations.

1. Resistance will be less if administrators and managers [and supervisors] feel that the project is their own—not one devised and operated by outsiders.
2. Resistance will be less if the . . . innovation clearly has whole-hearted support from top officials in the system.
3. Resistance will be less if the [organizational] participants see the change as reducing rather than increasing their present burdens.
4. Resistance will be less if the [innovative] project accords with values already acknowledged by participants.
5. Resistance will be less if the program offers the kind of *new* experience which interests participants.
6. Resistance will be less if participants feel their autonomy and security are not threatened.
7. Resistance will be less if participants have joined in diagnostic efforts leading them to agree on what the basic problems are and their importance.
8. Resistance will be less if the project is adopted by consensual group decision.
9. Resistance will be reduced if proponents are able to empathize with opponents; to recognize valid objections; and to take steps to relieve unnecessary fears.
10. Resistance will be reduced if it is recognized that innovations are likely to be misunderstood and misinterpreted, and if provision is made for feedback of perceptions of the project and for further clarification of need.
11. Resistance will be reduced if participants experience acceptance, support, trust, and confidence in their relations with one another.
12. Resistance will be reduced if the project is kept open to revision and

reconsideration if experience indicates that changes will be desirable. (Watson, 1966, p. 145–146)

One theme is apparent in all of Watson's recommendations: Overcoming resistance to change requires sensitivity by the supervisor to the personal concerns of people in the organization. In terms of proactive supervision, we cannot overemphasize the importance of knowing not only one's own priorities, values, philosophy, and action plan, but also those of the people who work in the organization. While such an awareness will not conquer all resistance to change, we can certainly assume that, the more we know about and are sensitive to the concerns of individuals, the less they will resist change.

SUMMARY

We assume in this chapter that "change for the sake of change" should not be promoted, but that innovation and change are inevitable and necessary for the continuing growth of any organization. Without periodic improvements, organizations will stagnate.

In the first part of the chapter we reviewed four conceptual models of change: problem-solving, social interaction, research-development-diffusion, and linkage. We suggested that all four models have strengths and weaknesses in terms of their potential to describe ideal strategies for implementing organizational change, but that the linkage model offers particular advantages because it incorporates elements from each of the other three.

We also examined a number of typical inhibitors to change, including general satisfaction with the status quo and lack of adequate rewards for participating in change. We also suggested that educational supervisors might find particularly helpful the recent efforts to define stages in the change process.

Finally, we concluded by suggesting a number of strategies that might be employed by supervisors who are intent on reducing, if not eliminating, resistance to change efforts in schools.

SUGGESTED ACTIVITIES

1. Talk with a group of teachers in a school to determine when they have seen some type of change introduced into their school, for example, a new reading curriculum. The actual change itself is not important, but try to ascertain the strategies that were used by supervisors, administrators, other teachers, or whoever was responsible for introducing the innovation to the school. Compare the strategy with the various change processes described in this chapter.

2. Visit three different schools and make an assessment, after interviewing the principal and two or three teachers in each school, as to whether the schools might be classified as belonging to any of the change phases or stages described in this chapter. Remember that a school does not necessarily have to have gone through a very dramatic change recently to qualify as having undergone change.

REFERENCES

Bennis, Warren G., Benne, Kenneth D., & Chin, Robert. (1969). *The planning of change* (2nd Ed.). New York: Holt, Rinehart & Winston.

Bhola, H. S. (1965, October). *The configuration theory of innovation diffusion.* Columbus: The Ohio State University College of Education.

Clark, David L., & Guba, Egor G. (1975, April). The configurational perspective: A new view of educational knowledge production and utilization. *Educational Researcher, 4*(4).

Fullan, Michael. (1973). Overview of the innovative process and the user. *Interchange, 3,* 1–46.

Hage, Gerald, & Aiken, Michael (1970). *Social change in complex organizations.* New York: Random House.

Hall, Gene, & Loucks, Susan. (1976). *A developmental model for determining whether or not the treatment really is implemented.* Austin: Texas Research and Development Center for Teacher Education.

Hall, Gene. (1987). *Taking charge of change* Alexandria, VA: Association for Supervision and Curriculum Development.

Havelock, Ronald G. (1969). *Planning for innovation through the dissemination and utilization of knowledge.* Ann Arbor, MI: Institute for Social Research, Center for Research on Utilization of Scientific Knowledge.

——— (1972). *Bibliography on knowledge utilization and dissemination.* Ann Arbor, MI: Institute for Social Research, Center for Research on Utilization of Scientific Knowledge.

——— (1973). *Training for change agents.* Ann Arbor, MI: Institute for Social Research, Center for Research on Utilization of Scientific Knowledge.

House, Ernest R. (1974). *The politics of educational innovation.* Berkeley, CA: McCutchan.

Lipham, James M. (1965). Leadership and administration. In Daniel Griffiths (Ed.), *Behavioral science and educational administration.* Chicago: National Society for the Study of Education.

Lipham, James M., & Hoeh, James. (1974). *The principalship: Foundations and functions.* New York: Harper & Row.

Lippitt, G. (1969). *Organizational renewal.* New York: Appleton-Century-Crofts.

Lippitt, R., Watson, J., & Westley, B. (1958). *The dynamics of planned change.* New York: Harcourt Brace Jovanovich.

Lovell, John T., & Wiles, Kimball. (1983). *Supervision for better schools* (5th Ed.). Englewood Cliffs, NJ: Prentice-Hall.

McLaughlin, Milbrey. (1976). Implementation as mutual adaptation: Change in classroom organization. *Teachers College Record, 77,* 339–351.

Owens, Robert (1986). *Organizational behavior in education* (3rd Ed.). Englewood Cliffs, NJ: Prentice-Hall.

Paul, Douglas. (1977). Change processes at the elementary, secondary, and post-secondary levels. In J. Culbertson & N. Nask (Eds.), *Linking processes in educational improvement.* Columbus, OH: University Council for Educational Administration.

Rogers, E. M. (1962). *Diffusion of innovations.* New York: The Free Press of Glencoe.

Rogers, E. M., & Shoemaker, F. F. (1971). *Communication of innovations: A cross-cultural approach.* New York: Free Press.

Ryan, B., & Gross, N. (1943). The Diffusion of hybrid seed corn in two Iowa communities. *Rural Sociology, 8,* 15–24.

Schmuck, Richard A., & Miles, Matthew B. (1971). *Organizational development in schools.* Palo Alto, CA: National Press Books.

Watson, Goodwin. (1966). Resistance to change. In Goodwin Watson (Ed.), *Concepts for social change.* Washington, DC: National Training Laboratories.

Zaltman, Gerald, Duncan, Robert, & Holbek, Jonny. (1973). *Innovations and organizations.* New York: Wiley-Interscience.

CHAPTER 10

Exercising Power and Authority

Although supervisory activities in schools and other organizations promote needed change, the concepts of "power" and "authority" inherent in supervision frequently evoke negative reactions. Classroom teachers intent on exploring alternative career options seem particularly concerned about the need for supervisors to exercise power and authority, perhaps because of a long-standing reluctance among educators to think in terms of trying to control others.

In this chapter we will explore the concepts of organizational power and authority in more descriptive and, it is hoped, less threatening ways. A formal leadership role such as that of a school supervisor or administrator carries with it the responsibility of authority, and that authority brings a degree of power, whether earned or delegated. In short, anyone who finds it unpleasant to think in these terms should probably eschew a career in supervision or administration.

We will explore the twin issues of power and authority as well as how the judicious exercise of these by supervisory personnel may bring about more effective organizations. As we have done in previous chapters, we will first consider some definitions for power and authority and then present the characteristics of each concept in greater detail. The chapter concludes with a consideration of some of the immediate, practical applications of these concepts for the individual interested in engaging in more effective and proactive supervisory processes.

ALTERNATIVE DEFINITIONS

"Power" and "authority" are terms that occur often in discussions of organizational leadership, but they are used with a surprising lack of precision. Many people, classroom teachers frequently among them, express distrust of those who appear to possess either characteristic. However, any fundamental understanding of the nature of supervision, whether in schools or other organizations, must include an understanding of power and authority.

In fairly simple terms, Max Weber (1947) defined *power* as "the probability that one actor within a social relationship will be in a position to carry out his own will despite resistance" (p. 52). Power, then, is the fundamental ability of one person to command some degree of compliance on the part of another person. By contrast, *authority* suggests a much less general concept. Resser (1973) defined authority as "a right granted to a manager to make decisions, within limitations, to assign duties to subordinates, and to require subordinates' conformance to expected behavior" (p. 311). Based on the distinctions suggested in these definitions, we can make some important generalizations about the distinctions between power and authority.

Everyone has power, or at least the *potential* for exercising power. Each of us potentially has the ability to encourage another person to behave in some particular way. Even a person whose role in society seems most unimportant may effect some change in others or in society in general. When we speak of power we tend to think in terms of its use. We think first of those whose roles automatically provide a potential for influencing others. Everyone has power, but not everyone makes use of it or develops the know-how required to exercise power effectively from a position that does not appear to be strong. This observation is true regardless of the way in which power was acquired in the first place, whether by assuming a position where formal authority is normally delegated, or by demonstrating competence in a typically "nonpower" role.

Not everyone, on the other hand, has access to authority, which is a condition possessed by a relatively small percentage of people. According to Herbert Simon (1945), a person with authority has and "uses the formal criterion of the receipt of a command . . . as his basis of choice" (pp. 108–109). Authority is a legitimized statement of one or more person's formal designation to control the behaviors in an organization, and it derives from certain societal sources to be reviewed later in this chapter.

The primary distinctions between authority and power are fairly straightforward. *Power* is the *ability* to make others behave in certain ways and is available to most people in society, regardless of whether or not they have formal authority. *Authority* is the *right* to make others behave in certain ways and is not available to everyone but rather is formally conferred on some.

Interestingly, however, the fact that people have authority does not necessarily guarantee that they will exercise power.

In the next two sections we will consider some specific features of these two characteristics of organizational life, beginning with the unique properties of power.

CHARACTERISTICS OF POWER

In this section we examine the broader concept of power by looking at its traditional sources. French and Raven (1960) suggested five sources of social power, and we will look at how these are related to the role of an educational supervisor.

French and Raven: Sources of Social Power

Reward power is the capacity to provide rewards to others in the organization as a way to influence their behavior. In a school setting, for example, a school board might offer bonus pay to teachers who perform at a level consistent with established district goals. Merit-pay proposals are fairly clear examples of attempts to exercise reward power in schools. In the context of our earlier discussion contrasting supervision with administration, we should note that supervisory personnel are traditionally thought to have very limited access to the use of reward power in organizations, whereas administrators generally are thought to control it. This perspective is limiting, however, because the concept of "rewards" can mean things other than the financial incentives usually controlled by school administrators or boards of education. Supervisors often exercise reward power in more subtle ways, such as assigning some teachers to more attractive committees, or distributing newer, more attractive curricular materials. Richard Gorton (1980) identified the following assumptions inherent in the use of reward power:

1. The strength of the reward power will increase with the magnitude of the rewards that the other person perceives another can obtain for him or her.
2. The strength of the reward power will depend on the *actual* rewards that a person can produce, not on what he or she hopes or would like to produce.
3. Unsuccessful attempts to exert reward power will tend to decrease the perceived strengths of that power in the future.

Coercive power is the capacity of one person to provide punishment or negative consequences to another, in a deliberate attempt to control the other person's behavior. Again, this form of power is normally associated with administrators, not supervisors. However, supervisory personnel make use of coercive strategies when they do such things as write negative evaluations of teacher performance, or reject new curricular programs that may be desired by some teachers. Gorton noted the following assumptions related to the use of coercive power:

1. The strength of coercive power will increase with the magnitude of the punishments or costs which the other person perceives that the person exercising power may apply.
2. The strength of the coercive power will depend on the *actual* sanctions or punishments that are applied, not only on what one hopes to apply.
3. Unsuccessful attempts to exert coercive power will tend to increase the perceived strength of that power in the future.

Legitimate power is most similar to what shall later be described as formal authority. Control of one person by another is based on the assumption that the person exercising the power has a legitimate right to do so, and is supported by a statement of law, policy, or even historical precedent and tradition.

Referent power is the tendency of other individuals to be attracted by and to identify closely with the person who exercises the power. A certain emphasis is therefore placed on the charismatic qualities of the supervisor, administrator, or other person who is making use of the power. Simply stated, this is power derived largely from the extent to which people "like" or respect the person in charge. Gorton's assumptions related to this source of power include:

1. The greater the perceived attractiveness of the person exercising power by another person or group, the more likely that there will be identification with the leader.
2. The stronger the identification with the leader by another person, the greater will be the likelihood that referent power can be successfully utilized by the leader.

Finally, *expert power* is the ability to influence others' behavior based on special knowledge. This is the power source most often linked to the supervisor's role. Because supervisors do not enjoy formal authority, the belief is that they must rely on public perceptions of their expertise and competence as a way to influence others. Teachers yield to the power of a supervisor of language arts, for instance, because they believe that the supervisor has special knowledge in the field of language arts. Gorton's assumptions concerning the application of expert power follow:

1. The strength of the expert power of a person will vary with the actual knowledge and skill that he or she might possess, along with others' perceptions of his or her expertise.

2. The stronger the perception by others that the leader possesses expert power, the higher will be their satisfaction and evaluation of him or her as a leader.

French and Raven's five sources of social power can be understood from both a descriptive and a normative perspective. They provide certain insights into how power may be classified for further analysis, and they can also provide the supervisor with a way of understanding the implications to be derived from reliance on one source or another. Understanding the differences that exist between referent power and reward power, for example, and the likely effect that each is likely to have on people who work in organizations, is a powerful guide to behavior. Consider the probable response to a supervisor who worked at increasing his or her expert powers by learning more about a particular topic as contrasted with the probable response to a supervisor who tried to "pull rank" by using threats, punishments, or other efforts associated with coercive power strategies.

Compliance Theory

Amitai Etzioni (1961) analyzed power relationships in organizations through the concept of *compliance theory,* which suggests that power sources should be matched with organizational types for more efficient use. Etzioni identified three major types of organizations, defined by their fundamental goals as "economic," "order," or "cultural." If the primary goal of an organization is to preserve order (political, moral, financial, or any other type), for example, the most appropriate source of power would be coercive. To understand this, we can look at how police use coercive (or impled coercive) power in their work, which is primarily directed toward fostering order and control. In a similar vein, an assistant principal in charge of student discipline for a high school would make much greater use of coercive power than of any other type, according to Etzioni's theory.

CHARACTERISTICS OF AUTHORITY

The legitimized and sanctioned use of power normally referred to as *authority* may also be understood according to certain characteristics.

Authority Types

The German sociologist Max Weber, whose definition of authority we noted earlier, suggested that there are three major types of authority utilized in different organizations:

1. *Traditional Authority*: Authority derived from tradition. People accept the control of others because it is assumed that those "others" have some sort of traditionally legitimate, absolute right to exercise that authority with no challenge. In school settings, for instance, a parent may tell a child to obey a teacher for the simple reason that the person *is* a teacher, and a teacher always deserves respect. Although this may not hold true in classrooms on a day-to-day basis, many such forms of reliance on traditional authority types may still be seen.

2. *Charismatic Authority:* Authority based on the assumption that the leader has some special gift, or even supernatural powers. Examples of this type of authority are religious leaders and some televangelists who, despite apparent inconsistencies in their personal lives, continue to attract millions of followers and their money because they have successfully established in the minds of their adherents that they possess special gifts from God.

3. *Legal Authority:* Authority derived from laws, policies, or statutes. Military officers have authority because such authority is decreed by regulation. As many enlisted personnel recognize, superior officers may lack identifiable skills or charisma; they are, however, in charge simply because they *are* officers.

Educators can use these descriptions of different types of authority in understanding why we defer to certain individuals. In addition to determining *type* of authority, however, we also need to determine whether it is "formal" or "functional."

Formal versus Functional Authority

Robert Peabody (1962) defines *formal* authority as authority derived from such sources as the organizational hierarchy, laws, a person's position in an organization, or office. *Functional* authority comes from such things as a person's professional expertise and competence, interpersonal skills, and suggestion of great experience in handling a particular situation. The tendency to assume that functional authority is "softer" or "better" is really not warranted. People who exercise authority make use of both approaches. On the other hand, one person may deliberately select a particular strategy in order to effect a desired goal. A school superintendent, for example, who might easily rely on his or her formal authority in order to bring about changes in the behavior of the teaching staff, might choose instead to seek a more indirect way to influence changes in behavior. The superintendent, in other words, might consciously seek to exercise functional rather than—or in addition to—formal authority.

I do not mean to suggest that an effective supervisor should shift between formal and functional authority patterns. Such inconsistency is unwise, if not impossible. For one thing, deliberate switches from a formal to a functional approach are often perceived by staff members as attempts to manipulate behavior in playing the game of "good cop–bad cop" with prisoners. Selecting one pattern rather than the other might very well be impossible for those supervisors who have no, or at best limited, access to formal authority strategies. The critical issue for the practitioner of proactive supervision is always to recognize the strengths and limitations of both formal and functional authority patterns.

IMPLICATIONS FOR SUPERVISORS

Power and authority are central issues in understanding the field of educational supervision. In Chapter 3 we noted the continuing controversy in the study of supervision over whether or not supervisors ever really get anything done. We suggested that the critical concern in assessing a supervisor's potential power rests in our appreciation of how much the supervisor can motivate *others* to do something.

Supervisors and others involved with supervisory activity can in fact be very effective, and they can be effective without any formal authority. Supervisory effectiveness can rest in functional authority and power. If the supervisor learns to engage primarily in behaviors that influence others, then he or she will bring about change. In school settings, the adoption of techniques designed to have an impact based on expertise, competence, and interpersonal skills will probably result in longer-lasting change on the part of teachers and other staff members who are well-educated, sophisticated, and accustomed to performing in settings where they must think for themselves. The supervisor who relies solely on formal authority and "pulls rank" to try to make others perform in a particular way will rarely be effective and, with professional employees, will often actually do more harm than good. Teachers who are "told" what to do will often rebel from what they perceive as an effort to manipulate their behavior.

Proactive supervision assumes that a practitioner will carefully weigh the outcomes likely to result from the use of different types of power and authority. Proactive supervision is an effective approach because it leads us toward finding ways of influencing as many people as possible within an organization. Power and authority are central to the questions of motivation or influence, and anyone who is uncomfortable with analyzing these topics in a school setting might well be advised to look at alternative professional roles.

SUMMARY

In this chapter we considered some definitions of two inescapable concerns of supervisory personnel—power and authority—and we emphasized the supervisor's need to understand and appreciate the most appropriate and judicious ways to exercise power and authority in school settings.

We reviewed the salient characteristics of power, including the sources of power offered by French and Raven and compliance theory as developed by Etzioni. The section dealing with authority included a brief overview of Weber's definitions of three types of authority—traditional, charismatic, and legal—and a discussion concerning the distinction between formal and functional authority. Finally, we noted how the concepts of authority and power are germane to the development of understanding educational supervision, particularly proactive supervision.

SUGGESTED ACTIVITIES

1. Interview a group of supervisors and a group of administrators and ask them to describe the strategies and techniques that they would all follow in trying to encourage teachers to comply with a new school district policy. As each group describes its practices, make an assessment of the types of power (according to French and Raven's conceptualization) that are being used. Are there differences between what the supervisors would do, as contrasted with the administrative group?
2. Talk with four or five teachers and present brief descriptions of the different authority types presented in this chapter. Ask each person to identify those situations in which they would expect supervisors or administrators to rely on one or another type.

REFERENCES

Etzioni, Amitai. (1961). *A comparative analysis of complex organizations.* New York: Free Press.

French, J. R. P., & Raven, B. (1960). The bases of social power. In D. Cartwright & A. Zander (Eds.), *Group dynamics: Research and theory* (2nd ed.). Evanston, IL: Harper & Row.

Gorton, Richard A. (1980). *School administration and supervision: Important issues, concepts, and case studies.* Dubuque, IA: Brown.

Peabody, Robert L. (1962, March). Perceptions of organizational authority: A comparative analysis. *Administrative Science Quarterly, 6*(4).

Resser, Clayton. (1973). *Management: Functions and modern concepts.* Chicago: Scott, Foresman.

Simon, Herbert (1945). *Administrative Behavior.* New York: Macmillan.

Weber, Max. (1947). *The theory of social and economic organization* (Talcott Parsons, Trans.). Glencoe, IL: The Free Press.

CHAPTER 11

Conflict as a Supervisory Reality

A lot of "pop" management literature features self-improvement prescriptions for leaders and would-be leaders to follow, and among the most frequently stated is the notion that effective managers must learn to reduce, or even totally eliminate, conflict from their lives. These books suggest simple steps, similar to time-management techniques, that may be followed to clean up conflict-riddled lives.

I am always amused by these "sure-cures" for managers. It is, simply put, impossible to take on a leadership role in an organization without confronting conflict. In fact, the more successful a manager or supervisor becomes, the more likely it is that he or she will experience more intense, frequent, and visible forms of conflict. Even for those not in formal organizational leadership positions, conflict is an unavoidable fact of life.

Some organizational theorists argue that conflict is not only an *inevitable* feature of organizational life but is also a *desirable* ingredient of functioning organizations. Life without periodic change is stagnant, this argument suggests, and the development of conflict is one way to force necessary change. Leaders are legitimately held responsible not for reducing or eliminating organizational conflict, but rather for using it to promote institutional improvement and growth.

The issue that I will address in this chapter, then, is not how to avoid conflict, but rather the ways in which a supervisor can minimize the negative consequences of conflict. First we will explore what conflict is, in conceptual terms, and present four standard types of conflict. In the second half of the chapter we will focus on a model designed to help us understand how to handle conflict in our lives.

WHAT IS CONFLICT?

Morton Deutsch (1973; cited in Owens, 1987) noted that "a conflict exists whenever incompatible activities occur" (p. 133). For Deutsch, then, conflict is little more than a state of disagreement between two parties. The word can describe a range of phenomena all the way from a simple difference of opinion to war. Kenneth Boulding (1962) suggests that the factor that distinguishes types of conflict is the amount of hostility present in the disagreement. Conflict between two people who want to drive their cars in the same space on an expressway may range in potency from simple annoyance (low hostility) to the violent and destructive behavior seen recently in some cities, where drivers have actually shot at one another (extremely high hostility). We cannot avoid this kind of conflict entirely, unless we decide never to drive, and the fact is that we must drive on freeways in order to get around cities like Chicago, Boston, or Los Angeles. Therefore we must put ourselves "at risk" to encounter conflict. The key is to remain at the annoyance or low end of the continuum.

Owens (1987) further distinguishes among low- or high-hostility events by noting that the major difference

> lies in the motivation behind them, often not easily discernible. Although considerable (and often vigorous) conflict may erupt over such issues as improving school performance, ways of desegregating a school system, or how to group children for instruction, the parties to the conflict may well be motivated by essentially constructive goals. The key is whether or not the parties involved want to work with the system or are motivated by a wish to destroy it. (p. 246)

If conflict is an inevitable organizational reality, what effects will it have? Obviously there may be good or bad consequences of any institutional characteristic, including conflict. When disagreements occur marked by either high or low hostility, two things may happen. The lack of consensus may lead to improvement in the organization, because communication takes place, and compromise or further appreciation of opposite views is achieved. In this case, the consequence of conflict might be described as "good." On the other hand, disagreement may result in polarization of viewpoints, the end of communication, and personal animosity among members in the organization. Here, the results of the conflict are clearly "bad." The responsibility of the leader, particularly a proactive educational supervisor, is to guide the conflicts that will always be present toward a lower level of hostility and therefore a higher probability of serving as positive forces for the organization. To try to avoid or eliminate conflict is, simply put, to avoid a legitimate supervisory responsibility, and the results of such an activity will almost always be negative. Think, for instance, of the school principal who wants to avoid conflict and therefore simply sits in an office all day with the door closed, shutting out the potential disagreements taking place in the corridors and classrooms. This behavior may be satisfying to the principal, whose blood pressure does not rise in response to the things going on outside the office, but its consequences to the organization, which consists of both children and teachers, are ultimately truly negative; opportunities for growth through resolution of conflicts are lost. In short, schools where the principal's door is always closed are rarely exciting schools. I am not suggesting that supervisors should deliberately stir up conflict. But when conflict appears, no effective leader should run from it.

TYPES AND SOURCES OF CONFLICT

The proactive supervisor needs to understand two additional dimensions of organizational conflict: the sources of conflict, and the types of conflict most frequently faced by educational supervisors.

Sources of Conflict

Educational supervisors typically face conflict from three sources: from people and things within an organization; from people and things outside the organization; and from within the individual. Owens (1987) defined the sources of conflict in this way:

> Conflict can occur *within* persons or social units; it is *intra*personal or *intra*group (or, of course, *intra*national). Conflict can also be experienced *between* two or more people or social units: so-called *inter*personal, *inter*group, or *inter*national conflict. (p. 92)

The only conflict described above that does not appear almost daily in the school leader's life is international, although even here there are probably situations where conflict is felt by supervisory personnel.

In the context of our overall goal of identifying ways to reduce the negative consequences of conflict, each source suggests strategies for the supervisor to follow. Fundamentally, the effective supervisor is one who develops the capacity to remain aware of what is going on within the organization so that potential conflicts may be identified in advance whenever possible. Developing a sensitivity to potential conflicts both inside and outside the organization does not guarantee the prevention of future conflict, but it does ensure that the supervisor will not be surprised (and frustrated) when something happens. There will never be, for example, a school in which every teacher gets along with every other teacher, or is totally satisfied with every decision made by the supervisor or administrator. When a leader makes a decision, someone will inevitably disagree. Poor leadership practice is anticipating neither the likely source nor the potency of the conflict that a decision will engender. Proactive supervisors have a sense of where the "land mines" are located, not in order to defuse them all in advance, but rather to find a path among them which will cause the least damage.

Analyzing conflict that arises from within the individual necessarily grows from an individual's ability to "know thyself." As was indicated in Chapter 2, many very important values can be defined in the process of developing and reviewing an individual philosophy of education. One of the greatest benefits of such continuous self-assessment is that it can alert us both to our values and to likely sources of personal conflict.

Types of Conflict

In the discussion of Jacob Getzels's social systems model in Chapter 5, we indicated that organizations are best understood as the products of an ongoing and dynamic interactive process involving individual (idiographic) and institutional (nomothetic) dimensions. Getzels defined effectiveness as the extent to which congruence (or lack of disagreement and conflict) was present in the interactions between the component elements of the theoretical model. From this view of effectiveness we can identify four major types of organizational conflict: *interrole, intrareference group, interreference group,* and *role-personality.*

Interrole conflict is the "disagreement between two or more roles simultaneously fulfilled by one person" (Lipham and Hoeh, 1974, p. 133). The supervisor feels the effects of trying to "wear too many hats."

High school subject department chairpersons often suffer from interrole conflict. Some released time from teaching is normally provided for chairpersons to engage in supervisory and administrative duties, but chairpersons are still usually expected to teach classes, advise students, serve on assorted governance and planning activities in the school or district, and, in many cases, do a duty assignment each day, coach a sport, or moderate some type of student activity. These assignments and expectations are only those encountered during the work day; personal and professional commitments— family, graduate education, community activities, and so forth—add fuel to feelings of conflict and stress. Naturally, the many competing demands cannot always be kept separate from one another. At some point, for example, the department chair may find it impossible to grade student papers before the next class and also fill out a purchase order to get materials requested by department faculty before the deadline imposed by the district business office. These professional pressures are often accompanied by additional demands from personal activities and responsibilities, the department chairperson may also owe a paper for a university course, have two children who need attention, and be a soloist in the church choir.

Such situations, where people are trying to "juggle several balls at once," are by no means infrequent. Most of us occasionally find that we have more commitments than time, and we sense some degree of interrole conflict. The more competent we are at what we do, the more likely we are to feel this type of pressure; the conflict serves almost as a recognition of ability. Nevertheless, the consequences can be negative. Important jobs are not completed, psychological stress intensifies, and our ability to fulfill our responsibilities is greatly impaired. We *can* take steps to reduce this type of conflict as well as its negative consequences.

For one thing, people facing interrole conflict need to take stock of their various competing professional and personal commitments to set priorities and decide which activities may be removed from their personal agendas. Must we sing in the church choir while taking graduate courses, or can we look forward to solos after completing the degree? Sometimes things that are important must be dropped, at least temporarily, to provide time for activities of greater personal or professional value.

Another way to reduce interrole conflict is to engage in time-management activities. Many schemes exist to help people control their uses of time. Larry Hughes (1984) offers one that I find particularly useful:

1. *Analyze your job* to clarify precisely what it is you are supposed to do in a particular setting. Formal job descriptions should be viewed as starting points in determining what is *really* expected in a school or district.
2. *Determine the difference between managing and doing.* Remember that efficiency (doing things well) must be consciously combined with effectiveness (getting the right things done well).
3. *Set personal goals and objectives* and develop strategies for achieving them. Define the goals precisely enough so that they may serve to guide continuing behavior.
4. *Conduct a personal time audit* as a way to see how you have really been using your time.
5. *Avoid interruptions on the job.* Watch out for "drop-in visitors" and unwanted telephone calls that divert you from your focus on effective use of available time.
6. *Delegate.* Organize yourself, your subordinates, colleagues, and bosses to accomplish necessary work most efficiently.
7. *Plan and conduct effective meetings.* Meetings should serve the needs of the organization and the people who work in it, and not as roadblocks to effective use of time. Consider how meetings might be arranged to reduce interrole conflict.
8. *Organize productive committees and task forces.* A primary cause of interrole conflict is that one person tries to do too many things. Increase effectiveness not only by delegating particular responsibili-

ties to others but also by assigning tasks and projects to well-organized committees. Consider how others in the organization might be enlisted to reduce competing demands.

No matter how efficient your use of time-management techniques, ultimately you can gain control over your commitments and the dysfunction caused by interrole conflict only through reviewing and assessing the personal principles that guide your choices. No one can do everything. At some point you need to decide which involvements are most important, and which may be ignored.

Intrareference group conflict is "conflict or disagreement within a reference group in their expectations for the role of the supervisor" (Lipham and Hoeh, 1974, p. 133). The supervisor is "caught in a crossfire." Once again, we might focus on the chairperson of a high school subject department. There may be a dozen or more teachers in the department, some of whom believe that the chair is simply "one of the teachers" who happens to hold a title, and others who may look at the department head as a stock clerk, responsible for doing nothing more than securing materials and equipment for the teachers. Yet another group of teachers may expect direct instructional monitoring from the chair, such as observing teachers in their classrooms. No clear, common vision of the role of the department chair exists, and intrareference group conflict may well be the result.

Interreference group conflict is the "disagreement in two or more (different) reference groups in their expectations" for the role of the supervisor (Lipham and Hoeh, 1974, p. 101). Here, the supervisor is "caught in the middle." A central office supervisor, for example, who visits teachers in schools may be seen by these teachers as a trusted colleague who can help them address their instructional concerns. But the same supervisor may be viewed by administrators in the central office as a perfect person to get out into the schools and "get the dirt" on the teachers. The supervisor is thus viewed as a potential "snoopervisor" by one group, and a "human relations specialist" by another group. This is a precise example of interreference group conflict.

Conflicts that arise from a supervisor's relationships with groups can be particularly frustrating and damaging to supervisory effectiveness. When groups have differing expectations about how a job will or should be carried out, the conflict is rooted in the perceptions of others; it is beyond the supervisor's immediate control. Nevertheless, some techniques can help reduce the potentially negative consequences of conflicts involving groups.

Many group conflicts can be headed off if jobs are precisely defined before they are begun. What are the formal, stated expectations listed as part of a high school subject department chairperson's position? Is there any suggestion that it is appropriate to be a "gofer"? An instructional leader? Is the job defined so vaguely that such wildly divergent expectations might exist? If so, try to clarify those expectations—and your own—at the outset. For the central office supervisor mentioned above, find out how teachers have traditionally viewed the responsibilities of central office supervisors, and ask central office administrators directly about their views concerning proper performance by supervisors.

Group conflict can also be reduced if the individual supervisor has a well-developed concept of what it means to be a supervisor. Again, there is no real substitute for a well-articulated personal philosophy. We can rarely be forced to juggle many competing expectations for a job if we have clearly defined our own role. This personal clarity may have the immediate consequence of angering some people in the organization who do not appreciate the supervisor's self-definition of role. This anger will typically be relatively short-lived, however, and considerably less dysfunctional over time than chronic uncertainty over what is proper behavior in a job.

Role-personality conflict is the "disagreement between the expectations for the role of the . . . [supervisor] and his [or her] personality need-dispositions" (Lipham and Hoeh, 1974, p. 133). Here, recalling the characteristics of Getzels's social systems model is particularly helpful. Figure 11.1 indicates that considerable incongruence can exist between the two elements of role and personality: The job may not fit the person.

Role-personality conflict may be the most frustrating of all, because it suggests that a person has made an error in judgment by selecting the wrong career path. A teacher, for example, decides to leave the classroom and go into a supervisory or administrative position based on some assumptions of what that position will be like, only to find that those assumptions were misguided. We might argue, of course, that the new supervisor can simply return to being a teacher, but the fact is that going back may be extremely difficult. A teacher who goes into a supervisory role has typically invested a lot of time and money in additional university courses, and has moved into a position with greater financial rewards. Turning away from the new status and prestige of a leadership role may be next to impossible—achievable, certainly, for some, but hard for most.

Again, there are ways in which the negative impact of this kind of conflict

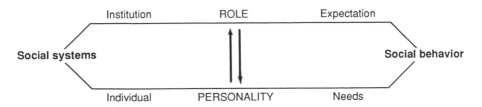

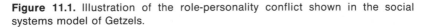

Figure 11.1. Illustration of the role-personality conflict shown in the social systems model of Getzels.

can be reduced. First and most importantly, of course, serious attention should be paid to the nature of a position *before* assuming it. We need to question the personal asssumptions and review the motivations that underlie a choice of a new job. Are our expectations realistic? Do our assumptions match the actual tasks performed?

Those who are responsible for training people for new roles also have an opportunity—and a responsibility—to acquaint applicants with the realities of their intended positions well in advance of a move. Apprenticeships, training in clinical settings, and numerous other forms of field-based situations help people understand their future roles before assuming their new job on a full-time basis. Lawyers go through clerkships, and physicians do residencies and clinical internships. In professional education, aspiring teachers must take part in student teaching and, increasingly, future administrators and supervisors engage in internships, planned field experiences, and numerous other activities that allow them to "taste" the new job before coming on board permanently. The primary purpose of these activities is to help people learn how to use certain practical skills that are related to the effective performance of their jobs, but I believe that a second, equally important purpose is fulfilled by a preservice practicum: It is to allow people to see and try a job in a *low-risk* setting, where no "loss of face" is attached to a decision, based on a glimpse of a career, not on the intention to pursue that position in the future. Preservice "tryouts" provide opportunities for people to drop out before experiencing the type of role-personality conflict that damages not only the organization but also the future administrator or supervisor. Those responsible for such programs must emphasize and safeguard their low-risk status, and must condone in nonjudgmental ways the decisions that some participants may make *not* to continue.

CONFLICT-HANDLING STYLES

We have reviewed techniques for reducing personal conflict and for decreasing potential negative impact on the overall organization. In addition, I would propose that the destructive power of conflict can be reduced by further analysis of the nature of conflict and the ways in which people address conflict situations in their lives.

One of the most frequently employed diagnostic procedures for analyzing organizational conflict is a model that assesses the nature of conflict-handling styles. The model, designed first by Kenneth Thomas (1974), suggests that people react to conflicting settings in one of two basic ways: (1) People deal with conflict assertively, by becoming aggressive about their own rights, needs, and interests; they exercise their own needs above those of others; or (2) people deal with conflict cooperatively, by playing down their own needs and trying to satisfy the concerns of others. Figure 11.2 illustrates

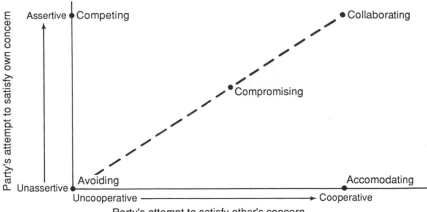

Figure 11.2. Model of conflict-handling modes. (Jamieson, D. W., & Thomas, K. W. (1974). Power and conflict in the student-teacher relationships. *Journal of Applied Behavioral Science, 10* (3): 326. Published by permission of JAI Press, Greenwich, CT.)

how conflicts may be handled along a continuum, from addressing one's own needs to addressing the needs of others.

As the Thomas model suggests, people may engage in behavior of five different types: avoiding, competing, collaborating, accommodating, or compromising. The three points at which there is a balance between equal efforts toward assertiveness and cooperativeness are represented by the points along the dotted diagonal line in Figure 11.2: avoidance, compromise, and collaboration. Owens (1987) describes these three points in the following ways:

Avoidance (low assertiveness and low cooperativeness) suggests withdrawal, peaceful coexistence, and indifference. Avoidance is useful when (a) the latent conflict probably cannot really be resolved ("live with it"), or (b) the issues are not so important to the parties as to require the time and resources to work them out. As Blake and Mouton (1964) pointed out, avoidance can serve as a form of "cease fire." Ultimately, however, this is not a valid way to deal with unresolved conflict; it only serves to suppress conflict momentarily.

Compromise (medium assertiveness, medium cooperativeness) suggests "splitting the difference." Compromise has some elements in common with collaborative problem solving: (a) the parties must be willing to engage in the process; (b) there is some move toward collaboration; and (c) the process is basically conciliatory and not in flagrant conflict with the organization's well-being. Compromising behavior is useful because it does represent an effort to find a set of long-term behaviors that will reduce conflict, but it essentially looks at the parties in conflict as adversaries. Compromising behavior does not move toward resolution; it tries to "keep a lid on" the problem.

Collaboration (high assertiveness and high cooperativeness) suggests that the conflicting parties work together to define their problems and then engage in mutual problem solving. This process requires, first, that the parties involved must actively want to use problem-solving techniques and second, that the parties possess (a) the necessary skills for communicating and working in groups, and (b) attitudes that support a climate of openness, trust, and frankness in which to identify and work out problems.

Thomas's model does not provide a prescription to deal with conflict. Indeed, there is no suggestion that one conflict-handling style is necessarily better than others all the time. On the contrary, I believe that the model suggests that a wide range of behaviors may be needed to deal effectively and positively with whatever conflicts arise in the life of the educational supervisor.

SUMMARY

Conflict is a very real—and unavoidable—part of organizational life. We noted that, because conflict is inevitable, supervisors need to know how to *work with* or *reduce* conflict, not how to eliminate it totally from their lives.

We defined conflict as disagreement between two parties. Conflict becomes more intense with the introduction of additional emotional commitment and hostility, so an important supervisory skill is the ability to reduce the *emotional level* in all conflicts. In this chapter we reviewed typical sources and types of conflict and suggested how each type of conflict might be rendered less harmful. We suggested throughout this discussion that a key element is the supervisor's ability to know his or her personal educational values and philosophy. We concluded with an explanation of Thomas's theoretical model, which was designed to enable us to diagnose the nature of conflict.

SUGGESTED ACTIVITIES

1. Using the list of time-management techniques proposed by Hughes, put together a survey questionnaire and distribute it to a number of administrators in your district. Ask people to check the items that they believe they do exceptionally well, and also the items that they do not follow. See if any patterns exist in the responses.

2. Find examples of conflict that are found in the local newspaper over a few days. Classify these conflicts according to the typologies presented in this chapter.

3. Use the concepts found in Thomas's model of conflict-handling styles and ask a group of teachers, supervisors, and administrators to estimate the predominant strategies that they use, according to the model, when faced with conflict in their professional lives. Do the same thing regarding personal conflicts. Are there differences in the ways in which people believe they handle conflict "at work" as contrasted with "at home"?

REFERENCES

Blake, Robert, & Mouton, Jane. (1964). *The managerial grid.* Houston: Gulf Publishing.
Boulding, Kenneth. (1962). *Conflict and defense: A general theory.* New York: Harper & Row.
Deutsch, Morton. (1973). *The resolution of conflict: Constructive and destructive processes.* New Haven, CT: Yale University Press.
Hughes, Larry W. (1984). *Organizing and managing time.* In James M. Cooper (Ed.), *Developing skills for instructional supervision.* White Plains, NY: Longman.
Jamieson, David W., & Thomas, Kenneth W. (1974). Power and conflict in the student-teacher relationship. *Journal of Applied Behavioral Science, 10*(3), 326.
Lipham, James M., & Hoeh, James A. (1974). *The principalship: Foundations and functions.* New York: Harper & Row.
Owens, Robert G. (1987). *Organizational behavior in education* (3rd ed.). Englewood Cliffs, NJ: Prentice-Hall.
Thomas, Kenneth W. (1974). Power and conflict in the student-teacher relationship. *Journal of Applied Behavioral Science, 10*(3).

ADDITIONAL READINGS

Blake, Robert R., Shepard, Herbert A., & Mouton, Jane S. (1964). *Managing intergroup conflict in industry.* Houston: Gulf Publishing.
Likert, Rensis, & Likert, Jane Gibson. (1976). *New ways of managing conflict.* New York: McGraw-Hill.
Thomas, John M., & Bennis, Warren G. (1972). *Management of change and conflict.* Baltimore: Penguin Books.

PART IV

Working With People:
Process and Evaluation

Much of what educational supervisors do involves organizing, motivating, understanding, and evaluating the people around them. In Part IV we will discuss strategies for working with teachers, staff, and others who are engaged in or around school settings in order to improve the educational climate and, ultimately, to provide a better education for our children.

CHAPTER 12

Groups

We often think of the educational supervisor as working almost exclusively with one-to-one contacts. Up to now in this book we have, in fact, emphasized the individualistic dimensions of supervision—the personal action plan, leadership, the need to deal with conflict as an ingredient of individual effectiveness. Proactive supervision places great emphasis on the actions of a single person engaged in shaping a more effective organization. We need to remember, however, that a large proportion of the proactive supervisor's professional life is in fact spent working *with, for, and through groups*. This reality tends to complicate organizational life—after all, it *is* easier for most people to work on a one-to-one basis—but there is a compelling need to develop insights into the nature of groups, both as components of larger organizations and as organisms unto themselves.

The purpose of this chapter, then, is to explore the nature of groups, which are in fact the building blocks of organizations. We will examine some alternative definitions of groups and then explore group characteristics and some of the ways in which they can be classified, along with some of the roles and responsibilities within them. We will consider characteristics of group effectiveness and conclude with some specific suggestions about how the analysis of groups may apply to the process of proactive supervision.

DEFINITION OF A GROUP

There are many "bunches" of people in society. Not every one of these may accurately be called a group, however. For our purposes, we will define a group quite simply as a condition wherein two or more people join together in the pursuit of a common, shared purpose. This definition is similar to a classic view offered by Michael Olmstead and Paul Hare (1978) in their oft-cited work on the nature of small groups: "A group . . . may be defined as a plurality of individuals who are in contact with one another, who take one another into account, and who are aware of some significant commonality" (p. 51).

I would suggest that the "commonality" that must knowingly be shared by all members of a group is an overriding sense of purpose. Further, the more strongly that the purpose is established and accepted by all, the stronger a group will be; it is relatively simple to tear apart a group when its members are uncertain why they have been brought together in the first place.

Groups exist throughout schools and school systems, some strong and some weak. Consequently, educational supervisors need to develop a sensitivity to various kinds of groups. Our definition is simple enough and general enough not to exclude groups currently in place. On the other hand, it provides a distinction between what may legitimately be called a "group" and what are simply "bunches of people," or what sociologists commonly refer to as "collectivities." The key difference is the extent to which there is a clearly identified emphasis on a common purpose. Collectivities can *become* groups; a number of people who happen to be in the same place at the same time may quickly form a shared identity and purpose. Passengers on a cruise ship who begin simply as people getting on the same boat, for example, often develop a commonality of identity and purpose by the third or fourth day at sea. On a very simple level, a group is formed. The group may become increasingly powerful and well-defined as an organization, based on both the length of the voyage and the number of common experiences shared by group members along the way. If an emergency forces the cruise passengers to abandon ship and stay together in lifeboats for several days, the group will form even greater definition based on their intense focus on the shared purpose of survival.

By contrast, groups can also become collectivities as once-shared common visions and purposes diminish. This occurs all too frequently in a school setting; a faculty that has existed as a strong and cohesive group for a long time eventually loses its identity and sense of purpose, and finally becomes nothing more than a collection of individual teachers "doing their own thing." This kind of disintegration often follows a struggle to achieve some common goal, perhaps the adoption of an innovative program such as team teaching or Individually Guided Education (IGE). When the goal is achieved, teachers start to lose interest and commitment to that goal and begin to drift apart. Suddenly, the strong "group" of teachers is simply a collection of individuals who work in the same building but go about doing their jobs in different, unconnected ways.

BASIC CONSIDERATIONS OF GROUPS

Now that we understand, in general terms, what a group *is*, we need to explore more specifically its typical characteristics. In the following section we will review some commonly accepted classifications of groups and then look into the special properties of groups and the behavior of people who belong to them.

Classification of Groups

Researchers have tried to develop classifications for groups as a way to understand some of their essential features. One of the most famous of these efforts is the work of Charles M. Cooley (1909), who noted the existence of *primary* and *secondary* groups.

> By primary groups I mean those characterized by intimate face-to-face association and cooperation. They are primary in several senses, but chiefly in that they are fundamental in forming the social structure and ideals of the individual. . . . Primary groups are primary in the sense that they give the individual his earliest and completest experience of social unity, and also in the sense that they do not change in the same degree as more elaborate relations, but form a comparatively permanent source out of which the latter are ever springing. . . . (p. 212)

Olmstead and Hare (1978) suggest that primary group members tend to have warm, intimate, and personal ties with one another; family, for instance, is a clear and immediate example of a primary group. However, other primary groups are formed in society when individuals are drawn together in highly personalized settings. What does the effective supervisor need to know about primary groups? First, primary groups are never created artificially; the supervisor cannot create a primary group, regardless of whatever sincere desire exists to knit strong bonds among individuals. Second, primary groups are rarely found in school settings, but supervisors still need to understand how primary groups work because when they *do* exist, they represent powerful forces that supervisors may use to channel organizational energy toward the attainment of organizational goals. Some school faculties have worked together for so long and so well that they have truly become a "family unit," in Cooley's terms. Supervisors who are not sensitive to such a group's strength will soon learn how it may subvert or support their agendas.

The *secondary* group complements the primary group. Olmstead and Hare (1978) noted:

> Relations among (secondary group) members are "cool," impersonal, rational, contractual, and formal. People participate not as whole personali-

ties but only in delimited and special capacities; the group is not an end in itself but a means to other ends. (p. 94)

Most groups are best classified as secondary groups. They gather to achieve some identified objective, and then they dissolve. They are not necessarily unfriendly settings, but members do not serve together as a matter of personal survival or fulfillment. People drift in and out according to highly personalized agendas. Most school faculties form secondary groups. Cordial and professional relations exist among group members, but the absence or presence of the group has little long-term effect on the satisfaction of the needs of its members. What are the implications for supervisory practice? When working with most school staffs, supervisors need to recognize that, while teachers may show commitment to the goals of the group, they probably have stronger allegiances to other groups outside the school.

Groups may also be classified as "formal" or "informal." Formal groups tend to be sanctioned by a particular organization to carry out one or more of the functions and responsibilities associated with that organization. In a school setting, examples of such formal groups might be the school board, the district administrative team, the local teachers' association, the PTA, a subject department in a high school, or the National Honor Society chapter. Membership requirements to such groups tend to be firmly established and identified, and it is relatively simple to determine who is and who is not a member. English teachers are not members of the math department; building principals are not members of the school board. In addition, the practices and behaviors of these groups tend to be well-defined and openly shared with members. Formal groups, then, display generally clear standards of both membership and behavior.

Informal groups tend to arise out of the immediate needs or interests of individuals. Such groups may or may not have titles. They are fairly constant in their lack of precision concerning membership; people tend to drop in and out of informal groups in somewhat erratic and unpredictable fashion. Finally, informal groups tend to have short lives due to the frequency with which their purposes and memberships fluctuate. Some informal groups do last for several years, but typically "here today, gone tomorrow" is an appropriate description of their fundamental character.

For the researcher, formal groups are easier to identify, name, track, and analyze than are informal groups; as a result, we know a considerable amount about the nature of formal groups but little about the precise nature of informal groups as organizational components. This lack of knowledge could be disastrous for the practitioner of supervision, of course. Imagine a situation where the supervisor assumes that a formal, recognized group (e.g., a subject department in a large high school) is the only group with an interest or stake in the subject area it represents. Unhappily, such assumptions are frequently made, rarely correct, and the source of almost inevitable conflict. The effective proactive supervisor is aware of who *really* has control of and interest in issues, not merely what responsibilities are listed on a formal organizational chart or job description.

W. J. Reddin (1967) also attempted to classify groups and suggested that the following eight types might appear at any time within any organization:

1. *Problem-solving group:* All group members demonstrate deep commitment to each other and to finding best solutions for whatever problems they face. This group, generally viewed as the most desirable, is high in both *interaction* effectiveness and *task* effectiveness.

2. *Production group:* This group is focused on accomplishing the task, with little or no emphasis on the needs of group members as people.

3. *Creative group:* The purpose of this group is the development of group members and their ideas. It is generally seen as a direct reverse of the production group, because little emphasis is placed on the completion of identified tasks.

4. *Procedural group:* Group members are more interested in complying with stated guidelines and procedures established for group behavior than in successfully completing a task, promoting individual growth and development, or keeping the group together in a harmonious fashion. Meeting the letter of the law and following regulations are critical goals for the group.

5. *Mixed group:* This group's behavior is typified by compromise and vascillation between hurting the feelings of group members and getting a particular job done. As a consequence, such a group achieves very little in terms of either interaction or task effectiveness.

6. *Fight group:* This group exhibits almost constant conflict, argument, and disagreement, usually based on the personalities and values of individual group members rather than the substantive issues being considered by the group. Virtually nothing of substance is accomplished.

7. *Dependent group:* Similar to the creative group, this group focuses almost exclusively on achieving interaction effectiveness. The critical difference here is that discussion regarding even slightly controversial substantive issues is altogether avoided. Only issues on which the group is likely to achieve immediate and absolute agreement are ever introduced. This lack of risk taking can quickly lead to group stagnation.

8. *Group in flight:* This group barely qualifies for the title of group in the first place. Members are not committed to any common purposes, and there is a general corresponding avoidance of participation.

We should make two observations concerning Reddin's group types. First, despite the images evoked by the descriptions of the eight classifications, we do not mean to suggest that under *all* conditions in *all* organizations one group is necessarily and absolutely "better" than another. The problem-solving group may appear more efficient, and being a member of such a group might seem more appealing than participating in a fight group: But there are times when disagreement might actually be more appropriate.

Second, we should note that these descriptions are not absolutes. Any grouping of people, formal or informal, goes through a periodic metamorphosis from one classification to another. For example, a board of education might be characterized as a fight group because its members frequently engage in much conflict and petty bickering. That same group of five or seven people, however, might quickly close ranks and become a productive group or a problem-solving group when forced to deal with a commonly felt challenge. Personal feuds might cease when the district needs to develop a policy concerning AIDS, for instance. By contrast, a subject department might normally appear to be a creative group, devoting most of its attention to providing for the continuing professional development of faculty, but the introduction of certain issues that require absolute adherence to district policy might turn the department into a procedural group. Any group, regardless of its longstanding tradition of behavior, will become an in-flight group if it loses its common purpose and shared vision.

Properties of groups: Regardless of classification, any group tends over time to take on characteristics similar to those of individual human beings. We can talk about "mature" groups, for example, in the same way we discuss mature people. A mature group might be one that has been in existence for a long time, or one that demonstrates particularly well-reasoned patterns of behavior, or both. An "immature" group, by contrast, might be a newly formed or particularly unpredictable one. As in the case with a person, of course, a group may become increasingly mature over time.

Groups also possess certain identifiable value orientations, defined as norms. In some groups it is acceptable for members to be argumentative; in others, members tend to nod and agree with everyone else. All members of some groups are expected to go to lunch together each day and behave as a unit at all times in public; other groups allow members to act independently and expect them to come together only on rare occasions. At some universities, for example, professors come to the office every day and keep consistent and predictable hours for student contact. In other institutions, the norm calls for faculty to "stay home and write" and rarely come into the office at all. A supervisor's ability or inability to identify accurately the existing norms of a particular group may be particularly relevant to successful interaction. If the supervisor assumes that a particular group is loosely knit and that one person speaks for everyone, the implications he or she draws from a conversation with that person may be absolutely false.

Group value patterns may shift rapidly at times, or they may not move for many years. The introduction of new members of a particular group may or may not have an immediate and observable impact on established beliefs and practices. As Cartwright and Zander (1960) explained in their classic analysis, *Group Dynamics,* group norms or standards must be understood both by members of the group and also by outsiders (such as educational supervisors) who work with the group for at least three reasons:

1. Norms are consciously utilized by the group to help accomplish its goals;
2. The norms are part of an ongoing self-maintenance process used by groups;
3. Norms help group members develop validity or "reality" for their opinions.

In addition to *human characteristics* and *norms,* groups possess a third common property: They always have *leaders,* or at least exhibit the pretense of something termed leadership. Herbert Thelen (1954) considered leadership as the ultimate focusing agent of groups: "Leadership is a set of functions through which the group coordinates the efforts of individuals" (p. 6). The implication is that groups would fail to exist if no evidence of leadership toward goal achievement were present.

Although formal leaders may be designated to serve groups, informal leaders may emerge in these same groups. This phenomenon begs the attention of the practitioner of proactive supervision. Consider, for example, a high school foreign-language department with a formally named chair, but one or more teachers who wield such influence over their colleagues' behavior that they also enjoy group leadership status. In fact, these individuals may wield considerably more power than does the formal leader. An outsider must then be extremely sensitive to the nuances of leadership—to the fact that the formal leader may not really be in charge, or that multiple sources of leadership may exist in the group. Determining who is really in charge is a critical task in any organization, whether it is a huge city school system or a four-member teaching team in an elementary school. Assuming that the person at the top of an organizational chart is always in fact in charge could be an embarrassing error that makes effective contact and working relations with a group nearly impossible to achieve.

Properties of people in groups. People in groups tend to play identifiable roles. Benne and Sheats (1948) noted three major classifications for group roles:

1. *Group Task Roles:* Individuals primarily concerned with "getting the job done" usually take on one of the following roles: initiator-contributor—developing and contributing new ideas or in some other way stimulating the group to undertake new directions; information-seeker; information-giver; coordinator; energizer; procedural technician; or recorder.

2. *Group Maintenance Roles:* People particularly attentive to the business of "keeping the group together" take on the following specific roles: gatekeeper—helping the group to "keep on track" and to move forward toward the achievement of group objectives; or clarifier—helping group members understand what is being said or what is happening in the group.

3. *Individual Roles:* People interested almost exclusively in their own self-interests take on these roles, including that of blocker (preventing the group from making progress toward its goals).

People in groups often play different roles in different groups or even shift roles over time in the same group. Most people belong to many different groups in society. Teachers are also members of church congregations, parent associations, bridge clubs, community councils, and other formal and informal groups, some of which have been around for years, and others of which have popped up overnight to accomplish a specific task. The same person may serve one group as a compromiser (Group Maintenance Role), trying to help others achieve agreement and harmony, and another as an information-giver (Group Task Role), committed to helping the group become productive. That same person may leave a meeting of either group and move directly to a third setting where he or she is so "tuned out" from the proceedings that personal recognition-seeking (Individual Role) is the only identifiable activity. We all serve as members of many groups, and we perform different functions at different times. This complex shifting of roles occurs for many reasons, including the extent to which a person feels personal affiliation with other group members, the level of acceptance demonstrated by the group members toward the individual, and external issues such as the amount of time available to participate in group activities.

The fact that people serve different roles in different groups has certain serious implications for the supervisor. A teacher, for example, might be perceived by the supervisor as "out of it" and uninvolved in the larger group of the school faculty, and the supervisor might make assumptions about how that teacher might be treated (or ignored) based on those assumptions. This same teacher might play an entirely different, more positive (and more powerful) role as a member of a curriculum committee, however. A supervisor who is unaware of the frequency with which such shifts occur runs the risk of ignoring a very important contributor to the goals of the organization.

GROUP EFFECTIVENESS

As we have noted throughout this chapter, an important responsibility for the effective supervisor is to analyze the ways in which groups function. Supervisors also play a critical role in assisting existing or newly created groups to find ways to attain their goals.

For Bernard Bass (1960), group effectiveness consists of two characteristics: *interaction* effectiveness and *task* effectiveness. Interaction effectiveness measures the extent to which group activities reduce conflict and enhance harmony within the membership of the group. A group is "good" or effective to the degree that positive, open, and friendly interaction occurs among its members. Task effectiveness measures the extent to which group activities promote, define, clarify, pursue, and accomplish the group's goals. Groups high in task effectiveness focus on "getting the job done," almost at any cost.

The balance between these two dimensions of group effectiveness determines a group's success. A *creative* or even *dependent* group may result from too high emphasis on interaction effectiveness; while these designations are acceptable for brief periods and may even be highly desirable under specific conditions, groups generally cannot exist merely to satisfy members' personal needs for affiliation with others. On the other hand, a group too high in task orientation might be cold and impersonal and ultimately might become an absolute productive or even fight group, with members so caught up in doing a job that they ignore the needs of others. Effective groups balance an appropriate amount of both interaction and task effectiveness.

The relevance of this is important for the practitioner of school supervision. Educational personnel and classroom teachers, in particular, tend to look at the quality of interaction patterns as a primary indicator of the effectiveness of a particular group. If things are going smoothly and no one is angry with anyone else, then the group is likely to be judged "good," and no further effort made to analyze that group. Whenever complacency sets in, whenever a school staff, task force, committee, subject department, or any other group is satisfied with positive interaction as an outcome, the effective supervisor prods the group by demanding to see outcomes and concrete results of the group effort. The operating theme needs to be, "So you like each other, but what have you *done?*"

On the other hand, supervisors must be able and willing to introduce strategies for more positive interactions among group members when the group becomes so blindly focused on accomplishing a given task that all concern for other group members is ignored. The danger in totally ignoring interpersonal needs is that, once a given task is completed, group members will rarely want to work together again toward achieving another goal. Such situations often occur in fields such as engineering where a high premium is placed, perhaps stereotypically, on purely technological skills. Engineers may join forces to design a new product and focus so intensely on the project that no one on the team gets to know anyone else. When the job is done, which may take months, the group immediately dissolves, although maintenance of the group might be useful for the organization to deal with future tasks. This phenomenon was witnessed many times in the aerospace industry during the early 1970s, where engineers who had worked side by side to send the first astronauts to the moon found that they knew little about their co-workers when the mission was accomplished. Great isolation and, frequently, personal depression resulted. The educational supervisor facing such a situation must encourage group members to look at each other as people from time to time so that task accomplishment does not block communication.

APPLICATIONS TO SUPERVISION

Supervisors need to understand how groups function, for they will spend a considerable part of their professional lives working with people in this social pattern. Effective supervisors are able to do a number of things regarding groups:

1. *Supervisors know how to "read' groups.* Educational supervisory personnel often work with the teaching staffs of many different schools or even school districts, with frequent shifting from one setting to another and many brief encounters with different groups. The luxury of spending a lot of time getting to know groups is rarely available. Supervisors need to be able to determine quickly whether a group is truly a group or merely a collectivity, who is really in charge, whether a group is too high in either task orientation or interaction orientation, and who is playing what role for what purpose in the group.
2. *Supervisors need to create groups.* Supervisors often need to pull together people to engage in a particular task—an ad hoc committee to review the math curriculum for the district, for example. The first responsibility in creating a group is to establish as firmly as possible the purpose for convening it. If members don't understand the group's purpose from the outset, little further progress will be possible.
3. *Supervisors need to keep groups going.* Once a group has been fashioned from a collectivity, the supervisor needs to keep it moving toward its shared purpose. As we have noted earlier, groups will periodically shift from problem solving to groups in flight. When this happens, and group members lose their focus on the group's goals, the supervisor must intervene to reestablish the structure and purpose of the group. As a result, knowledge of group-process skills and group-developmental activities is extremely useful for effective school supervision.

SUMMARY

In this chapter we emphasized the vital need for educational supervisors to understand groups. The reason for this emphasis is that groups are found everywhere in the supervisor's environment—in administrative and teaching teams, subject departments, school boards, parent associations, student councils, and the dozens of formal and informal staff groups that are constantly forming and reforming. Supervisors must recognize the powerful potential that groups have for contributing to the school environment and the quality of organizational life in schools. Supervisors who do not recognize this potential will rarely be entirely effective.

We began by considering some definitions of groups and settled on one that defines a group as two or more people assembled for a common, shared purpose. We considered some basic features of groups and of the people who form their memberships, and we reviewed the concepts inherent in group effectiveness. Finally, we listed some essential skills needed by any supervisor who wishes to build and maintain groups that will effectively aid in reaching the stated goals and objectives of the school in which the groups operate.

SUGGESTED ACTIVITIES

1. Analyze any group (at school or in your personal life) of which you are a member to determine if it conforms to the characteristics of groups described throughout this chapter.
2. Interview a practicing supervisor or administrator to determine the numbers and types of groups with which he or she interacts during a typical work week. To what extent are the various types of groups listed by Reddin present in this listing?

REFERENCES

Bass, Bernard M. (1960). *Leadership, psychology, and organizational behavior.* New York: Harper & Row.

Benne, Kenneth D., & Sheats, Paul. (1948, Spring). Functional roles of group members. *Journal of Social Issues, 4*(2), 41–49.

Cartwright, Dorian, & Zander, Alvin (Eds.). (1960). *Group dynamics: Research and theory* (2nd ed.). Evanston, IL: Harper & Row.

Cooley, Charles H. (1909). *Social organization.* New York: Scribner.

Olmstead, Michael S., & Hare, A. Paul. (1978). *The small group* (2nd ed.). New York: Random House.

Reddin, W. J. (1967). *Team analysis.* Fredericton, New Brunswick: Managerial Effectiveness.

Thelen, Herbert A. (1954). *Dynamics of groups at work.* Chicago: University of Chicago Press.

CHAPTER 13

Teachers and Supervisors

In 1974, Arthur Blumberg published his analysis of the nature of working relationships between teachers and supervisors. The title of that book, *Supervisors and Teachers: A Private Cold War,* is a straightforward description of a truly unfortunate reality in the area of supervisory practice. The fact is that the relationships that have existed historically between teachers and supervisors in schools have tended to be negative or, at best, typified by uneasy tolerance. There are many probable explanations for this fact. For one thing, the earliest historical image of supervision as a form of inspection ("snoopervision") has provided a powerful continuing image of how supervisors view teachers (i.e., mostly as incompetent and untrustworthy employees). More recently, the lack of friendly relations between supervisor and teacher has been reenforced by collective-bargaining agreements that require clear distinctions to be made between "labor" and "management." General societal factors also play a role. For example, recent financial constraints and enrollment declines have raised anxieties for many teachers, creating automatic adversarial relationships in many school systems, and demands for greater accountability placed on social institutions including schools have further widened the gulf between teachers and supervisors. What we must recognize, however, is that whatever the undue emphasis on the differences between teachers and formal school leaders, this emphasis cannot ultimately prevent cooperation. Supervisors must develop strategies that permit teachers, supervisors, administrators, and other school staff members to work together as colleagues. Collaboration is clearly an essential ingredient in the proactive supervisory process.

In this chapter we want to look at the world of teachers and teaching to provide you with some insights into the professional life of the people with whom you will work. Virtually everyone who serves as a supervisor or school administrator has spent some time working as a classroom teacher; nearly every state requires at least three years of teaching experience as a prerequisite to qualifying for a supervisory or administrative certificate. Living the life of a teacher, however, does not necessarily provide the kind of understanding required by a *leader,* who must appreciate those subtle features of the world of teaching that will affect the relationships between supervisors and teachers. This chapter will not deal with analyses of the activity of teaching per se; the emphasis here is on *who* teachers and supervisors *are,* not *what* teachers *do.*

To begin, we will review some characteristics of teachers identified by numerous demographic studies and emphasize particularly those factors identified as having attracted people to the field of teaching in the first place. Finally, we will examine the professional environment in which teachers work on a daily basis and look at those strategies that may be employed by supervisors who are interested in finding more effective ways to work with teachers as colleagues. For those of you preparing to serve as supervisors, our goal in each section will be to provide insights into the nature of the life of teachers—the people who ultimately "make things happen" for children in schools.

WHO ARE TEACHERS?

Researchers have tried to answer this question many times over the years. A classic, frequently cited review of the background characteristics of teachers was undertaken by Willard Waller (1932) in *The Sociology of Teaching,* and Blanche Geer (1965) and Dan Lortie (1975) carried out similar examinations. These reviews and many others have yielded remarkably similar observations, all of which are vitally relevant for those of us who invest a large part of our time and energy in working with teachers.

First, research has shown that teachers often come from humble backgrounds. Historically, teachers have been depicted as representatives of the middle class or lower middle class, but these designations are generally meaningless in present-day society; what is clear is that the majority of teachers today do *not* come from wealthy families, or the upper class.

Unsurprisingly, then, a large number of teachers have traditionally represented the first generation of college graduates in their families. Some evidence suggests that this is changing, as more people in society are able to pursue university studies. Nevertheless, while physicians and attorneys often come from families with a long tradition of access to higher education, the same thing cannot generally be said of teachers. Lortie (1975) suggested that controlled access to a college education is indeed an important characteristic of the teaching field. Socioeconomic constraints typically reduce the range of career choices that are available to those who will eventually become teachers.

> Few occupations are in as good a position (as teaching) to take advantage of socioeconomic constraints which limit access to college education. The system of colleges for teacher training turns out to be more than an institution of socialization—it also recruits. One finds a kind of "entrapment" as such colleges draw in students of limited opportunity whose initial interest in teaching is low. (p. 48)

Lortie's observation suggests not only that teachers often come from families who cannot be selective when it comes to choosing a college, but that this characteristic serves to entice people into teaching in the first place. People from humble family backgrounds who can barely pay for postsecondary education are still able to look at teaching as a realistic professional goal. The extent of the financial outlay required for medical school or law school effectively prevents most people from pursuing those careers. Professional preparation for teachers, however, is widely (and relatively cheaply) available at public universities; any able student can aspire to a teaching career.

Not surprisingly, this observation has come into play in the controversies surrounding recent reports such as that of the Holmes Group (1986), which recommended an increase in status and professionalism for teachers, often including postbaccalaureate education. Critics of such proposals have suggested that efforts to force prospective teachers to undergo significantly greater formal preservice preparation at the university level will automatically close access to teaching for those unable to afford such advanced training. An old inner-city saying suggests that the only career options available to ghetto residents are those of "preacher, teacher, or social worker." Clearly this situation is changing, but the fact remains that teaching is more easily accessible to more people than most other professional fields.

Research also suggests that teachers select the classroom as a career goal fairly early in their lives. Women tend to identify teaching as a likely career while still in elementary school, and men at least tentatively choose teaching by the time they leave high school. More recent surveys suggest that current teachers made these choices at a slightly later point in their lives, in part, no doubt, because women now have significantly more options available than they once did. Evidence continues to suggest, however, that people who select teaching as a career choice tend to stay with it, even if that choice is made slightly later in their lives than it once was.

Profiles of the teaching field in the United States, which have been developed by state departments of education and professional organizations such as the National Education Association, substantiate several other enduring characteristics:

1. *Racial characteristics:* Overwhelmingly, teachers in the United States are white, although the 10 percent of teachers who are black come close to proportionately equalling the nearly 12 percent of the general population that is black. Of black teachers, more are female than male. Further, members of nonwhite or nonblack racial groups make up even smaller percentages of the classroom teacher population in this country.

2. *Sex distributions:* Nearly 60 percent of American teachers are female. In addition, the historic tendency for the percentage of male teachers to increase at more advanced levels of schooling (i.e., as one moves from elementary to secondary schools) continues.

3. *Age levels and teaching experience:* Although recent shortages of teachers in some areas of the country and in some subject specializations are beginning to have an impact on the average ages and years of experience of teachers in the United States, those averages continue to rise. In 1911, the average age of teachers was 24, and the typical teacher had five years' experience in the classroom (Rodgers, 1976). Today, the typical teacher is slightly more than 35 years old, with approximately 11 years' experience. These figures are higher in larger school systems where there is traditionally less turnover among teachers.

These assorted characteristics provide us with an interesting snapshot of the people who work in America's classrooms. Teachers generally do not come from wealthy backgrounds, and they often work hard to pay for the education that will enable them to reach their goal—a goal they have typically established relatively early in life. The "typical" teacher is white, female, in her mid-thirties, and usually married. For the most part, then, teachers come from a relatively homogeneous pool of people; they tend to be more similar to, than dissimilar from, one another. Research also suggests that most are politically conservative but registered Democrats, Protestants, and regular churchgoers. Obviously these "typical" traits go only a short way toward providing valid and usable data to educational leaders; they tend to obscure the huge numbers of teachers who are liberal Republicans (or unaffiliated anarchists), Jewish or Catholic or atheist, unmarried—who deviate, in other words, from the statistical norm. To some extent, however, such research-based information can inform supervisory "hunches" or guesses about how teachers may react in different situations.

WHY DO PEOPLE BECOME TEACHERS?

Once again, we can identify patterns in response to this question, but the differences that exist are as wide-ranging as the number of people who are teaching. Still, supervisors can gather some insights into the nature of teachers from the research available.

An extremely important study of why people become teachers was carried out by Dan Lortie during the 1960s and reported in his famous work, *Schoolteacher,* published in 1975. In this work, five major attractors to teaching were identified:

1. *The interpersonal theme.* Perhaps the response most frequently given by teachers to questions about their selection of teaching as a career is based on their desire for continuing contact with young people. Other professions also enable people to maintain steady interactions with the young but, as Lortie (1975) noted, "Unlike other major middle-class occupations involving children, such as pediatric nursing and some kinds of social work, teaching provides the opportunity to work with children who are neither ill nor especially disadvantaged" (p. 27).

2. *The service theme.* Some people select careers in teaching because they believe that, by devoting their lives to this work, they can fulfill some special mission in society. The aspiring teacher is taking on a responsibility to provide service by engaging in what in many societies in the world is an honored (if not always well-compensated) vocation.

3. *The continuation theme.* Some individuals become teachers because they were very comfortable as students sheltered in the world of schools. As they grew, they continued to be so attached to life in schools that they could not bear to leave that environment. Lortie summarized this phenomenon by observing: "Some [teachers] said they 'liked school' and wanted to work in that setting; others mentioned school-linked pursuits and the difficulty of engaging in them outside educational institutions" (Lortie, 1975, p. 29). Supervisors should recognize that those who choose to teach because they wish to stay where they are comfortable are unlikely to engage in activities that will change the status quo of schools.

4. *Material benefits.* Surprisingly (especially to many teachers!), Lortie discovered that some people selected careers in teaching for reasons of money, prestige, and employment security. This seems to contradict the general perception that teachers suffer anxiety because they lack these things, and this anxiety may in fact be a major feature in the attitudes of teachers now in the classroom. But we can understand

how "material benefits" can motivate some people to become teachers if we recall that reviews of background characteristics have traditionally shown that teachers come from relatively modest socio-economic groups, and that they are often among the first members of their families to attend college. The opportunity for a steady, relatively secure job that offers an average beginning salary in excess of $16,000 for *ten months* of work might indeed be appealing. For many, an entry-level teaching job may be considerably more lucrative than a job held by a parent for many years. In short, entering teachers may sometimes look at their chosen profession not as one that "pays well" but rather as one that "pays better." The more time spent as a teacher, however, the less powerful this motivation becomes; teachers see neighbors and friends who are able to move toward financial rewards at a rate and level far beyond that available to a classroom teacher.

5. *Time compatibility theme.* An old saying suggests that the three best reasons to go into teaching are "June, July, and August." Lortie and many others have found considerable truth in this notion: People find teaching appealing because it does, when compared to most professions, offer more time for the pursuit of other interests and responsibilities. Although teachers may not always admit it, the fact remains that teaching appeals to many because one can go to work each day before most other people get on the expressways, arrive home or go shopping before others, and enjoy protracted vacation periods throughout the year. Teaching has traditionally been recognized as a job that allows women to raise children while working full-time: They can put their own kids on a school bus in the morning, go to work, and return home at about the same time their children do.

Lortie's study of the reasons why people enter teaching remains a milestone for those interested in learning more about the realities of classroom life. Other motivating factors have been identified in other studies. Armstrong, Henson, and Savage (1981) suggest the following ideas:

1. *Nice working conditions.* Many teachers comment on their favorable impression of both the physical environments within which they work and the kinds of people with whom they work. In addition, teaching is perceived as a job that allows for considerable personal autonomy, which many people find appealing.
2. *Lack of routine.* Teachers who have had to depend on other jobs at other points in their lives, often jobs with great monotony attached, find teaching refreshingly unpredictable. Students are diverse, and, as a result, each day in the classroom is to some extent different. In

addition, teachers control some of what they do in their classes and can "program in" variety. Finally, the typical school year "life cycle" contains many natural peaks and valleys, sometimes predictable and sometimes not.

3. *Importance of teaching.* As Lortie's "service" theme suggests, some teachers do what they do because they view their work as a way to transmit culture to new generations, provide information to youngsters, serve as positive role models, and achieve scores of other important goals that will ultimately serve as part of the design of a more positive society.

4. *Excitement of learning.* Many teachers were eager learners when they were in school, and they continue to believe in the fundamental value of learning. Many recall their own sense of excitement as they acquired new knowledge, and they assume that, as teachers, they will stimulate the same learning and bring about similar challenges for new generations of students.

What other answers can we provide to the question "Why do people teach?" In addition to his list of attractors, Lortie also identified certain other factors that tend to direct people toward teaching. He noted, for example, that people become teachers because they have identified with a significant teacher at some point in their schooling, because someone in their family had been a teacher, through "labeling" by significant others, or because aspirations to some other field (e.g., medicine or engineering) have been blocked by socioeconomic or other factors. What is remarkable in most reviews of the reasons people become teachers is the virtual absence of what might be called "negative influences." For example, virtually no teachers suggested that their own early experience with poor teachers had compelled them to try to "do something better" than what they had seen in classrooms. This contrasts, incidentally, with the reasons often cited by teachers who move into administration or supervision that they can do better than what they see others do.

Regardless of what factors motivate people to teach in the first place, the significance for supervisors is the pattern of similarities, which suggests some data that might be used in developing more effective working relationships.

WHAT DO TEACHERS DO?

Teachers instruct students. In addition, they learn how to function in an environment with some very special characteristics—characteristics that need to be appreciated by supervisors who wish to find strategies for enhancing the effectiveness of school staff.

The General Nature of Teaching

Ann Lieberman and Lynne Miller (1984) carried out an extensive analysis of what teachers' lives are like, and they considered the implications of these "social realities" of teaching for supervisors and others who wish to improve the quality of educational practice. Lieberman and Miller noted that to understand teaching we must appreciate the *nature* of teaching; thus, they identified the following features:

1. Teaching style is highly personalized. Because teachers must constantly work with large groups of students (often 25 or more at a time) but must do so in as individualized a fashion as possible, teachers often develop highly personalized and idiosyncratic strategies. When teachers settle upon their own ways of dealing with the contradiction between group and individual, they become quite defensive and even militant regarding their strategies. What they do often becomes "the right way" to do things.

2. Teachers' rewards are derived primarily from students. Lieberman and Miller (1984) noted that "the greatest satisfaction for a teacher is the feeling of being rewarded by one's students" (p. 2) and these rewards tend to be found in the affirmation by students that a teacher is doing his or her job properly. Students show support for teachers by participating in class discussions, studying more diligently for exams, or volunteering for special projects. Teachers recognize these behaviors and perceive them as signs that what they are doing is "good." Importantly, teachers usually do *not* receive this type of approval as a regular part of their contact with peers, superiors, or other colleagues in their schools.

3. Teachers are uncertain of the link between their teaching and student learning. Teaching is much like "shooting an arrow into the air, never knowing where it may fall." Most teachers find continually frustrating their inability to see the ultimate effects of their work. Not knowing "the final product" has for years been one of the most often discussed limitations on teaching as a profession. Teachers never really know whether what they did in the past, or what they are doing now, will serve any truly positive purposes. According to Lieberman and Miller, "A teacher does his or her best, develops curricula, tries new approaches, works with individuals and groups, and yet never knows for sure what are the effects. One hopes the children will get it, but one is never sure. A teacher operates out of a kind of blind faith" (Lieberman and Miller, 1984, p. 3). This characteristic of the workaday life of teachers was also recognized by Alan Tom (1984), who, in developing the metaphor of "teaching as a moral craft" made the following observation:

> This . . . (relationship of) teacher behavior to student learning . . . is what I
> call the billiard ball hypothesis. The pool player (teacher) aims the cue ball
> (his behavior) so that it will strike the target billiard ball (the student) at
> exactly the right angle to cause the billiard ball to go into a pocket (the
> achievement of what the student is supposed to learn). (p. 55)

This analogy is flawed only in its failure to recognize the teachers' traditional
perception that, just as they strike cue to ball, they are forced to turn their
backs to the table and never see if they have met their targets.

4. *The knowledge base of teaching is weak.* Teaching, unlike medicine,
law, engineering, and other professions, possesses no unified and highly
codified body of knowledge that provides clear direction to those who wish to
"cover what is important." Educators agree neither on what should be taught
nor on what methods should be used to teach. Is Rubin (1985) correct in
emphasizing the "artistry of teaching"? Are the "scientific" approaches to the
analysis of teaching more appropriate? This general lack of consensus
concerning the content and techniques of "good" teaching provides a weak
knowledge base that in turn impacts negatively on the sense of commitment
felt by many classroom teachers.

5. *The goals of teaching are vague and often conflicting.* What are
teachers "supposed" to do? Disseminate a fixed body of knowledge? Enter-
tain? Baby-sit? The lack of clarity about a teacher's true role leaves teachers
with no true understanding of a single purpose. "When all goals are
addressed, no goals are met." Lieberman and Miller noted that, because of
this vagueness and corresponding conflict concerning purpose, "individual
teachers make their own translations of [educational] policy" and this
contributes directly to the lack of consensus often found in schools.

6. *Control norms are seen as necessary features of schools.* Educational goals are not always clear, but the end result usually is: Schools are
expected to exercise strong control over young people to guarantee that
social order is maintained. This educational "fact of life" is demonstrated
almost daily in schools where parents, other teachers, supervisors, administrators, and, often, students hold in high esteem those teachers who "keep the
kids in line." By contrast, the inability to "control" students is typically
viewed as a serious flaw in a teacher's professional performance, and is in fact
often seen as grounds for dismissal.

7. *Professional support is lacking.* Paradoxically, although contact between people (i.e., teacher-to-student, student-to-teacher) is a primary
feature of teaching, teachers are remarkably isolated as workers, particularly
from colleagues and other adults. This lack of collegiality usually begins with

the first classroom assignment, where "rookie" teachers who have just completed teacher training are thrown into the same setting—with the same expectations for professional performance—as considerably more experienced teachers.

Stuart Palonsky left his position as a university professor to spend two years teaching social studies in a suburban high school. In his fascinating analysis of that experience, *900 Shows a Year: A Look at Teaching from a Teacher's Side of the Desk* (1986), Palonsky provides a poignant description of the loneliness of teaching:

> Lou was one of the teachers who had retreated from the mainstream of the faculty, and he defined teaching personally and in isolation from other teachers. At one time he had played tennis with Sal, and he considered one of the French teachers to be his friend, but these teachers were now married, and Lou was divorced. He claimed he no longer maintained social relationships with his colleagues, and he rarely went to faculty parties. From our conversations, it did not appear that he liked most of the other teachers, but he enjoyed teaching.

Lou is not unique. I remember talking with an experienced teacher, a man with more than 15 years' experience teaching math, who in all those years had never had anyone except an administrator—fulfilling the requirements of a master contract for periodic class observation—drop in to see him teach. Even more remarkable, and equally lamentable, was the teacher's next statement that, during those 15 years, he had never seen another teacher teach, either.

8. Teaching is an art. Lieberman and Miller conclude by suggesting that the efforts to turn teaching into a precise science are wrong; ". . . in the long haul, more artistry . . . is practiced as teachers struggle to adjust and readjust, to make routines, and establish patterns, only to recast what has been done in a new form to meet a new need or a new vision. Teachers are best viewed as craftspeople; the reality of teaching is of a craft learned on the job" (p. 94). Efforts to make teachers conform to behavioral patterns that represent "good teaching" are usually futile because artists struggle to express their uniqueness and resist conformity.

Louis Rubin (1985) provided the following list of features normally associated with "artistic teaching." Artistic teachers:

1. Focus on the subtleties of teaching—how to motivate, pace, and control students—which invigorate basic instructional methods and subject matter.
2. Improvise tactics for reaching objectives and overcoming difficulties. They are creative, inventive, and know how to "go with the flow."

3. Take advantage of unexpected opportunities to clarify ideas and reinforce concepts.
4. Make use of their intuition and hunches to guide the modification of routine practices and have a special sense of when to throw away the lesson plan.
5. Set high expectations for themselves and their students.
6. Find the most efficient and expedient ways of getting things done.
7. Are good storytellers and are sensitive enough to know how to use temporary digressions on related topics to enrich lessons, stimulate interest, and increase student involvement.
8. Base their control of learning activities on the nature of student behavior.
9. Take great pride in what they do and in the achievements of their students.
10. Concentrate on a few dominant goals that they believe to be central to their purpose as teachers.
11. Respect their own convictions.
12. Devote as much time as possible to whatever they enjoy most in teaching.

The "Dailiness" of Teaching

Supervisors and others who wish to understand the teacher's world must appreciate, according to Lieberman and Miller, not only its general nature but also its "dailiness."

Predictability. They note, for example, that the life of a teacher follows certain predictable cycles and rhythms—as anyone who has spent time around schools will agree. Teachers begin each day at the same time, drink coffee at the same time, even go to the bathroom at the same time each day; all of these activities are regulated by the need to provide "coverage" for students. "For the majority of the day, they are bound in space and time. In most instances, teachers need the permission of the principal to leave the building during school hours" (Lieberman and Miller, 1984, p. 5). The predictable rhythms of each school day occur in the context of the larger rhythms of the school year. Every year, the excitement of September slows until the holiday season begins at the end of October and continues through early January. Winter doldrums set in and days are dull until March or April when spring break occurs. The weeks after that vacation are almost always marked by the increasing fatigue of teachers who are trying to cope with the decreasing interest of students, who are working toward summer vacation. This same annual cycle is found in virtually every school—public or private, elementary or secondary—across the nation each year, and significant changes in its peaks and valleys are highly unlikely.

Interestingly, the observable and predictable nature of the normal teaching day and year contradicts the perception of many entering teachers that the classroom represents a way of life free from routine and predictability. Teacher-student relationships within individual classrooms may indeed be unpredictable, but that spontaneity is not characteristic of the large picture of teachers' lives. Palonsky provides a noteworthy portrait of the "grind" of daily school life:

> For the most part, one day blended in with the next, with little to distinguish one from another. I saw the same students at the same time every day. I passed the same teachers and students in the hall at the same place and time every day, said hello to the same people as often as a dozen times a day, but rarely engaged any of them in more substantive conversation. I arrived at school at the same time; I ate lunch at the same time; and I left at the same time every day. (Palonsky, 1986, pp. 81–82)

Regulation. The daily world of teachers is also a highly regulated one. Some of these rules are the official policies and procedures specified by the local board of education. In this sense, teaching differs little from other occupations where employees are told when to start work, how many sick days are available, how to complete certain forms, or what to do in dealing with emergencies or crises.

Other "rules" associated with teaching, as Lieberman and Miller point out, are not formal policies but rather informal norms that serve to govern the behavior of classroom instructors. Two important norms are the expectations that teachers will always be *practical* and *private.*

Teachers are expected to be *practical* and to find immediately applicable solutions to whatever problems they encounter in their classroom activities; perhaps the worst thing that can be said about an educator's ideas is that they are "theoretical." As we noted in Chapter 2, most educators have a strong antitheoretical bias, which both results from and reenforces the practicality norm found in most schools. More research on how this norm has developed over time might help us determine if teachers tend to be people who view the world in concrete and nonabstract terms in the first place, or if the nature of teaching forces its practitioners to look for practical solutions rather than theoretical concepts.

Privacy in teaching "means not sharing experiences about teaching, about classes, about students, about perceptions" (Lieberman and Miller, 1984, p. 8). Unfortunately the norm of collegiality is not found in most schools; teachers, of course, lose something by not having the opportunity to share their work with co-workers. The strong pull toward privacy derives at least in part from the face that unobserved people cannot be judged as incompetent. Do teachers believe that they have had inadequate preservice preparation for their roles, and consequently spend a large percentage of their professional lives trying to disguise what they fear are inadequacies in their performance? Or do teachers close their classroom doors to others because they have learned, either through personal experience or via oral tradition, that anyone who sees you teach will inevitably find fault? In short, is retreat to privacy one of the strategies employed as part of Blumberg's "cold war"?

Limitation of contact. Interactions among teachers are typically quite limited. The vast majority of interpersonal contact experienced by classroom teachers is with children, not with co-workers. For years, I have asked teachers who come to my classes after spending the day at work in schools to indicate the amount of time that they spent in talking with adults that day at work. The average time was about 25 minutes. If teachers are asked to indicate the time spent in "meaningful talk" with adults (i.e., not lounge chit-chat concerning yesterday's football game, upcoming television shows, or momentary gossip, for example), the average amount of time is greatly reduced. Teachers live in a world surrounded by people, but with little opportunity for discussion with peers. A serious consequence of this lack of contact is that teachers assigned to classes with difficult students live daily lives filled to overflowing with negative human contacts. No wonder that teachers at the end of many school days have trouble being animated in discussions about organizational theory. As Lieberman and Miller (1984) suggest:

> For most teachers in most schools, teaching is indeed a lonely enterprise. With so many people engaged in so common a mission in so compact a space and time, it is perhaps the greatest irony—and the greatest tragedy of teaching—that so much is carried on self-imposed and professionally sanctioned isolation. (p. 11)

SO WHAT CAN SUPERVISORS DO?

Throughout this chapter I have painted a picture of the lives of teachers and the business of teaching, which, while fairly honest and accurate, is also fairly depressing. We could add other brush strokes to this picture including the "poor public image and inadequate public appreciation" (Geer, 1965, p. 6) faced by teachers, and the general lack of esteem, low pay, and social status afforded them. These latter characteristics clearly have a serious impact on the daily lives of educators, but I prefer not to dwell on them simply because a supervisor, proactive or otherwise, can do little to modify societal perceptions that have emerged over many years. A supervisor alone cannot make the public value teachers and pay them more money. A supervisor *can,* however, modify some of the daily conditions faced by teachers on his or her staff. And even if changes are not always possible, the supervisor who really wants to make a difference will be more effective, and more readily accepted by teachers, if he or she appreciates the characteristics of teachers' lives.

Daniel Duke's thoughtful analysis, entitled *Teaching: An Imperiled Profession* (1984), found many of the same conditions we discussed above not only to be present but also likely to cause paralysis in both teachers and schools. In Duke's view, the greatest constraints to teacher effectiveness are rooted both in *ambiguity* (teachers must cope constantly with the lack of rationality and consensus surrounding goals and purposes) and *insecurity* (teachers face instability in jobs, social status, assignments, and finance). In response to these issues and others raised in this chapter, Duke proposes a serious reconceptualization of teaching as a profession, guided by the following "What if . . ." considerations:

1. *What if we stopped acting as if there were one best type of teacher and began valuing diversity?* If educators believe firmly that schools must deal with the uniqueness of individual children as learners, why do many of these same educators assume comparability and similarity among all teachers? Particular teachers might best be matched with particular students who possess the same values and perspectives on learning. Policymakers and other educational leaders need to acknowledge the true value of diversity among teachers. Some supervisors spend as much time learning about the individual qualities of the teachers with whom they work as in watching those same teachers perform in classrooms and thus more completely appreciate the diversity and richness of their teaching staff.

2. *What if teaching were reconceptualized as a set of complex technical skills, including problem solving, hypothesis testing, decision making, information processing, logical analysis, and resource allocation?* We need to define teaching as an activity that requires as much skill as it does pure emotional commitment to children. The latter is clearly important, but society values skills and knowledge as well as commitment. Some supervisors work with their teaching staffs to design and implement action-research projects that not only increase the knowledge base regarding local school issues, but also promote thinking and acting by teachers that goes beyond traditional patterns and limitations.

3. *What if teachers would be regarded as discipline-based scholars as well as instructors?* Would not the consequence of this reconceptualization of teaching further enhance the strength and positive image of the profession? As Duke noted, "such action might also help bridge the gulf now separating public school teachers from professors" (Duke, 1984, p. 139). In this way, too, teachers may become more actively involved as researchers in their professional fields.

4. *What if part of a teacher's time was spent teaching adults?* One of the traditional limitations on the teaching profession is that teachers work only with children. Could we not redefine schools as total learning communities, where adults and younger people come to-

gether on occasion to partake in mutual learning experiences? Teachers might then be seen not only as true specialists with important bodies of knowledge, but also as possessors of special skills for disseminating that knowledge.

5. *What if students came to school with questions and teachers helped them find answers?* Would not such a turnaround in traditional student-teacher roles decrease the familiar patterns of passive learning now found in most schools? Can teachers be viewed increasingly as *facilitators* of the learning process for students, rather than *providers* of all knowledge to students? Such a pattern might be an important step toward the goal of making students control their own learning.

6. *What if teachers at age 55 did not have to perform the same functions that teachers perform at age 22?* Is it not reasonable to assume that some teachers do some tasks better when they are younger, and others have different insights when they are older? In most schools, a beginning teacher is as likely to be assigned an Algebra I class as a 30-year veteran. Interchangeability of teaching assignments (and teachers) is a time-honored tradition in schools, but some creative placement of teachers might benefit the quality of interactions between students and teachers, and might also serve to make teachers more satisfied with their professional status. Increasingly, supervisors are aware of the particular needs of adults as learners at different times during their lives and realize that beginning teachers and experienced teachers are not "the same."

Duke's suggestions are a good way to begin the process of thinking about ways in which the teaching profession might be changed over time. There are also some very concrete and immediate things that supervisors and administrators may do on a daily basis to enhance the quality of teachers' work life in schools.

First, supervisors and administrators must find ways of restructuring teachers' daily schedules so that more prolonged, if not more frequent, contact is possible among the adults on the school staff. At present, teaching assignments are almost universally constructed in ways that make contact impossible; teachers see colleagues only during the mad dash that usually represents a "duty-free lunch period." Prep times, when provided, are rarely arranged so that teams of teachers can get together. In many schools, duty assignments appear more highly valued than opportunities for communication and professional dialogue among peers.

Second, supervisors should examine those factors that attract teachers to the field and use that information in promoting a more effective learning environment. What I am suggesting here is that supervisors can structure some elements of the teacher's world so that the factors that attracted teachers to the field in the first place are more evident. As we noted earlier in this chapter, one of the strongest drawing points to teaching for many people is the opportunity to have contact with students. In reality, however, a teacher's life is often filled with so many administrative and "task" responsibilities that the ability to spend much meaningful time with young people is severely constrained. I believe that a supervisor who could find ways of cleaning administrative tasks off a teacher's desk would go far toward encouraging that teacher to feel much happier about his or her job. And the long-term result of this satisfaction would be improved teaching and greater student learning. This same strategy may not work for all teachers, but the same basic premise—that the supervisor needs to become more aware of teachers' real characteristics and concerns—is always an effective way for supervisory and administrative personnel to work with staff.

Finally, the supervisor or administrator who is intent upon getting better performance out of teachers needs to spend time analyzing any conflict between teacher and supervisor that is linked only to the nature of the *roles* rather than to the *people* who fulfill those roles. At many times in the life of any organization, people will not get along, but these times should not be based solely or even largely on job titles. Supervisors and teachers do not *have* to live in a state of constant war, cold or otherwise.

SUMMARY

In this chapter we reviewed the world of teaching and teachers as it relates to the responsibilities of the proactive supervisor. I began by looking at who teachers are and noting that, for the most part, those of us who have spent time in the classroom are more similar than not in terms of our socioeconomic backgrounds, value orientations, and stated reasons for having gone into teaching in the first place. Next, we reviewed the general characteristics of the life of a teacher, including isolation from one's colleagues and other adults, and the expectation that teachers will enforce certain norms not always supported in their own minds. Finally, we considered some of the ways in which supervisors or administrators can increase their sensitivity toward the realities of teaching in order to enhance the quality of the teaching-learning process in their schools.

SUGGESTED ACTIVITIES

1. Conduct a series of brief interviews with a group of teachers to determine such things as their backgrounds, reasons for becoming teachers, and reasons for continuing in the classroom. Compare your findings to those presented in this chapter concerning the characteristics of teachers. What generalizations can you make from the similarities and differences found?
2. Using the features of the lives of teachers described by Lieberman and Miller,

construct a survey instrument and ask that a group of teachers in your school or district respond in terms of their agreement or disagreement with the views of the authors. Are teachers, for example, as lonely in their work as suggested?

3. Review the propositions for improvement listed by Daniel Duke with two or three practicing supervisors and administrators to determine if they have any concrete suggestions for ways in which those strategies for improvement might be implemented in their schools or districts.

REFERENCES

Armstrong, David G., Henson, Kenneth T., & Savage, Tom V. (1981). *Education: An introduction.* New York: Macmillan.

Blumberg, Arthur (1974). *Supervisors and teachers: A private Cold War.* Boston: Allyn & Bacon.

Duke, Daniel L. (1984). *Teaching: An Imperiled Profession.* Albany: State University of New York Press.

Geer, Blanche (1965). Teaching. In Sils (Ed.), *International encyclopedia of the social sciences.* New York: Free Press.

The Holmes Group (1986). *Tomorrow's Teachers: A report of the Holmes Group.* East Lansing, MI: The Holmes Group.

Lieberman, Ann, & Miller, Lynne. (1984). *Teachers, their world, and their work: Implications for school improvement.* Alexandria, VA: Association for Supervision and Curriculum Development.

Lortie, Dan C. (1975). *Schoolteacher.* Chicago: The University of Chicago Press.

Palonsky, Stuart B. (1986). *900 shows a year: A look at teaching from a teacher's side of the desk.* New York: Random House.

Rodgers, Frederik A. (1976). Past and future of teaching: You've come a long way. *Educational Leadership, 34.*

Rubin, Louis J. (1985). *Artistry in teaching.* New York: Random House.

Tom, Alan R. (1984). *Teaching as a moral craft.* White Plains, NY: Longman.

Waller, Willard. (1932). *The sociology of teaching.* New York: Russell and Russell.

ADDITIONAL READINGS

Cherniss, C. (1980). *Professional burnout in human service organizations.* New York: Praeger.

Goodlad, John. (1984). *A place called school.* New York: McGraw-Hill.

Jackson, Philip W. (1968). *Life in classrooms.* New York: Holt, Rinehart & Winston.

Lightfoot, Sarah L. (1983). *The good high school: Portraits of character and culture.* New York: Basic Books.

McPherson, G. (1972). *Small town teacher.* Cambridge, MA: Harvard University Press.

Sarason, Seymour. (1982). *The culture of the school and the problem of change* (2nd ed.). Boston: Allyn & Bacon.

CHAPTER 14

Evaluation

Educators often assume that *educational supervision* is virtually synonymous with *evaluation*—that supervisors do little more than evaluate teachers and curricular programs. And when we talk about an administrator's supervisory responsibility, we often mean how that administrator goes about evaluating teachers.

As we have seen throughout this book, supervision in schools is in fact much more than evaluation. To be sure, a strong relationship exists between supervision and evaluation. Supervisors *do* have a responsibility to carry out evaluation. In this chapter, however, we will establish a *context* for the evaluation duties of the proactive educational supervisor. We will see that evaluation is simply one important aspect of the effort to match individual human abilities with organizational goals, objectives, and priorities, and we will try to defuse the notion that educational evaluation automatically and necessarily involves evaluation of the teaching staff for the purpose of making employment decisions.

How does the proactive supervisor carry out evaluation responsibilities? To answer that question, we begin with a brief overview of three different types of evaluation, which we match to common educational foci, or objectives. Then we will look at the most prevalent problems in the area of staff evaluation and conclude with suggestions to supervisors on how to deal with common problems.

Evaluation is simply the process of determining the worth—goodness or badness—of something. Blaine Worthen and James Sanders (1987) provide further explanation of the basic concepts of educational evaluation by noting:

In education, [evaluation] is the formal determination of the quality, effectiveness, or value of a program, product, project, process, objective, or curriculum. Evaluation uses inquiry and judgment issues, including: (1) determining standards for judging quality and deciding whether those standards should be relative or absolute; (2) collecting relevant information; and (3) applying the standards to determine quality. Evaluation can apply to either current or proposed enterprises. (p. 22)

Evaluation implies the necessary existence and use of a *criterion* or standard to which the "something" being evaluated may be compared to determine relative worth. Evaluation thus differs from another term with which it is often confused, namely *assessment,* which describes a process of judging something with or without an external standard or guide. All evaluation, therefore, is assessment, but not all forms of assessment are examples of evaluation. Organizational evaluation and assessment both have basically the same purpose, and that is to collect data that people in the organization may use to make decisions. In *educational* evaluation the purpose is to enable decision makers to determine the value of certain activities and processes used in educating children.

TYPES OF EVALUATION

The three basic types of evaluation are *diagnostic, formative,* and *summative.*

Diagnostic Evaluation

Diagnostic evaluation is normally used to determine the *beginning* status or condition of something. It is carried out prior to the application of intervention or treatment in order (1) to determine what intervention or treatment may be needed (as a physician diagnoses a patient to establish necessary medical treatment), or (2) to determine what an object or person is like *before* something is done to it so that, after that intervention is completed, its effectiveness can be assessed (as physical scientists note the nature of an environment before they conduct an experiment so they know what effect their experiment has had at its conclusion). Social scientists make use of this same research strategy that, in turn, increases the overall importance of precision in the conduct of diagnostic evaluation.

The educational supervisor frequently uses diagnostic evaluation procedures for both purposes. Supervisors are often called upon to suggest treatments, remedies, or other approaches to "fixing" things that are going wrong in schools. In the same way that a physician uses diagnostic data to determine treatment, then, the supervisor is expected to prescribe solutions on the basis of a diagnosis. Diagnostic evaluation also provides a picture of conditions before anything is done, so the effect of an intervention can be determined. In both cases, care and precision in the diagnosis are vital, or the treatment and/or its results will be in error. A physician must have precise data concerning a patient's weight, heart beat, blood pressure, and so forth before the patient undergoes any medical procedure. Only in this way can the attending physician ascertain if critical aspects of a patient's condition have changed over time. Observed changes provide the diagnostician with a place to look for the cause of the malady.

Similarly, in a school setting, the supervisor can profit considerably from a careful and precise analysis of changes that occur in, for instance, student achievement on some evaluation instrument after a period of instruction. The whole concept of pretest and post-test measurement is based on the logic of using preliminary diagnostic evaluation information as a *baseline* to examine the net effect of instructional intervention.

Formative Evaluation

Michael Scriven (1967) first distinguished between "formative" and "summative" evaluation, and Worthen and Sanders (1987) noted the importance of keeping these two evaluative forms, which appear similar in practice, apart.

Worthen and Sanders (1987) point out that "formative evaluation is conducted during the operation of a program to provide program directors evaluative information useful in improving the program" (p. 34). We use formative evaluation to gain intermittent feedback concerning the nature of some activity or practice *while* it is in progress. Activities can be evaluated many times, and feedback from this kind of evaluation is usually supplied to whoever is in control of the activity being evaluated. Unfortunately, formative evaluation is the least frequently employed of the three forms of evaluation reviewed, and when educational supervisors do employ it, they rarely follow through with appropriate feedback to their teaching staffs. Supervisory and administrative personnel have not traditionally worked with teachers in formative ways.

Formative evaluation implies that the project or activity being reviewed could be improved if properly analyzed and assessed. Business and industry have long used the concept of formative evaluation, particularly in assembly lines. Consider, for example, the supervisor who oversees the production of automobiles. It is this person's responsibility to note minor flaws in the assembly process before the automobile proceeds too far down the line and major revision is necessary, or a flawed total product results. "Mid-course correction" does not always occur on assembly lines, and evaluative feedback is not always acted upon, but the value of periodic formative evaluation is clear. For the most part, this conscious effort to employ continuous evaluation has not been implemented in the field of education.

Educational supervisors would do well to find more opportunities for formative evaluation procedures. Supervisors need to become "sensors," or monitors of work in progress, and need also to develop the skills and strategies necessary to feed information gained in this way back to the teaching staff. In most schools, such practices have not traditionally existed.

Summative Evaluation

"Summative evaluation is conducted at the end of a program to provide potential consumers with judgments about the program's worth or merit" (Worthen and Sanders, 1987, p. 34). Summative evaluation is the process of collecting data in order to make final decisions about the future status of whatever is being evaluated. It is the "last chance," the final point where an ultimate disposition concerning a person or thing is made. Data collected as part of summative evaluation is directed exclusively toward the goal of final judgment.

In both private corporations and public organizations such as school systems, newly hired employees are generally given a standard probationary period during which the new person can decide if the organization is the kind of place in which he or she wants to work, and the organization can look at the performance of the new person and decide if, over time, he or she can "fit in" and be successful in the organization. Some type of formative evaluation is probably carried out from time to time to let the new employee see if his or her work is generally proceeding up to the expectation levels of the company. Finally, at the conclusion of the agreed-upon probation period, the organization takes one last serious look at the employee's work. That summative evaluation is a final, "go–no go" decision point. Virtually every summative evaluation we undergo in our lives represents a major milestone, because of the final nature of the decision that is made.

Summative evaluation differs from diagnostic and formative evaluation precisely in its emphasis on finality. Because it represents an absolute endpoint or a final decision, summative evaluation typically carries with it a sense of anxiety and seriousness, whether or not these feelings are warranted.

OBJECTIVES OF EVALUATION

The four major educational areas most frequently evaluated are students, curricular programs, curricular materials (which are often evaluated with programs), and staff. In this section we will examine each of these objectives and provide examples of each of the evaluation types matched with these objectives.

Student Evaluation

Students are evaluated almost continuously in most schools, and all three processes are employed. *Diagnostic* student evaluation might involve a simple pretest administered by a classroom teacher at the outset of a chapter or unit, to determine the level of students' awareness of central concepts to be taught; this pretest might then guide the teacher in selecting appropriate instructional strategies. Special-education teachers use multiple techniques to diagnose the nature of individual learning handicaps so that future instruction can be directed more precisely. And standardized achievement test scores serve as a baseline to plan instruction.

Formative student evaluation is an ongoing practice in most schools. Teachers give "pop quizzes" precisely because they want to get some sense of how well students are learning during the course of instruction, and also to give students some hints concerning the teacher's expectations for student mastery of course content. Formative evaluation need not necessarily be confined to written tests or other evaluative instruments. Good teachers use formative evaluation techniques constantly; they watch student behavior patterns, and they invite particular students to participate in class discussion to assess their progress. Teachers can then adjust instruction accordingly.

A typical example of *summative* student evaluation is the traditional final exam that concludes a marking period, the results of which are used to make a summary "pass/fail" decision for a student. Similar judgments are made at the end of instructional units in subject areas, and at the end of the entire school year, when most schools use comprehensive examinations to evaluate student success across all subjects. Standardized achievement tests are frequently used to make summative judgments about student learning—an undesirable and perhaps invalid form of evaluation, but one we must recognize is widespread in schools.

Curricular Programs and Materials

Schools frequently assess the quality of their overall curriculum as well as the materials available to assist students in attaining the stated goals of the curriculum. Committees of teachers and administrators may work togather to review the adequacy of the curriculum and the books that fit it. These activities are all basically *diagnostic* in nature.

A school or department might also review a new textbook midway through the year in which it is initially used. The results of that review would be used, not to decide whether to continue using the text, but rather to determine if it could be used more effectively. Do students need supplementary readings? A workbook? Should the speed with which teachers cover the material be varied? This "mid-course" evaluation is *formative.*

At the end of the school year, teachers and administrators who suggested new curricular programs or products earlier in the year might reconvene to decide if their recommendations were effective. *Summative* evaluation would provide data to assist the committee in making its final decisions and recommendations.

Staff Evaluation

Many educators believe that making decisions about staff is the supervisor's sole evaluative responsibility. Staff evaluation is clearly a critical area and one that may cause considerable anxiety for both the supervisor and the people supervised. But as we have seen in the previous sections of this chapter, it is far from being the only area of evaluative responsibility for supervisors.

The traditional employment interview carried out before an individual is hired by a school district is an example of *diagnostic* evaluation. Other methods frequently used to determine if an individual is suited for a particular job include employment exams to determine basic competency, psychological profiles, or in recent years for teachers in some states, statewide teacher competency tests. Districts also review letters of recommendation submitted on behalf of candidates for staff positions, academic records, and employment files from earlier positions. Most of these forms of diagnostic evaluation provide information for the employing school system about potential staff members before they are hired. In addition, such evaluation also allows the candidate to learn more about a particular school system.

Formative evaluation of staff is one of the most poorly developed features of the entire range of supervisory responsibilities. Periodic evaluation designed to provide teachers and other school staff members with feedback to encourage better performance sounds like a simple thing to do. In practice, however, few schools provide constructive criticism to their staffs in an open, nonthreatening fashion. Several explanations account for this. First, a high percentage of supervisors and administrators are untrained in how to provide feedback to staffs that would encourage "mid-course correction" and improvement. For administrators and supervisors to assume an "improvement" responsibility is foreign to the traditional image of supervisor as authority figure, making final judgments about job performance. Second, when administrators and supervisors *do* provide formative assistance, they are generally expected to make final judgments concerning staff competence at the same time. This dual responsibility means that, when supervisors offer feedback, ask teachers to share problems, or urge them to take "creative risks" to improve their performances, supervisors are expected at the same time to be "filing away" information on which to base future decisions on adequacy or inadequacy of performance. It is virtually impossible for the same practitioner of supervision to engage in both formative and summative evaluation responsibilities with equal effectiveness, yet school systems tend to hold supervisors and administrators accountable for making the difficult decisions associated with summative evaluation. Finally, formative evaluation is a time-consuming process that emphasizes interpersonal skills and communication between the supervisor and the persons being supervised. In many cases, supervisors do not have—are not willing to invest—enough time or interpersonal skills to make formative techniques effective. Whatever difficulties formative staff evaluation may engender for supervisors, it is important and well worth doing frequently and regularly in schools. Various

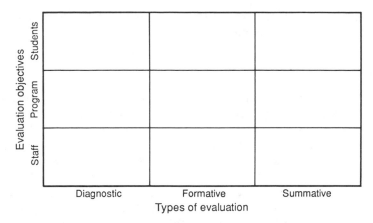

Figure 14.1. Model depicting three different types of evaluation in relation to three typical objectives of educational evaluation.

models have been developed to help supervisors increase opportunities for this type of evaluation.

As we noted above, supervisors are often perceived as engaging in *summative* evaluation of teachers and others. Principals, for instance, regularly make class observations for teachers being considered for tenure or a continuing contract. Because tenure decisions are normally made only once in a teacher's professional life, the evaluation process carried out in this case is clearly summative in nature. In reality, it is generally administrators with formal personnel responsibilities who make summative career decisions for those on their staffs. There is no doubt that summative evaluation is important in the traditional job descriptions of supervisors, but it is typically a rarely employed skill for a person classified as a supervisor.

Figure 14.1 suggests the potential relationships between types and objectives in school evaluation.

CURRENT PROBLEMS AND ISSUES IN EVALUATION

The area of staff evaluation presents some very tangible and special concerns to the practitioner of educational supervision. On the one hand, we generally accept that, to improve practice, we need to determine the worth and effectiveness of that practice. On the other hand, we are all aware of the trauma that frequently surrounds discussions of evaluation. This paradox will probably never completely be resolved. The supervisor may, however, reduce the negative stigma associated with evaluation of educational personnel by remaining aware of significant current problems in the area, as well as suggested ways of avoiding these problems.

Mixing Purposes

Evaluation effectiveness often suffers because the objectives of evaluation are mixed. This is particularly true of formative and summative staff evaluation. Formative evaluation suggests a climate of openness and trust between supervisor and staff member, to the extent that staff members can admit their deficiencies openly and request feedback that might lead to improved performance. If staff members suspect that information collected as part of the formative evaluation will come back to haunt them during a summative, personnel decision-making part of the evaluation cycle, trust and openness will be either destroyed or damaged to the point where open communication between supervisor and staff member is no longer possible. Consequently, supervisors should strive to separate formative and summative evaluation as completely as possible, even to the extent of involving different people at each stage.

For staff evaluation to be truly an effective activity, and one that conforms to our idea of proactive supervisory processes, we must first clearly understand what evaluation is supposed to do. Gary Borich (1977) suggested five legitimate functions of evaluation, the first two of which are formative in nature, and the last three summative. According to Borich, evaluation may be used to:

1. Guide self-improvement efforts by the teachers;
2. Assist a supervisor in the process of improving someone else's teaching;
3. Advise potential "consumers" of teaching, particularly students;
4. Guide personnel decisions by present or potential employers or superiors;
5. Provide data to external audiences interested in cost-effectiveness, accountability considerations, or the success of a particular project.

Lack of Teacher Involvement

Teachers often report that they feel they have not had significant involvement in the development of district staff evaluation programs. This problem is on the wane in many school systems where teachers have become more and more involved with committees and task forces convened to review evaluation practices. The fact is increasingly recognized that, as primary consumers of the evaluation process, teachers have a legitimate stake in the design of procedures.

Lack of Self-Evaluation

Traditionally, little consistent emphasis has been given to the concept of staff self-evaluation. The predominant view suggests that evaluation is "done to" staff by administrators or supervisors. In fact, evaluation conducted by a person regarding his or her own performance is a much more powerful activity than evaluation conducted by an external source. Supervisors designing formal staff evaluation programs need to emphasize self-evaluation as well as the review and evaluation carried out by supervisors and administrators.

Inadequate Evaluation Criteria

Criteria used for staff evaluation often come from personal preferences. Some supervisory personnel, for example, tend to judge the effectiveness of teaching performance according to the extent to which the teacher's activities resemble how the supervisor would have taught the same material. An example of reliance on personal-preference criteria, or at least on criteria that are extremely subjective, is illustrated in the teacher-evaluation checklist shown in Figure 14.2. Note the number of items that are to be interpreted solely by the supervisor.

In fact, staff evaluation criteria and instruments should be based primarily on *teacher effectiveness research* rather than on personal preference. Berliner and Tikunoff (1976) proposed the following list of effective teacher behaviors:

1. The teacher reacts constructively (in overt, verbal, or nonverbal ways) to students' feelings and attitudes.
2. The teacher actively listens to what a student is saying, reading, or reciting.
3. The teacher gives a direction or a threat and follows through with it.
4. The teacher seems confident in teaching a given subject and demonstrates a grasp of it.
5. The teacher checks a student's progress regularly and adjusts his or her instruction accordingly.
6. The teacher expresses positive, pleasant, and optimistic attitudes and feelings.
7. The teacher seems to perceive the learning rate of students and adjusts his or her teaching pace accordingly.
8. The teacher encourages students to take responsibility for their own class work.
9. The teacher capitalizes instructionally on unexpected incidents that might arise during class time.

CLASSROOM OBSERVATION

Always	Frequently	Seldom	Hardly Ever

Teacher _____ Subject _____ Date _____

1. Shows specific interests in students as they enter and leave the classroom.

2. Calls students by name.

3. Looks at class when in discussion with them.

4. Makes an effort to involve all students.

5. Provides a variety of classroom activities and experiences.
6. Provides a comfortable and attractive environment for the students.
7. Uses room arrangements appropriate to the teaching-learning techniques employed.

8. Displays disturbing mannerisms and expressions.

9. Directions are clear and understandable.

10. Learning materials are readily available.

11. Responds appropriately to unplanned occurrences.

12. Goals for activities are clearly communicated.

13. Teacher is enthusiastic.
14. Contacts students individually to observe, answer questions, etc.

15. Maintains adequate supervision for activities.

16. Encourages and develops each student's point of view.
17. Demonstrates interest in activities of students (curricular and co-curricular).

18. Displays an appropriate sense of humor.

19. Handles classroom management efficiently.

20. Maintains order and discipline within the class.

Figure 14.2. Typical example of items utilized in a checklist designed to guide teacher observation and evaluation.

10. The teacher prepares students for a lesson by reviewing, outlining, explaining objectives, and summarizing.

Research has shown that all of these behaviors have a high relationship with student outcomes, as measured by performance on standardized achievement tests in mathematics and reading. This is certainly not intended as a "perfect" listing of all characteristics shown by effective teachers, but these behaviors may be observed in a more objective fashion than the items presented in the checklist we reviewed earlier in Figure 14.2.

Effective teaching has been conceptualized recently as something other than specific in-class instructional behaviors that produce improved student outcomes on standardized achievement tests. Instead, researchers have emphasized a more subtle, "holistic" pattern. Elliot Eisner (1982) described "Artistic Supervision" as an approach to evaluation that requires the following:

1. Attention to the muted or expressive character of events, not simply to their incidence or literal meaning;

2. High levels of educational connoisseurship; that is, the ability to see what is significant yet subtle;

3. Appreciation of the unique contributions the teacher makes to the educational development of the young, as well as those contributions a teacher may have in common with others;

4. Attention to the process of classroom life and observation of this process over extended periods of time so that the significance of events can be placed in a temporal context;

5. Establishment of rapport between the supervisor and those being supervised so that dialogue and a sense of trust can be established between the two;

6. An ability to use language, to exploit its potential so as to make public the expressive character of what has been seen;

7. An ability to interpret the meaning of events so that their educational importance may be fully appreciated;

8. Recognition of the fact that the individual supervisor with his or her strengths, sensitivities, and experience is the major "instrument" through which the educational situation is perceived.

These basic principles of artistic evaluation are further developed by Louis Rubin (1986), who defined a series of behaviors that suggest artistic teaching. In Rubin's view, "artistic teachers" are those who:

1. Focus on the subtleties of teaching (i.e., motivation of student, pacing, control), which invigorate basic instructional methods and subject matter;

2. Improvise tactics for reaching objectives and overcoming difficulties;
3. Take advantage of opportunities to clarify ideas and reinforce concepts;
4. Make use of intention and hunch in modifying routine practice;
5. Set high expectations for themselves and their students;
6. Find the most efficient and expedient ways of getting things done;
7. Use temporary digressions on related topics to enrich lessons, stimulate interest, and increase pace;
8. Base their control of learning activities on student behavior;
9. Take pride in what they do and in the achievement of their students;
10. Concentrate on a few dominant goals that are central to their purpose;
11. Respect their convictions;
12. Devote as much time as possible to whatever they enjoy most in teaching.

Whatever perspective the supervisor values—artistic or more scientific—the point here is that a *consistent, research-based,* and *objective* set of standards should serve as the basis for evaluation of staff.

Evaluation Procedures Not Communicated

In many schools, the purposes, criteria, and processes of staff evaluation are not adequately communicated to staff. School systems often take great pains to improve the quality of their evaluation procedures; committees of teachers and supervisory personnel work diligently to put together effective evaluation programs, efforts are made to find objective evaluation criteria, and the evaluation program is excellently "packaged." But many of these attempts fail simply because, once the new evaluation program is designed, it is not sufficiently communicated to the entire staff. Districts frequently develop new evaluation procedures one year and then fail to "reeducate" staff to these procedures in following years, assuming that "we all know about those practices around here." Unfortunately, that assumption is often incorrect. Supervisors should ensure that the purposes, criteria, and procedures of any staff evaluation program are clearly communicated periodically to all staff. Such practice increases the likelihood that staff will "buy into" evaluation practices and, more importantly, will raise suggestions for improving the status quo from time to time.

Insufficient Expertise

Staff evaluation procedures often experience difficulties because the administrative or supervisory personnel called upon to implement these procedures lack sufficient technical expertise in the area of evaluation. For years, school administrators were trained to serve as *managers* of their buildings. As we noted in Chapter 6, the expectation that administrators and supervisors will engage in behaviors more reflective of instructional leadership is relatively recent. Thus, few present educational leaders have had extensive training in evaluation practices. Those who do have a background in this area tend to have had specific training primarily in summative staff evaluation procedures. Aspiring administrative and supervisory personnel currently in training must receive additional specialized training and preparation in all types of evaluation and for all objectives. Present administrators and supervisors who feel that they lack sufficient knowledge about *how* to evaluate or *what* to evaluate must utilize the expertise of others in evaluating staff. In secondary schools, for instance, a principal with a teaching background in math may need to observe and evaluate a teacher of Spanish. The obvious solution here is to ask help from someone with greater subject area expertise—a department chairperson, subject supervisor, or senior teacher—in providing both criteria for the evaluation and specific feedback regarding mastery of the instructional content.

Due-Process Issues

Considerable evidence suggests that, with the advent of negotiated teacher contracts and other more sophisticated efforts to take into account the rights of teachers as employees, the concern that due process is not always observed in staff evaluation has been alleviated. The concern is particularly powerful, predictably, in the area of summative evaluation, from which final decisions concerning employment may result. Effective supervisors ensure that due process is always observed in staff evaluation by following these recommended procedures:

1. Whenever a teacher is evaluated, provide to that teacher a *written* identification of strengths as well as a diagnosis of weaknesses. In addition, provide specific recommendations for the ways in which weaknesses might be improved.
2. Offer intensive follow-up to the teacher so that he or she can, in fact, implement the specific recommendations provided by the supervisor or administrator. The supervisor or administrator is responsible for documenting this follow-up.
3. If the results of the evaluation and improvement plan still warrant an unfavorable or adverse personnel decision, communicate advance notice of this decision in writing to the staff member. Also provide notice of the staff member's right to a hearing with the supervisor or administrator responsible for making the adverse recommendation.
4. Specify appeal procedures should the staff member be dissatisfied with the outcome of the hearing.

5. Communicate all these procedures in writing, as well as any additional information unique to the local setting, to all staff members.

In addition to following the specific procedures listed above, adherence to a few general principles will alleviate much of the anxiety supervisors and administrators may feel about this issue of due process and legal responsibilities in general.

1. Evaluation of teaching must be *based on a sense of equal respect* between supervisor and teacher. (Teachers and other staff members are human beings who possess certain rights. All evaluation procedures must respect the simple human dignity of school staff members.)
2. Evaluation of teaching must be *reasonable.* (Evaluation procedures must be neither arbitrary nor capricious. Decisions based on information gathered for evaluation must be warranted by that information.)
3. The *purpose* of evaluation must be *clearly identified with educational effectiveness.* (Evaluation procedures must promote good education. Evaluation should assure that the aims of the school are being met in an effective manner.)

Inadequate Follow-up

Throughout this discussion we have assumed that the ultimate purpose of any educational evaluation (staff, student, or curricular; diagnostic, formative, or summative) is to enhance the quality of education available to children. To ensure that such enhancement actually occurs, sufficient follow-up about possible instructional improvement must be provided to teachers after they have been evaluated by administrators or supervisors. Unfortunately, current evaluation practice is often marked by a decided lack of feedback.

As we will see in Chapter 15, the *clinical supervision model* is designed largely as a formative evaluation technique that stresses direct feedback from supervisors to teachers. Keith Acheson and Meredith Gall (1987) note that effective feedback in postevaluation conferences requires three kinds of activities. The first of these must take place *before* and *during the observation* or evaluation session itself; the second and third must take place *during the postevaluation conference.*

The following activities, according to Acheson and Gall, must occur before and during the evaluation session:

1. In a preevaluation planning conference, the teacher and supervisor must set goals for the year, identify concerns, establish a rationale for working together, consider strategies the teacher has been using and intends to use, and translate abstract concerns into observable behaviors that the supervisor can record.

2. Before the observation session, the teacher and supervisor must identify the nature of the lesson to be observed, make the objectives explicit, discuss what the teacher will be doing, predict what the students will be doing, consider specific problems or concerns that the teacher anticipates during the lesson, and select appropriate observation techniques and recording systems.
3. During the observational visit, the supervisor must employ one or more devices from a repertoire of data-recording techniques, use appropriate recording devices for the specific situation as related to the goals and concerns, and record data unobtrusively and without disruption of the class.

The above activities are normally included in the first two stages of the clinical supervision model, and they represent what should occur in order for an effective feedback conference to take place.

For Acheson and Gall, the second set of activities that represent part of effective follow-up to evaluation are the following, which form the general, conceptual basis for postevaluation feedback:

1. The supervisor must provide the teacher with feedback using objective observational data.
2. The supervisor must elicit the teacher's opinions, feelings, and inferences about the observational data.
3. The supervisor must encourage the teacher to consider alternative lesson objectives, methods, and reasons.
4. The supervisor must provide the teacher with opportunities for practice and comparison.

Finally, Acheson and Gall suggest five specific activities that should occur at the postobservation feedback conference:

1. The observer *displays* the data recorded at the observation. This is done without evaluative comments.
2. The teacher *analyzes* what was happening during the lesson as evidenced by the data. The supervisor simply helps to clarify what behaviors the recorded data represent.
3. The teacher, with the help of the supervisor, *interprets* the behaviors of the teacher and students as represented by the observational data. At this stage the teacher becomes more evaluative because causes and consequences must be discussed as desirable or undesirable.
4. The teacher, with assistance from the supervisor, *decides* on alternative approaches for the future to attend to dissatisfaction with the observed teaching or to emphasize those aspects that were satisfying.
5. The supervisor *reinforces* the teacher's announced intentions for

change when the supervisor agrees with them or helps the teacher modify the intentions if there is some disagreement.

I do not suggest that such detail needs to be included in every case of postevaluation follow-up; indeed, effective conferences can consist of an informal chat in the hallway after an observation. There is a critical need, however, for *adequate* feedback to be made available to staff members *as soon as possible* after evaluation has been carried out.

We should also mention that, although Acheson and Gall use a clinical model that employs in-class teacher observation as the sole data-gathering technique, observation is certainly not the only way in which evaluative data may be collected. Self-evaluations by teachers (probably the most potent form of evaluation), student evaluations of teaching, and even informal discussions with staff members outside of their normal teaching responsibilities also represent ways in which information can be gathered and structured as part of staff evaluation.

Evaluation of Evaluation

Evaluation programs themselves are rarely evaluated. Procedures are often followed primarily because "we've always done it that way around here," rather than because a solid history of effectiveness argues for the continuation of existing practices.

Kunkel and Tucker (1977) suggested five criteria by which supervisors and administrators might evaluate the quality of their own evaluation activities, as we suggest these as an appropriate and natural starting point for the development of a strategy for periodic review of existing evaluation practices:

1. *Holism:* Does the evaluation activity look at the total picture without an undue emphasis on quantification, or on only a few variables?
2. *Helpfulness toward program improvement:* Does the evaluation program promote growth, improvement, increased effectiveness, and other similar types of positive benefits, rather than serving only as a ranking, judging, or criticizing technique?
3. *Acceptance of hard and soft data:* Does the evaluation process emphasize both empirical and intuitive methodologies?
4. *Evaluation vulnerability:* Is the person responsible for conducting the evaluation able to grow as much as the persons being evaluated?
5. *Vision of the future:* Does the evaluation activity have a future orientation, directed toward helping improve things later rather than "fixing" things now?

Regardless of the criteria selected, evaluation practices must be reviewed periodically to determine if they are continuing to serve the same purposes that they were originally designed to serve.

SUMMARY

Evaluation is a critical responsibility for the practitioner of educational supervision. Although evaluation is far from being the only duty for a supervisor, it is clearly one of the most important. Only through effective evaluation can data be obtained to assist the supervisor in making appropriate educational decisions; only through evaluation can the quality of instruction—and of education overall—be improved. Quality education demands continuing efforts at improvement, and improvement often implies changing existing practices. To make correct and effective changes, accurate evaluative information is vitally important.

We began this chapter by defining evaluation as a process for determining the basic worth of something by measuring that "something" against established standards or criteria. We described three types of evaluation: *diagnostic,* which determines the nature of something prior to an intervention; *formative,* which determines how well something is working in progress; and *summative,* which determines whether or not something has ultimately succeeded. All three types or stages are vital activities for improving schools—although, as we noted, too much attention is typically directed toward summative activities and too little toward formative activities.

Primarily, educational evaluation assesses students, curricular programs and materials, and staff. We provided examples in this chapter of evaluative activities directed at each of these three areas. Finally, we concluded with a review of some typical problems associated with evaluation in schools, including confusion over the purpose of evaluation, lack of objective criteria, and lack of strategies to evaluate the evaluation activities themselves.

The most important point in this chapter is this: We need to work to improve evaluation processes in education because effective educational evaluation will ultimately result in better teachers—and better education—for our children.

SUGGESTED ACTIVITIES

1. Collect descriptions for the teacher-evaluation procedures used in at least four school systems. Analyze these descriptions in terms of the criteria for determining the effectiveness of evaluation practices specified by Kunkel and Tucker.
2. Interview a sample of teachers from your school to determine what they believe are areas that need improvement in staff evaluation practices for your district. Engage in the same activity with a group of principals and other administrators in your

district. Make sure to ask people for suggestions regarding the ways in which improvement may be carried out.

3. Ask a number of administrators to estimate the percentage of their weekly time that is devoted to the different types and objects of evaluation described in this chapter. If they had more time to spend on evaluation, which types would they do more, and why?

REFERENCES

Acheson, Keith A., & Gall, Meredith D. (1987). *Techniques in the clinical supervision of teachers* (2nd ed.). White Plains, NY: Longman.

Berliner, David, & Tickunoff, W. (1976). The California beginning teacher evaluation study: Overview of the ethnographic study. *Journal of Teacher Education, 27.*

Borich, Gary D. (1977). *The appraisal of teaching: Concepts and process.* Reading, MA: Addison-Wesley.

Eisner, Elliot. (1982). An artistic approach to supervision. In Thomas J. Sergiovanni (Ed.), *Supervision of teaching* (1982 Yearbook of the Association for Supervision and Curriculum Development). Alexandria, VA: The Association.

Kunkel, Richard C., & Tucker, Susan. (1977). A perception-based model of program evaluation: A values-oriented theory. Paper presented at the Annual Meeting of the American Educational Research Association, New York.

Rubin, Louis J. (1985). *Artistry in teaching.* New York: Random House.

Scriven, Michael. (1967). The methodology of evaluation. In Robert E. Stake (Ed.), *Curriculum evaluation.* American Educational Research Association Monograph Series on Evaluation. Chicago: Rand McNally.

Worthen, Blaine R., & Sanders, James R. (1987). *Educational evaluation: Alternative approaches and practical guidelines.* White Plains, NY: Longman.

PART V

Models for Supervision: Now and the Future

In Part V we review *clinical supervision,* a supervisory model that many see as a cure-all for the ills of educational supervision, as well as other emerging models in the field. Finally, we will review the important issue of staff development and inservice training and look quickly at future trends and issues.

CHAPTER 15

Clinical Supervision

As we noted in the previous chapter, educators have rarely had a strong record in formative evaluative practices. Well-developed strategies guide diagnostic and summative staff evaluation, but strategies for formative evaluation are less clear. Even though researchers generally recognize that intervention to improve any activity is most effective if undertaken while that activity is in progress, formative evaluation of staff has not been given high priority in most school systems. This situation has begun to change during the last 20 years, and one reason is the general acceptance of the supervisory model we discuss in this chapter, *clinical supervision.*

UNDERLYING ASSUMPTIONS
OF CLINICAL SUPERVISION

Many educators endorse clinical supervision as a perfect approach to the supervision of teachers. In Ohio, for example, the most recent standards for certification of educational supervisors mandated by the state's department of education require candidates seeking a supervisory license to receive special, intensive training in the use of the clinical supervision model. I do not agree that clinical supervision will cure all our current ills, but I do think that it offers some very useful strategies for the improvement of supervisory practice. Throughout this chapter I will suggest that clinical supervision must be understood in an appropriate context, and that context is defined largely by the assumptions and historical background upon which this model is based.

Clinical supervision is typically presented as the brainchild of Robert Goldhammer and Morris Cogan, former faculty members at Harvard University, who worked during the late 1950s and early 1960s on the development of curriculum and instructional practices for Harvard's experimental Master of Arts in Teaching (M.A.T.) Program, normally referred to as the Harvard-Newton Summer School project (Cogan, 1961). Cogan and Goldhammer were charged specifically with the development of a practicum that would be a part of this new program. We need to point out here that the Harvard-Newton program was never designed to be available to all teachers; it was, basically, a highly selective project designed to refine the teaching skills of the *very best* teachers in the country. From its initial planning, the Harvard effort was directed toward refinement of existing excellence, never at "fixing" mediocre or poor teachers, and the practicum was an important way in which excellent, experienced teachers could become even better.

Goldhammer and Cogan, primary designers of the Harvard-Newton program practicum, were faced with a critical dilemma. How could they design a field-based learning program that was not established, like traditional student-teaching arrangements, to provide basic hands-on learning opportunities in real, live classrooms? The participating teachers were often "master" teachers in their own districts, and were often called on to work with weaker colleagues. How could anyone hope to provide feedback to people of this quality who were returning to student teaching?

The answer to this was what Cogan and Goldhammer—later joined by Robert Anderson and Robert Krajewski—called "clinical supervision." Cogan (1973) defined their model as supervision "focused upon the improvement of the teacher's classroom instruction. The principal data of clinical supervision includes records of classroom events: what the teacher and students do in the classroom during the teaching-learning process" (p. 9). The notion of "clinical" as opposed to "general" supervision was selected to suggest an emphasis on supervision related specifically to classroom observation, analysis of events taking place within the classroom, and the in-class behavior of teachers and students. The primary goal of this model was to provide an opportunity for teachers to gain feedback that would allow them to improve already good teaching skills. Noreen Garman (1982) notes, "In the clinical approach to supervision, the supervisor provides the practitioner with a service that is concerned with the quality of his or her practice" (p. 35).

Weller (1977) identified the following elements of clinical supervision:

1. To improve instruction, teachers must learn specific intellectual and behavioral skills.
2. The supervisor should take responsibility for helping teachers to develop:
   skills for analyzing the instructional process based on systematic data;

skills for experimentation, adaptation, and modification of the
curriculum;
a broader repertoire of teaching skills and techniques.
3. The supervisor should emphasize what and how teachers teach: to
improve instruction, not to change the teacher's personality.
4. Planning and analysis must center on making and testing instructional hypotheses based on observational evidence.
5. Conferences should deal with a few instructional issues that are
important, relevant to the teacher, and amenable to change.
6. The feedback conference should concentrate on constructive analysis and the reinforcement of successful patterns rather than on the
condemnation of unsuccessful patterns.
7. Feedback must be based on observational evidence, not on unsub-
stantiated value judgments.
8. The cycle of planning, observation, and analysis should be continuous and cumulative.
9. Supervision is a dynamic process of give-and-take in which supervisors and teachers are colleagues in search of mutual educational
understanding.
10. The supervisory process is primarily centered on the analysis of
instruction.
11. The individual teacher has both the freedom and the responsibility
to initiate issues, analyze and improve his or her own teaching, and
develop a personal teaching style.
12. Supervision can be perceived, analyzed, and improved in much the
same manner as teaching can.
13. The supervisor has both the freedom and the responsibility to
analyze and evaluate his or her own supervision in a manner similar
to a teacher's analysis and evaluation of his or her instruction.

Acheson and Gall (1987) noted five major goals implied by the clinical
supervision model. Clinical supervision is designed to

1. Provide teachers with objective feedback on the current state of their
instruction.
2. Diagnose and solve instructional problems.
3. Help teachers develop skill in using instructional strategies.
4. Evaluate teachers for promotion, tenure, or other decisions.
5. Help teachers develop a positive attitude about continuous professional development.

All of these assumptions and goals accurately reflect the nature of
supervisory practice that follows the clinical model. In addition, I want to
point out two other considerations. First, clinical supervision is not for

everyone; it is designed to support and provide feedback to *experienced, reflective,* and generally very *good* classroom teachers. Second, clinical supervision presumes that teachers should direct the supervisory process precisely because, as users, they *are* experienced and effective. This teacher-controlled model should not be used to *judge* teaching quality, but rather as a *resource* for good teachers to refine their instructional techniques. Effective supervisors should be capable of making these practices available to teachers at any time they are requested to.

Clinical supervision is best viewed as a collegial practice, not as something that a superordinate (an administrator or supervisor, for example) does *to* a teacher, but as a peer-to-peer activity. Thus, some practitioners suggest that the clinical supervision model is best used between teachers, and that supervisors or administrators have no real ongoing role in it.

I do not mean to reduce the potential value of this model: Rather, I wish to emphasize that the best use of clinical supervision must be based on its documented strengths, and not on assumptions that have in fact never been present. The clinical model, for instance, cannot be used effectively with a first-year teacher, and I doubt that true clinical supervision is an appropriate way to provide feedback to a teacher judged as incompetent. Because of these limitations, we must approach with considerable caution those wholesale suggestions that clinical supervision should automatically be used with all teachers in all schools under all circumstances.

DEVELOPING AN APPROPRIATE CLIMATE

Before we can legitimately consider the structure of the clinical supervision model, we need to define those conditions that must exist to make the use of that model effective. Just as clinical supervision is not appropriate for every teacher, it is also not appropriate for every school setting. Under certain conditions, clinical supervision may cause more harm than good.

Clinical supervision is collaborative, collegial, and teacher-directed. As a result, clinical supervision can only be effectively used if supervisors or administrators truly trust the teachers in the school, to the extent that they are willing to allow those teachers to define and control the analysis of their own instructional behavior. Moreover, teachers must feel comfortable enough in the school environment to "act naturally." Improvement can only take place among those who are willing to admit to their own imperfections.

If no climate of trust exists, then any clinical practices employed in supervision will be without substance. Lovell and Wiles (1983) noted the importance of this condition in discussing potential pitfalls of clinical supervision:

> Sometimes supervisors are not willing to take the time, or do not have the
> ability, to establish a basis of mutual trust. Such a condition is essential.

However, there is also a need for mutual respect for professional competence. Without these two conditions, it is impossible to have effective clinical supervision. (p. 182)

Many supervisory schemes make use of the structural steps of clinical supervision. Without the proper climate, however, true clinical supervision simply is not taking place. As Lovell and Wiles observed:

Some organizations like the "sound" and the "glamour" of clinical supervision but do not have the conviction and/or the ability to provide the human and material resources. To implement clinical supervision, it is essential that supervisors and teachers have *time* to participate in various kinds of activities on a continuing basis. Time is needed for pre-observation conferences, observations and analysis of teaching, and post-observation feed-back and corrective procedures. Clinical observation requires in-depth thinking and working together over an extended period of time. If it is going to work, the organization must provide the necessary personnel, arrangements, rewards, equipment, leadership, and support. (Lovell and Wiles, 1983, p. 211)

STAGES OF THE CLINICAL SUPERVISION MODEL

Cogan's (1973) initial design of a clinical supervision model included eight steps:

1. Establishing the teacher-supervision relationship.
2. Planning with the teacher.
3. Planning the strategy of observation.
4. Observing instruction.
5. Analyzing the teaching-learning process.
6. Planning the strategy of the conference.
7. The conference.
8. Renewed planning.

Mosher and Purpel (1972) reduced these eight steps to three stages or process activities:

1. Planning
2. Observing
3. Evaluating or analyzing

Acheson and Gall (1987) also simplified the clinical supervision model by suggesting only three stages:

1. Planning conference
2. Classroom observation
3. Feedback conference

Peter Oliva (1984) summarized these competing descriptions of the component elements of clinical supervision by suggesting that, regardless of the particular approach, all possess certain essential ingredients: (1) contact or communication with the teacher prior to an observation; (2) classroom observation; and (3) follow-up of the observation.

Practitioners will no doubt continue to disagree over the "official" number of steps in the clinical supervision model. For our purposes, I find useful the five-stage description first presented by Goldhammer (1969), and maintained in the more recent work of Goldhammer, Anderson, and Krajewski (1981):

1. Preobservation conference
2. Observation
3. Analysis and strategy
4. Supervision conference
5. Postconference analysis

Preobservation Conference

This first stage allows participants to form a mental framework in anticipation of the observation of teaching that is to follow. This stage has the following specific purposes:

1. Communication can be opened (or reopened) between supervisor and teacher. Goldhammer suggested that "it can be useful for [the] teacher and [the] supervisor to talk together . . . to renew their habits of communication, their familiarity with one another's intellectual style and expressive rhythms . . ." (Goldhammer, 1969, p. 57).
2. Supervisor and teacher may become familiar with each other's goals and intentions, as well as reasons, premises, doubts, motives, and ultimate expectations, and interpersonal communication may become more fluent.
3. Teacher and supervisor can rehearse what will take place during the actual episode of classroom observation.
4. Last-minute revisions of the teacher's goals, objectives, and lesson plan may be carried out.
5. The nature of the specific practices to be followed in the observation can be determined and a "contract" regarding the ground rules (i.e., how long the supervisor will observe, at what time during the school day, when the supervisor will enter the classroom, and so forth) made between the teacher and supervisor.

In short, this first stage is when teacher and supervisor plan the clinical supervision cycle. It is here that the teacher articulates (often in a vague and ill-defined way) his or her reasons for requesting someone to observe a class. During this step, supervisors should avoid any tendency to make demands and place restrictions on teachers in anticipation of the observation. Instead, the supervisor primarily listens to the teacher specify what is wanted. If this is not well-defined, the supervisor helps the teacher articulate concerns more completely. The following outline, developed by Goldhammer, Anderson, and Krajewski (1981), offers a sample agenda for a well-designed preobservation conference.

1. Establish a "contract" or "agreement" between the supervisor and the teacher to be observed, including:
   a. Objectives of the lesson.
   b. Relationship of the lesson objectives to the overall learning program being implemented.
   c. Activities to be observed.
   d. Possible changing of activity format, delivery system, and other elements based on interactive agreement between supervisor and teacher.
   e. Specific description of items or problems on which the teacher desires feedback.
   f. Assessment procedures of activities and problems.
2. Establish the mechanics or ground rules of the observation, including:
   a. Time of the observation.
   b. Length of the observation.
   c. Place of the observation.
3. Establish specific plans for carrying out the observation:
   a. Where shall the supervisor sit?
   b. Should the supervisor talk to students about the lesson? If so, when? Before or after the lesson?
   c. Will the supervisor look for a specific action?
   d. Should the supervisor interact with students?
   e. Will any special materials or preparations be necessary?
   f. How shall the supervisor leave the observation? (Goldhammer, Anderson, and Krajewski, 1981, p. 55.)

Observation

This step, so simple to describe (the supervisor observes the teacher), may be the most difficult and complicated for the supervisor actually to carry out. Observation is difficult and complicated because it requires the supervisor to make use of many different skills, which we can cluster into two basic categories: determining *what* to observe, and determining *how* to observe.

Deciding *what* to observe should be guided by the discussion between supervisor and teacher at the preobservation conference. As Oliva (1984) notes:

> If we follow through with the cycle of clinical supervision the teacher and supervisor in the preobservation conference have decided on the specific behaviors of teacher and students which the supervisor will observe. The supervisor concentrates on the presence or absence of the specific behaviors. (p. 502)

This is, at least in theory, the proper focus for classroom observation—but only if what the teacher indicated in advance is in fact an accurate description of the major issues that exist in the classroom. If the teacher suggested, for example, that his or her major problem is knowing whether or not he or she is using sufficiently demanding questions to elicit high-level thinking skills from students, and if the observer finds that this indeed is the major classroom issue, then the observation can be classically nondirective. If, however, the observer finds many other classroom problems that need to be addressed, then the observer needs to make an immediate decision: Will he or she observe the teacher's stated problem, or will he or she note instead the true problems that the observer perceives in the classroom?

The issue of *how* to observe also deserves attention. The best intentions of supervisors will be pointless if their efforts at observation are not guided by the overriding realization that data must be gathered in an efficient and objective fashion. The ultimate goal of data gathering is to obtain information to share with the teacher after the observation has concluded, so that the teacher can analyze his or her own activities in the classroom. One recent development of use to us in refining classroom observation techniques is the research focus on analyzing classroom activities. Researchers with no particular interest in supervision (or for that matter in any processes the goal of which is to modify teaching behavior) have nevertheless developed instruments that enable supervisors to engage in more sophisticated in-class observations. Acheson and Gall (1987) reviewed many of these techniques and suggested their potential application for clinical supervision:

1. *Selective verbatim:* The supervisor makes a written record of exactly what is said, in a verbatim transcript. Not all verbal events are recorded; the supervisor and teacher, as part of their conference, have decided what kinds of verbal events ought to be written down in a "selective" fashion. For example, if a teacher believes that he or she is not asking sufficiently difficult questions to challenge the very bright students in a class, the supervisor may spend the entire observation doing nothing but transcribing the questions used by the teacher. This transcription can take place while the class is in progress, or from a review of a taped recording of a class.

2. *Observational records based on seating charts:* The supervisor docu-

ments the behaviors of students as they interact with a teacher during a class session. A considerable amount of complex behavior and interaction can be described pictorially. An application of this approach might be in a case where, during a preobservation conference, a teacher expresses concern about the fact that some students are more involved in class discussions than others. Using a seating chart observation form, the observer may document graphically that the teacher is in fact interacting more frequently with a handful of students, suggesting that some students are not receiving much attention. This may serve as an explanation for why some students are not as involved as others.

3. *Wide-lens techniques:* The observer makes brief notes of events in the classroom that answer, in very broad fashion, the question, "What happened?" Wide-lens notes are also called *anecdotal records.* The observer makes no effort to record precise events, but rather writes down overall impressions and big events. This technique might be particularly appropriate when the teacher does not have a precisely defined concern or problem related to teaching. Often a teacher will simply recognize that "something just isn't going well in my class." The wide-lens technique might then be employed by a supervisor who wishes to collect data that reflect broad impressions of what is going on in the classroom. These broad impressions might then serve to assist the teacher in more precisely describing his or her concerns.

4. *Checklists and timeline coding:* The supervisor observes and collects data about the teaching behavior being observed and categorizes these activities according to predefined classifications. A famous example of this procedure in supervisory observation is the Flanders Interaction Analysis scale (Flanders, 1970), which suggests that teaching behavior may be understood in terms of the extent to which classroom activities fit into three broad categories—Teacher Talk, Student Talk, and Silence. Each of these categories is further divided into more precise descriptive classifications, as indicated in the illustration of the Flanders Interaction Analysis Categories (FIAC) instrument in Table 15.1.

Another checklist used to guide classroom observation is the *timeline coding technique* developed over the past 20 years, principally as part of research designed to study teaching strategies. Here, the observer notes certain predetermined behaviors of either teacher or students at particular times during a class. These techniques, once again, can provide data to teachers who are unable to articulate precisely what they feel should be observed in their classes. These widely validated instruments can guide supervisors in their observations and provide specific feedback within accepted classifications.

As I have attempted to indicate here, a wide variety of techniques may be

TABLE 15.1. FLANDERS INTERACTION ANALYSIS CATEGORIES.

Teacher Talk	**Response**	1. *Accepts feeling.* Accepts and clarifies an attitude or the feeling tone of a student in a nonthreatening manner. Feelings may be positive or negative. Predicting and recalling feelings are included.
		2. *Praises or encourages.* Praises or encourages students; says "um hum" or "go on"; makes jokes that release tension, but not at the expense of a student.
		3. *Accepts or uses ideas of students.* Acknowledges student talk. Clarifies, builds on, or asks questions based on student ideas.
		4. *Asks questions.* Asks questions about content or procedure, based on teacher ideas, with the intent that a student will answer.
	Initiation	5. *Lectures.* Offers facts or opinions about content or procedures: expresses his own ideas, gives *his own* explanation, or cites an authority other than a student.
		6. *Gives directions.* Gives directions, commands, or orders with which a student is expected to comply.
		7. *Criticizes student or justifies authority.* Makes statements intended to change student behavior from nonacceptable to acceptable patterns; arbitrarily corrects student answers; bawls someone out. Or states why the teacher is doing what he is doing; uses extreme self-reference.
Student Talk	**Response**	8. *Student talk—response.* Student talk in response to a teacher contact that structures or limits the situation. Freedom to express own ideas is limited.
	Initiation	9. *Student talk—initiation.* Student initiates or expresses his own ideas, either spontaneously or in response to the teacher's solicitation. Freedom to develop opinions and a line of thought; going beyond existing structure.
Silence		10. *Silence or confusion.* Pauses, short periods of silence, and periods of confusion in which communication cannot be understood by the observer.

SOURCE: Based on Flanders, Ned A. (1970). Analyzing teaching behavior, as printed in Keith A. Acheson & Meredith Damien Gall (1987). Techniques in the clinical supervision of teachers, 2nd edition. White Plains, NY: Longman.

used to direct the observation stage of clinical supervision. The effective supervisor should be aware of many approaches in order to choose one that fits the concerns of the teacher. What I see from time to time is, unfortunately, the reverse. In many settings, supervisors learn about one technique such as the Flanders Interaction Analysis and become wedded to it. Techniques have clear strengths, but these strengths quickly disappear when a supervisor insists on using a single approach to guide every observation process, rather than allowing the teacher's instructional concerns to dictate the tool for observation.

Despite the limitations inherent in this stage, observation is absolutely critical for many reasons. As Goldhammer noted when he first described the purpose and rationale for observing teaching in classes:

> In the most general sense, observation should create opportunities for supervisors to help teachers to test reality, the reality of their own perceptions and judgments about their teaching. I have argued that supervision should result in heightened autonomy for teacher and, particularly, in strengthened capacities for independent, objective, self-analysis, and that supervision which increases teacher's dependency upon supervisor to know whether his teaching is good or bad, that is, supervision in which supervisor's unexamined value judgments predominate, is bad supervision. But the supervisor's perceptions and evaluations, rather than counting for nothing, represent a potentially excellent source of data from which consensual validation can be obtained: given his own perceptions of what has taken place, Teacher can test "reality" by ascertaining whether Supervisor's observations (and later his value judgments) tend to confirm or to oppose his own. (Goldhammer, 1969, p. 61)

This description of the potential value of observation suggests another issue: Is clinical supervision in fact primarily an activity of staff *development* rather than staff *evaluation?* One theme that permeates existing explanations of the model is that teachers may use clinical supervision to assume increasing control over their own professional development. Not surprisingly, then, recent programs directed at developing teachers' capacities for helping their colleagues, such as the Toledo, Ohio, collegial evaluation model, the Peer-Assisted Review (PAR) program in Columbus, Ohio, and other similar efforts across the nation, make use of the structure and assumptions of the classic clinical supervision model.

Analysis and Strategy

In the third stage of the clinical supervision model, supervisor and teacher independently reflect on the nature of what has just transpired and assess the extent to which the observation was related to the goals and objectives developed during preobservation. Goldhammer's initial description of this stage noted that there are two general purposes to be addressed. The first, *Analysis,* involves making sense out of the observational data. In the second, *Strategy,* supervisor and teacher plan the agenda of the conference that will follow; "that is, what issues to treat, which data to cite, what goals to aim for, how to begin, where to end, and who should do what" (Goldhammer, 1969, p. 63).

Supervision Conference

As soon as possible after the actual observation, supervisor and teacher meet for a follow-up conference primarily designed to permit the two actors in the clinical model to "de-brief" about what has taken place to that point: Were the goals and concerns of the teacher identified during the preobservation conference accurate? What was seen during the observation? What do we now know as a result of the observation?

Lovell and Wiles (1983) identified the following specific goals of the supervision conference:

1. Anticipated teacher and student behavior and actual teacher and student behavior are compared.
2. Discrepancies are identified between anticipated teacher and student behavior and actual teacher and student behavior.
3. Decisions are made about what should be done about discrepancies and congruencies between anticipated and actual behavior.
4. Comparisons are made between projected use of subject content, materials, equipment, physical space, and social environment with their actual use, with emphasis on the identification of congruencies and discrepancies, and plans for their future use.
5. Comparisons are made regarding desired learning outcomes with actual learning outcomes within the context of other appropriate factors in the situation, as described by observation. (p. 179)

Goldhammer, Anderson, and Krajewski (1981) acknowledge that, in addition to providing feedback to the teacher and a basis for the improvement of future teaching, the conference can meet at least five additional goals:

1. Teachers can be provided with adult rewards and satisfactions. A supervisor may say to a teacher, in essence, "You are worth my time, and I value you as a colleague sufficiently that I am glad to work with you." As we noted in Chapter 13, teachers rarely receive this kind of signal from others with whom they work.
2. Issues in teaching may be defined more precisely. The supervisor can affirm that what the teacher sensed as a problem was indeed something that needed attention.
3. If appropriate, the supervisor can offer to intervene directly with the teacher to provide didactic assistance and guidance. Depending on a number of circumstances (particularly the level of trust between the supervisor and the teacher), the supervisor may usefully suggest specific changes to be made by the teacher.
4. The teacher may be trained in techniques for self-supervision. The clinical supervision model is, ultimately, to be replaced by the ability

of the individual teacher to "do without" the supervisor. Good teachers, of course, will always value feedback from colleagues. But an effective clinical supervisor aims at making teachers increasingly responsible for their own improvement. The postobservation conference can be used to increase capability in this area.

5. Teachers can be provided with additional incentives for increasing future levels of professional self-analysis.

Postconference Analysis

Four basic objectives may be achieved in this fifth and final stage, which is structurally part of the supervision conference. First, teacher and supervisor reconstruct the salient features of the conference so that they understand what took place and determine what agreements were made. Second, the participants assess the supervision conference to decide whether or to what extent the objectives of the observation were attained, and to what extent the conference was of value to the teacher. Third, supervisor and teacher consider whether or not the entire process of clinical supervision has had any value to the overall professional development of the teacher. Finally, teacher and supervisor assess the quality of the supervisor's skill in carrying out each of the stages in the model. In short, this final stage in the clinical supervision model allows teacher and supervisor to relax, reflect, and consider the strengths and weaknesses of the process in which they have just been involved. Was it worth all the effort? Did it have any payoff? Should it be done again in the future? In what ways might the process be changed? These questions and others might be considered by teacher and supervisor during the postobservation analysis phase.

These five stages of clinical supervision are not absolute requirements. As we noted earlier, different theorists have included more or fewer steps, but virtually all these descriptions can be logically structured into three stages: preobservation conferencing; observation; and postobservation conferencing. Adherence to every step in a model is not the critical issue; in fact, the specific steps are much less important than the precondition described earlier, namely the establishment of a climate of mutual trust and open communication.

Conversely, then, we can point out that merely employing the five stages (or eight, or three, or whatever particular description is selected) does *not* produce clinical supervision. Many evaluative programs require supervisors or administrators to hold conferences before observing staff, and also to conduct de-briefing conferences after the observation has taken place. Unless this sequence occurs in a setting where the *basic assumptions* of clinical supervision are observed (i.e., that it is a formative activity, teacher directed, and carried out in an environment where collegial trust is present), the model has not been implemented.

LIMITS OF CLINICAL SUPERVISION

As I noted in the opening of this chapter, the process of clinical supervision holds considerable promise as a technique for stimulating teachers to take more control of their own development and, as a result, improve the quality of their teaching behavior. However, clinical supervision is not a panacea to be applied to all teachers in all circumstances. I have already noted why some teachers might not be appropriate participants in the clinical model. Other basic limitations of the model also exist.

Ben Harris (1976) presented a precise review of the limitations inherent in the clinical supervision model. He suggested restrictions in three broad categories: the settings in which the model is deployed; the personal abilities of those involved with the model; and the strategies that need to be followed to make clinical supervision work.

Limitations in Settings

The day-to-day realities of life in schools make clinical supervision exceedingly difficult. As should be evident by now, the model requires considerable time to implement—from two to five hours to carry out in its entirety. If that amount of time is multiplied by the number of times any given teacher might wish to be clinically supervised (remember that the true model is "on demand"), little would go on in a school other than teacher conferencing and observations. This problem can be substantially reduced in situations where the role of supervisor is broadly enough defined to include the possibility of teachers observing other teachers in peer programs. And some educators suggest that, indeed, most supervisory and administrative time in schools *should* be devoted to precisely the activities of the clinical model. Nevertheless, the fact is that time is limited in schools, and this restricts the unbridled use of clinical supervision.

Harris (1976) also suggests that, because of the press toward conformity felt by teachers at most schools, the highly individualistic nature of clinical supervision makes the model unappealing to many who feel it sets them aside as "special" from their peers. From their initial preservice programs, teachers are trained to do what everyone else on the faculty does. Clinical supervision threatens to violate this norm by asking that teachers think of their own needs differently from those of their co-workers.

Personal Limitations

Not every teacher is motivated enough to make the intense time and energy commitment required of clinical supervision. Teachers can be quite talented, experienced, and generally fit the profile of those who may profit from the model, but they simply may not wish to go through all the bother.

Other teachers may simply not be, as Harris (1976) points out, "intelligent, creative, imaginative, open (or) uninhibited" (p. 87) enough to engage in the model. These teachers are not capable, for example, of reflecting on their teaching to the point of sophisticated analysis.

Personal limitations can also restrict the supervisor. Some supervisors are not sufficiently creative or reflective to use the clinical process. Also, the model implies a strong ability to be nondirective in encounters between supervisors and teachers; the fact is that many in supervisory positions have neither the patience nor the inclination to allow teachers to direct the supervisory process.

Strategic Limitations

The fundamental assumption of clinical supervision is that the quality of education in a school can be improved through intervention into the behaviors of teachers in classrooms. The model ignores the fact that other factors contribute to the quality of life in schools. More than observation and analysis of in-class phenomena must be taken into account in the strategies employed to supervise teachers.

Lovell and Wiles (1983) describe other "pitfalls" inherent in the ways in which the clinical supervision model is carried out in many schools:

1. Some organizations have yielded to the temptation to use "clinical supervision" as a system for evaluating teachers for personnel decisions. Such a decision precludes the use of privileged information, can be threatening and can limit willingness to share problems and concerns, can put teachers in a role of dependency and inferiority, and can limit the hoped-for outcome of teachers becoming better-functioning and self-improving professionals.
2. Sometimes clinical supervision is delivered in a rigorous and inflexible series of steps, which may not take into consideration the needs and concerns of a teacher, or his or her readiness to participate in things like observation and analysis of his or her teaching, feedback and corrective procedures. This practice could be a "turnoff" for some teachers and downright "shattering" for others. Supervisors need to be sensitive to the *individual* differences among teachers.
3. Sometimes supervisors think that the way they observe a situation is the way it is. It is impossible ever to see things as they are. We can only see them the way we think they are. Thus, it is necessary for supervisors to share their observations with teachers and get teacher feedback, with the hope of reshaping data toward agreement. The teaching situation is too complex and filled with stimuli to see everything. We need to remember that observational data are rough and incomplete at best, and we need to keep working to improve it.
4. The possibility of tenseness and fear are present when teachers are getting feedback about their behavior. Supervisors must take appropriate steps to ease these situations by stressing the positive aspects of a teacher's performance before making any statement that could be

perceived by the instructor to be negative feedback. (Lovell and Wiles, 1983, pp. 181–182)

SUMMARY

Clinical supervision is a powerful way to provide formative evaluative feedback to classroom teachers. In this chapter we reviewed assumptions of this model in the context of its original design and noted that, from the first, clinical supervision was not a practice intended for all teachers. A struggling first-year teacher who finds it nearly impossible to specify clearly what things are going *well* in the classroom let alone what things are problematic is hardly capable of engaging in clinical supervision. Only teachers able to articulate fairly specific concerns about their own instructional behavior can constructively enjoy the process of self-directed analysis. We also noted that clinical supervision's use in a school is always contingent upon the extent to which a climate of openness and trust exists in that school between supervisors and teachers. The model may be used only when teachers and supervisors share a fundamental respect for each other.

The chapter also described the stages normally included in clinical supervision and accepted Goldhammer's five steps as appropriate for our review. They are preobservation conference, observation, analysis and strategy, supervision conference, and postconference analysis. Finally, we considered some ways in which the effective application of clinical supervision is limited by ongoing conditions in schools.

SUGGESTED ACTIVITIES

1. Interview a group of practicing school principals to determine the extent to which they are familiar with the concepts and practices of clinical supervision in this chapter. Are they using the model in their schools? Why or why not, and to what extent?
2. Role-play a preobservation conference with a teacher and practice strategies for asking the teacher to articulate as clearly as possible the things that you might observe in his or her class.
3. Observe a teacher's class, using at least two different techniques described in this chapter.

REFERENCES

Acheson, Keith A., & Gall, Meredith D. (1987). *Techniques in the clinical supervision of teachers* (2nd ed.). White Plains, NY: Longman.
Cogan, Morris. (1961). Supervision at the Harvard-Newton Summer School. Unpub-

lished mimeographed paper, Harvard Graduate School of Education.
────── (1973). *Clinical supervision.* Boston: Houghton Mifflin.
Flanders, Ned A. (1970). *Analyzing teaching behavior.* Reading, MA: Addison-Wesley.
Garman, Noreen B. (1982). The clinical approach to supervision. In Thomas J. Sergiovanni (Ed.), *Supervision of teaching* (1982 Yearbook of the Association for Supervision and Curriculum Development). Alexandria, VA: The Association.
Goldhammer, Robert. (1969). *Clinical supervision.* New York: Holt, Rinehart & Winston.
Goldhammer, Robert, Anderson, Robert H., & Krajewski, Robert J. (1981). *Clinical supervision: Special methods for the supervision of teachers* (2nd ed.). New York: Holt, Rinehart & Winston.
Harris, Ben M. (1976). Limits and supplements to formal clinical supervision. *Journal of Research and Development in Education, 9*(2), 85–89.
Lovell, John T., & Wiles, Kimball. (1983). *Supervision for better schools* (5th ed.). Englewood Cliffs, NJ: Prentice-Hall.
Mosher, Robert L., & Purpel, D. E. (1972). *Supervision: The reluctant profession.* Boston: Houghton Mifflin.
Oliva, Peter F. (1984). *Supervision for today's schools* (2nd ed.). White Plains, NY: Longman.
Weller, Richard (Ed.). (1977). *Humanistic education: visions and realities.* Berkeley, CA: McCutchan.

ADDITIONAL READINGS

Bellon, Jerry J., Eaker, Robert E., Huffman, James O., & Jones, Richard V. (1978). *Classroom supervision and instructional improvement: A synergetic process.* Dubuque, IA: Brown.
Clinical Supervision. (Theme Issue). (1977, Fall). *Contemporary Education, 49.*
────── (Theme Issue). (1976). *Journal of Research and Development in Education, 9*(4).
Cooper, James M. (Ed.). (1984). *Developing skills for instructional supervision.* White Plains, NY: Longman.
Sullivan, Cheryl Granade. (1980). *Clinical supervision: A state of the art review.* Arlington, VA: Association for Supervision and Curriculum Development.

CHAPTER 16

Emerging Models of Supervision

An important consequence of recent reports and discussions about the importance of instructional leadership in schools has been an increasing focus on educational supervision. One by-product of this focus has been the development of some exciting new conceptualizations of supervisory practice.

In this chapter we will review two emerging conceptual models of supervision: Glickman's view of developmental supervision, and Glatthorn's description of differential patterns of supervision.

DEVELOPMENTAL SUPERVISION

The basic assumption in the developmental supervision model proposed by Carl Glickman (1981) is simple: Teachers are adults, and the supervision of adults must acknowledge the nature of their ongoing developmental process. This model suggests that any educational supervisor must recognize the individual differences among clients of supervisory behavior in schools. This relatively simple notion is nevertheless powerful, and Glickman's contribution has been significant because his is that rare formal system designed to take into account human development and individual differences.

The core of developmental supervision is the belief that two basic factors have an impact on whether supervisors provide more or less effective treatment: the supervisor's basic beliefs, and the teacher's characteristics.

Supervisory Beliefs

The first factor that influences supervision is those basic beliefs that any given supervisor holds when working with teachers. Ten different behaviors are indicative of these beliefs, which in turn suggest three basic orientations toward supervision: *nondirective, collaborative,* and *directive.* The behaviors and their associated orientations are as follows:

Orientation: Nondirective

1. *Listening.* The supervisor says nothing when working with a teacher; perhaps gives slight nonverbal cues such as a nod of the head to indicate that the teacher should continue to speak without interruption.
2. *Clarifying.* The supervisor asks questions but only to the extent that these will draw the teacher into giving information that provides fuller understanding of his or her problems.
3. *Encouraging.* The supervisor encourages the teacher to talk about those factors that may be a part of the problem.
4. *Presenting.* The supervisor offers a limited number of personal perceptions and thoughts about the difficulties that are expressed by the teacher.

Orientation: Collaborative

5. *Problem Solving.* The supervisor initiates discussions with the teacher by using statements that are aimed at exploring possible solutions to the teacher's problems.
6. *Negotiating.* The supervisor attempts quickly to get to the matter at hand by prodding the teacher to resolve his or her problem immediately.
7. *Demonstrating.* The supervisor physically shows a teacher how to act in similar circumstances, thus eliminating the teaching problem.

Orientation: Directive

8. *Directing.* The supervisor details simply and exactly what the teacher must do in order to address a problem and improve performance.
9. *Standardizing.* The supervisor explains to the teacher what must be done in order to comply with the behaviors of all others in the school.
10. *Reinforcing.* The supervisor specifically delineates the conditions and consequences for the teacher's improvement.

The relationship between specific supervisory behaviors and general orientations to supervision is shown in Figure 16.1. Note how behaviors

s Listening Clarifying Encouraging Presenting Problem solving Negotiating Demonstrating Directing Standardizing Reinforcing t
T   1   2   3   4   5   6   7   8   9   10   S

Orientation to
supervision: **NONDIRECTIVE**   **COLLABORATIVE**   **DIRECTIVE**

KEY:

T = Maximum teacher responsibility	t = Minimum teacher responsibility
S = Maximum supervisor responsibility	s = Minimum supervisor responsibility

Figure 16.1. The Supervisory Behavior Continuum in the Developmental Supervision Model. (Glickman, C. (1981). *Developmental supervision: Alternative practices for helping teachers improve instruction, 10.* Reprinted with permission of the Association for Supervision and Curriculum Development. Copyright © 1981 by the Assocation for Supervision and Curriculum Development. All rights reserved.)

signify a gradual shift of control over the supervisory encounter from the teacher to the supervisor. Those practicing supervision generally have a preferred approach to supervisory behavior, which is in line with some specific point on the continuum. Glickman refers to this as a *predominant supervisory belief.*

In order to understand the developmental supervision model more thoroughly, we need to look more closely at the three major orientations to supervision. These three orientations—directive, collaborative, and non-directive—have great impact on the ways in which an individual interacts with the teachers in a school.

Directive Supervision. In this orientation, the supervisor tends to exercise great control in the relationship with the teacher. This does not necessarily mean that the supervisor acts in an authoritarian or arbitrary fashion, but rather suggests that the supervisor sets very precise standards for teachers and then openly explains his or her expectations that those standards will be met. As Glickman (1981) noted, "The approach presumes that the supervisor knows more about the context of teaching and learning than the teacher does. Therefore, the supervisor's decisions are more effective than if the teacher is left to his or her own devices" (p. 21).

Collaborative Supervision. This approach suggests that either teacher or supervisor may appropriately take the initiative to require a meeting to discuss concerns. The critical issue is not who requests a supervisory contact, but that the product of the teacher/supervisor meeting is an actively negotiated plan of action. If negotiation between the two parties is not possible, then some third party must be invited to work with the teacher and supervisor to mediate any major differences.

Nondirective Supervision. The nondirective orientation is based on the primary assumption that teachers are capable of initiating their own improvement activities by analyzing their own instruction. The supervisor acts as a facilitator helping teachers control their own improvement. As Glickman notes, a "nondirective orientation ultimately assumes that the teacher makes the wisest and most responsible decisions for his or her own behavior; thus the final determination is still left with the teacher" (Glickman, 1981, p. 35). I believe that the true clinical supervisory model with its emphasis on teacher control of the supervisory process fits well with the inherent assumptions of nondirective supervision.

Teacher Characteristics

In addition to supervisory beliefs, a second important factor needs to be recognized in the analysis of supervisory practices: the characteristics of teachers—clients of the supervisory relationship. Glickman's model suggests that the characteristics of teachers are best understood as the product of two features: level of commitment and level of abstraction.

Level of Commitment. Based on research by Gould (1972), Loevinger (1976), and Levinson (1978), and observations of others such as Sheehy (1976), Fuller (1969), and Hall and Loucks (1978), we can identify a number of fairly specific stages through which teachers progress during their professional lives. Glickman has built his developmental supervision model upon these recognized stages of teacher development and has indicated that identifiable characteristics parallel the increasing intensity of individual commitment to a teaching career. "Low commitment" is demonstrated by such things as little concern for other teachers, little time or energy expended toward the job, and great emphasis directed toward simply keeping one's job. These "low commitment" characteristics interestingly parallel lower-level needs on Maslow's hierarchy (see Chapter 7). At the other end of the continuum, those teachers "high" in professional commitment display high degrees of concern for students and other teachers in the school, interest and willingness to spend more time and energy on job-related activities, and a primary concern with being able to do more for others.

Level of Abstraction. A continuum also defines the range of teachers' abstract thinking ability, which Glickman (1981) defines as "levels of cognitive development, where abstract/symbolic thinking predominates (as a way) to function with greater flexibility in the classroom" (p. 35).

Teachers described as low in level of abstraction are easily confused by the professional problems they face, tend not to know what choices can be made to solve problems, need specific instructions from others, and often have one or two habitual responses to problems, regardless of the complexity of issues involved. Teachers with a moderate level of abstract thinking ability are better at defining the problem at hand, can think of two or more possible responses to a professional problem, but have trouble developing a comprehensive plan for dealing with complex and multifaceted problems. These teachers can usually define a problem in their own terms and then develop a limited range of potential solutions. Finally, teachers with high levels of abstract thinking ability can look at a problem from many different perspectives; they can, for example, see things from the perspectives of other teachers, of students, and of parents. As a result, they are able to generate many alternative and viable solutions to complex problems, to choose a plan of action, and to think through each step in that plan.

The continuums of abstraction and commitment combine to form four typical teacher profiles that generally describe the staff of virtually any school:

Teacher Dropouts—low in both level of commitment and level of abstract thinking ability.

Unfocused Workers—high commitment, but low abstract thinking skills.

Analytical Observers—high thinking skills but low level of commitment.

Professionals—high in both level of commitment and abstract thinking skills.

Figure 16.2 demonstrates the relationships between teacher characteristics and supervisory orientations.

The developmental supervision model has great potential to help proactive supervisors do their job better and be more sensitive to the needs of the teachers in the school. At various points throughout this book I have suggested that certain conditions are likely to have an impact on how we engage in supervisory responsibilities. Your personal philosophy and platform, for example, have considerable importance in moving you to approach supervision from one point of view (perhaps "snoopervision") or another (perhaps human relations). I have also suggested that organizational and environmental features have an impact on our choice of a supervisory orientation. Practitioners in business-oriented communities with business-oriented school board members may be tugged toward those practices that are consistent with the beliefs and assumptions of scientific management.

I also have suggested that some supervisory practices and models, like clinical supervision, are appropriate only in fairly limited circumstances. The value of Glickman's model is that it suggests that the best and most appropriate supervisory strategies are those that recognize that not everyone should receive the same treatment under all circumstances. Developmental supervision is not an easy model to follow at all times, but, perhaps because of that, it is a good one. It stresses the need to develop sensitivity to the backgrounds, abilities, needs, and characteristics of a heterogeneous teaching staff that possesses many special skills and talents, which, properly analyzed, will provide excellent learning opportunities for children.

DIFFERENTIATED SUPERVISION

Allan Glatthorn (1984) developed an approach to appropriate supervisory strategies that was widely distributed by the Association for Supervision and Curriculum Development in a monograph entitled *Differential Supervision*. As was true of Glickman's work, the basic premise in differential supervision is quite simple: Different circumstances require different approaches. Research conducted by a number of workers, including Lovell and Phelps (1976), Young and Heichberger (1975), Cawelti and Reavis (1980), and Ritz and Cashell (1980), has made abundantly clear that teachers have traditionally viewed supervisory activities in schools as rigid and inflexible. Options are needed that will address a variety of needs, interests, skills, and backgrounds.

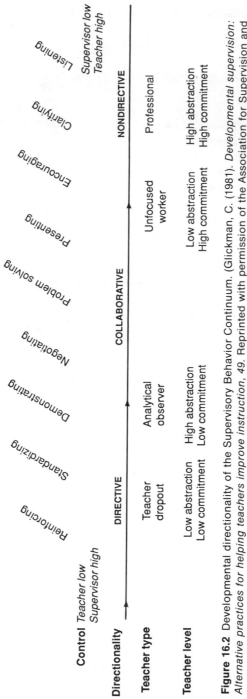

Figure 16.2 Developmental directionality of the Supervisory Behavior Continuum. (Glickman, C. (1981). *Developmental supervision: Alternative practices for helping teachers improve instruction, 49.* Reprinted with permission of the Association for Supervision and Curriculum Development. Copyright © 1981 by the Association for Supervision and Curriculum Development. All rights reserved.)

238

In response to these assumptions, Glatthorn proposes four types of supervisory practice for schools: *clinical supervision, cooperative professional development, self-directed development,* and *administrative monitoring.* He defines these approaches in the following ways:

1. Clincial supervision is an intensive process designed to improve instruction by conferring with a teacher on lesson planning, observing the lesson, analyzing the observational data, and giving the teacher feedback about the observation.
2. Cooperative professional development is a collegial process in which a small group of teachers agree to work together for their own professional growth.
3. Self-directed development enables the individual teacher to work independently on professional growth concerns.
4. Administrative monitoring, as the term implies, is a process by which an administrator monitors the work of the staff, making brief and unannounced visits simply to ensure that staff are carrying out assignments and responsibilities in a professional manner. (Glatthorn, 1984, pp. 4–5)

Certain situations arise in which each of these four models might effectively be used.

Clinical Supervision

Although we described clinical supervision in considerable detail in Chapter 15, we include it again here because Glatthorn suggests it as one of his alternative models. Many understand clinical supervision as a practice narrowly defined by Cogan or Goldhammer and requiring absolute adherence. Glatthorn, however, suggests that the structure of the clinical model is compatible with a number of other recently developed supervisory models including scientific supervision, accountable supervision, and artistic supervision.

Scientific supervision is typified most directly by the views of Madeline Hunter (Russell and Hunter, 1980), who has suggested that the activity of teaching might best be assessed according to the extent to which a classroom teacher engages in each of nine specific activities:

1. *Diagnosis:* Identifying a general objective and assessing pupils' present attainment in relation to it.
2. *Specific Objectives:* On the basis of the diagnosis, selecting a specific objective for the daily lesson.
3. *Anticipatory Set:* Focusing attention, reviewing precious learning, and developing readiness for what is to come.

4. *Perceived Purpose:* Clarifying the objective for the pupils, explaining its importance, and relating it to previous learning.
5. *Learning Opportunities:* Choosing learning opportunities that will help learners achieve objectives.
6. *Modeling:* Providing both a verbal and a visual example of what is to be learned.
7. *Check for Understanding:* Assessing the extent to which pupils are achieving objectives.
8. *Guided Practice:* Guiding pupils' practice of learning and checking to see that they can perform successfully.
9. *Independent Practice:* Giving pupils the opportunity to practice the new skill on their own.

This "scientific" approach to the supervisory evaluation of teaching has achieved considerable popularity in recent years in large part, I believe, because it appeals to our sense that there must be "right ways" to do certain things. It is reassuring to think that teaching can be assessed according to certain tenets that have been shown "by research" to be true. Hunter's views have also engendered criticism, however, from researchers who suggest that teaching involves many activities performed well beyond the boundaries of observable teacher-student interactions in a classroom setting (Fenster-macher, 1978; Peterson, 1979). Calfee (1981) provided the following criticism of the "narrowness" of the Hunter model:

> The investigations (from which the direct instruction model derives) have tended to be empirical, behavioral, correlational, and prescriptive: the typical study lacks theoretical foundation, focuses on action more than thought, entails interventions that are poorly controlled, yet proposes eventualities in advance to the teacher on how to conduct classroom instruction. (p. 53)

Accountable supervision emphasizes a supervisory focus not on the teacher's behavior as much as on the apparent student outcomes derived from the instructional activity. McNeil (1971) indicated that an accountable approach would involve the following steps:

1. The supervisor helps the teacher determine what learning objectives will be emphasized during a given lesson.
2. The teacher and supervisor agree on how student learning will be asssessed.
3. The supervisor visits the teacher's classroom for the primary purpose of observing and determining whether or not the pupils have achieved the intended objectives.

4. The overall assessment of the teacher's activity is made almost exclusively in light of whether or not students achieved stated objectives, not on whether or not there was any "goodness" or "badness" in the instruction itself.

Those who disapprove of this perspective suggest, once again, that it is a highly narrow view of what should take place in the teacher-student interaction. The notion that measurable student outcomes can serve as the criterion for whether or not a teacher is doing a good job is the basis of considerable criticism. Despite these objections, however, others suggest that the emphasis in the accountable approach is squarely where it should be, on the "bottom line." If students are not learning, then there must be something wrong with teaching.

Artistic supervision, the third current perspective that Glatthorn suggests, is compatible with clinical supervision. Artistic supervision was developed by Eliott Eisner (1982), who defined it in this way:

[Artistic supervision is] an approach to supervision that relies on the sensitivity, perceptivity, and knowledge of the supervisor as a way of appreciating the significant subtleties occurring in the classroom, and that exploits the expressive, poetic, and often metaphorical potential of language to convey to teachers or to others whose decisions affect what goes on in schools, what has been observed. (p. 59)

The fundamental value of the artistic approach to supervision is that it defines teaching much more holistically than other models do: Teaching is an art that changes according to a variety of conditions that do not always fit in to preconceived, lock-step models of how teachers must teach. Critics of Eisner's perspective point to its almost total emphasis on subjective assessment and ask, predictably, If the model does not say what *is right,* what can be *wrong?* Glatthorn (1984) and Sergiovanni (1982) both recognize limitations in the artistic view and suggest that, at best, it can function as a supplement to the scientific and accountable approaches, providing a kind of balance to the narrow foci implied in other views.

The basic assumptions of scientific, accountable, and artistic approaches to supervision are all compatible with the overall assumptions and structure of the clinical supervison process. The questions Glatthorn then asks are: Who should receive clinical supervision? Who should provide clinical supervision?

For Glatthorn, those who should *receive* clinical supervision include the following:

1. Experienced teachers who have just begun to teach at a particular school. They are unknown quantities—and should at least begin with clinical supervision until the supervisor is assured of their basic competence.

2. Experienced teachers who are encountering serious problems of teaching and learning. They need the intensive help that clinical supervision can provide.

3. Competent, experienced teachers who believe they can profit from intensive supervision. Even these teachers can learn from effective supervision—but, for them, clinical supervision should be an option that they choose. (Glatthorn, 1984, p. 35–36)

In answer to the second question, who should *provide* clinical supervision, Glatthorn suggests the following:

1. Ideally, a trained supervisor, not an administrator, should provide clinical supervision. Clinical supervision is an *improvement* model, not a form of evaluation, and administrators are typically charged with the duty of evaluating, so their involvement with this model is not advisable.

2. Experienced classroom teachers may be trained in the clinical model, and may be asked to provide this service to their colleagues. This solution is particularly useful in school systems that are too small to employ regular full-time supervisory personnel in addition to administrators.

3. If the school is large enough, one administrator may be assigned the single responsibility of providing clinical supervision to teachers, and be relieved of any teacher evaluation duties. This solution, however, ignores much recent research on instructional leadership, which suggests that such leadership will never be a forceful reality in schools if it is delegated to only one member of an administrative team (Liu and Daresh, 1985).

4. Following the recommendation of Sturges (1978), a specialized role of "consultative supervisor" might be created to designate one staff member who is always "on call" to provide clinical supervision.

5. Principals may "swap schools" and go to different buildings in the same district to provide clinical supervision, thus avoiding the assumed conflict between the clinical model and the administrative duty of evaluating staff.

6. Principals and other administrators might develop skills to do both jobs—clinically supervise and evaluate teachers—provided that they are able to avoid mixing these two very different practices.

All of these suggestions have apparent merit, but the realities of most present school systems, in my opinion, dictate that the currently typical solution, where principals do two jobs, will continue to prevail.

Cooperative Professional Development

Glatthorn defines cooperative professional development as "a moderately formalized process by which two or more teachers agree to work together for their own professional growth, usually by observing each other's classes, giving each other feedback about the observation, and discussing shared professional concerns. Often in the literature it is referred to as *peer supervision* or *collegial supervision*" (Glatthorn, 1984, p. 39). Four essential characteristics serve as the basis for a supervisory program of cooperative professional development:

1. The relationship that is developed between or among cooperating teachers is moderately formalized and institutionalized. It is not simply an informal exchange of occasional visits by a few teachers who are close associates.
2. At a minimum, the teachers agree to observe each other's classes at least twice and to hold conferences after the visits.
3. The supervisory relationship is among peers. Although an adminstrator or supervisor may be involved in organizing and occasionally monitoring the program, the observations, conferences, and follow-up discussions involve only teachers.
4. The relationship is purely nonjudgmental and nonevaluative. It is intended to complement, not take the place of, traditional evaluation systems. None of the observation or conference data are shared with administrators or made part of the evaluation process.

The approach to supervision inherent in this cooperative development model speaks to a very serious problem found in most schools. At a number of points in this text, I have commented on the unfortunate isolation of teachers from their colleagues in most schools. Cooperative professional development offers several ways for teachers to work cooperatively to improve their performance, thus considerably reducing this kind of professional separation.

In this model, for example, teachers—professional peers—can serve as informal observers and consultants to their colleagues. Teachers may also serve as true clinical supervisors of their colleagues, an approach that has become increasingly popular as evidenced by recent peer supervision programs in many communities. Peer clinical supervision has become a highly formalized program, negotiated between district administrators and local teachers' associations, with the particular purpose of helping new teachers or teachers experiencing difficulty on the job.

Yet another strategy for implementing cooperative professional development is the use of teachers as focused observers of classroom instruction. Perhaps the best example of this is the widely disseminated Teacher Expectations and Student Achievement (TESA) model designed by Kerman (1979), in an effort to formalize the exchange of observation data among teachers who interact frequently in coaching arrangements. An even more formal and institutionalized arrangement to encourage cooperative professional development can be found in what Lawrence and Branch (1978) describe as "peer panels," in which teachers guide the inservice and developmental activities for their colleagues in a school or district. The final strategy to encourage teachers to interact with each other is one that has existed in many schools for a long time, the result not of any intended plan for peer supervision, but rather of normal organizational patterns. Here, teachers who work together in instructional teams also observe each other as peers, plan together, and make suggestions for improvement.

Like most other models, the cooperative professional development approach to supervision has considerable potential value, but not necessarily for all teachers in all schools. It provides another option for some situations in some settings, most notably in those cases where a demonstrated climate of openness and trust already exists among the teachers of a school.

Self-Directed Development

Glatthorn defines self-directed development as a process for professional growth characterized by the following four basic features:

1. *The individual teacher works independently on a program of professional growth.* Although a member of a leadership team acts as a resource for the teacher, the teacher is not supervised by others, in the conventional sense of the term, and the teacher does not work cooperatively with other members of a team.
2. *The individual develops and follows a goal-oriented program of professional involvement.* The goals of this program stem from the teacher's own assessment of professional need; there is no need for the teacher's goals to be derived from organizational goals. It is assumed that any professional growth will contribute at least indirectly to the school's goals.
3. *The individual has access to a variety of resources in working toward those goals.* Based on the nature of the goals set, the leader and the teacher may decide that one or more of the following resources and experiences might be appropriate: videotapes of the teacher's teaching; feedback from students; professional books and computerized

information services; graduate courses and intensive workshops; support from school and district supervisors and administrators; intraschool visitation.

4. *The results of the self-directed program are not used in evaluating teacher performance.* The program is entirely divorced from evaluation; it is assumed that the teacher will be evaluated by whatever district program is in place. (Glatthorn, 1984, pp. 49–50)

A number of ways exist in which the basic concept of self-directed development may be effectuated. The most familiar approach is probably formal self-appraisal systems such as management-by-objective programs (MBO) or the Redfern evaluation plan (1980). The following appear to be common steps followed in most similar programs in use in school districts around the nation:

1. District goals are established for the following school year. (For example, a district's goal for the next year might be to increase student reading comprehension scores on standardized achievement tests.)
2. Individual staff members review the district goals and formulate individual performance targets and objectives that are in harmony with the district's priorities. (An individual teacher examines his or her instructional goals and priorities for the year and decides how the increase in reading scores might be supported.)
3. Individual members develop performance (or appraisal) contracts that specify how the individual job targets will be achieved and how they will be evaluated. (If, for example, a teacher suggests that he or she will spend 15 minutes more per day on activities related to the improvement of reading comprehension, the teacher's appraisal will be based on the extent to which this target is met.)
4. Staff members review their performance contracts with their organizational superiors. (In a nonjudgmental and nonthreatening fashion, teachers hold individual conferences with supervisors or administrators to see how well they followed their job targets.)
5. Progress toward the attainment of the stated goals is periodically reviewed.
6. The individual staff member meets with a superior at the conclusion of the cycle to evaluate, in a summative fashion, the extent to which the overall and specific goals were achieved. A new goal-setting cycle may then begin. (The ultimate question to be asked in this context is not whether the teacher was "good" or "bad," but rather whether or not the targets were appropriate, and if they were not achieved, what prevented their attainment.)

Teachers can also analyze their performances on the basis of videotape recordings. Once pupils (and teachers) lose their overawareness of the presence of cameras in classrooms, this technique is a powerful way for individual teachers to assess their performances under nonthreatening circumstances.

As with Glatthorn's other supervisorial approaches, self-directed development has both strengths and weaknesses. For example, critics cite research suggesting that teachers have not traditionally been very skillful in appraising their own teaching (Carroll, 1981). On the other hand, supporters stress the value in recognizing teachers as adult learners and of puting them in charge of their own learning and development. Further, teachers are individuals with distinct needs, and self-directed development allows for the highly individualized aspects of teacher development (Bents and Howey, 1981).

I would in no way suggest that self-directed improvement should serve as a replacement for all other forms of supervision. I would, however, concur that this strategy represents yet another potentially powerful way to foster improvement in schools.

Administrative Monitoring

Glatthorn recognizes that some situations call for a more directive approach to supervision by school administrators. He refers to this as administrative monitoring, or "drop-in supervision," the brief and informal observations of teachers made by principals or assistant principals. Glatthorn has identified four major characteristics as part of this supervisory approach:

1. *Administrative monitoring must be open.* This is not an activity based on the "supervision as inspection" assumptions defined in Chapter 1. The purpose here is to see teachers at work under normal conditions, not to catch them doing something incompetent. A basic assumption of administrative monitoring is that, from the outset, the principal and teacher will speak openly about issues such as:
   Who will do the monitoring?
   What kind of behavior can the teacher typically expect from the administrator who will drop in for visits?
   What kind of feedback may the teacher expect after a drop-in visit?
   What records will be kept of the monitoring?
   Will data from monitoring sessions be made part of the formal teacher-evaluation process?
2. *Administrative monitoring should be planned and scheduled, not done randomly and unsystematically.* Certain times during the school week might be established as those when the principal and assistant principals will generally be "out and about" the school building, and

teachers who are to receive administrative monitoring will be visited during those times.

3. *Administrative monitoring should be learning-centered.* If the "drop-in" is not based on the review of learning activities, the visit will not have much purpose. In fact, the arrival of a principal (or anyone else) in a class without any clear purpose will end up being a dysfunctional intrusion to the teacher's work rather than a help. The following questions may serve to guide an unstructured drop-in visit:

What is the teacher's purpose? To what extent is it definite? Attainable?

How suitable for achieving these purposes is the plan of instruction that the teacher has prepared?

To what extent do the learning experiences proposed promise to help realize the desired purposes?

To what extent have students been psychologically prepared, by assignment and otherwise, to participate in this learning experience?

What is the atmosphere of the classroom and what is the morale of the students as evidenced by their attitudes toward each other, toward the teacher, and toward the work they are doing?

Are abundant and rich materials prepared by the teacher or by the pupils in evidence?

Are the pupils gaining adequate guidance by the teacher in directing their own learning? Does each pupil know what to do?

To what extent is the presentation of new material adequate and clarified by explanation, by obvious order, by illustrations, by relation to the pupils' past experiences, and by application to pupils' needs, immediate or recognized as probable in the future?

How ready does the teacher appear to be to modify the instructional plan so as to seize the opportunity as it appears for student learning?

4. *Administrative monitoring is likely to be most effective when it is interactive across two dimensions: The administrator gives feedback to the teacher and uses the observational data as part of an ongoing assessment of the instructional program and the school climate.* The teacher involved should receive both negative and positive feedback as a result of the administrator's visit. Some questions that may serve as the basis for this interaction between teacher and administrator are the following:

Are there certain times during the day when pupils seem inattentive and are disruptive in class?

Are there certain paces in the building where pupils seem easily distracted?

How much direct instruction goes on across grades, ability levels, and subjects?

Is monitoring used excessively, insufficiently, or inappropriately?

To what extent are teachers giving attention to critical thinking and the higher thought processes?

How much do teachers vary content and method from group to group? (Glatthorn, 1984, p. 63–65)

Administrative monitoring is an essential activity in all schools, but *not* for *all* teachers under *all* circumstances. It may sound like a rather harsh concept—administrators wandering around in teachers' classrooms without any real warning. At the same time, considerable evidence suggests that, when supervisors and administrators know what is going on in an organization, everyone benefits.

SUMMARY

In this chapter we examined the basic assumptions and practices associated with two recent conceptualizations of educational supervision: Carl Glickman's developmental supervision and Allan Glatthorn's differentiated supervision. Both of these perspectives represent emerging views of the ways in which supervisors can work with teachers to achieve the goals of schools.

We selected two models because, in the author's judgment, they represent coherent *approaches* to supervision and not merely "packaged" models. The recent call for new supervisory and instructional leadership has produced a predictable bombardment of educators with all manner of quick-fix schemes to improve supervisory practices—videotape programs, books, and offers for workshops. These cure-alls flood the mailboxes of administrative and supervisory personnel with the promise of immediate improvement in teacher supervision. The fact is, however, that effective supervision is the product not of a weekend seminar but of hard work and serious thought. That is the message of the approaches I have reviewed in this chapter, and it is also the message that I have tried to share throughout this entire book.

SUGGESTED ACTIVITIES

1. Review Glickman's Supervisory Behavior Continuum presented in Figure 16.1. Ask several teachers to indicate the behavior that they prefer to receive from supervisory personnel (i.e., "listening," "encouraging," etc.) and also the behaviors they believe they actually witness in supervisory relationships. Do the same with two or three supervisors by asking them to indicate the ways in which they believe they interact with teachers, and also the ways in which they wish they *could*

interact. What are the differences and similarities among these various perceptions?

2. With the permission of a classroom teacher, observe a class and try to answer the questions listed under "Administrative monitoring should be learning-centered" on p. 247. Use the responses to these questions to focus a feedback session with the teacher after the class has concluded.

3. Using the various alternative approaches to supervision provided by Glatthorn, conduct a survey of practices used in your district to determine the percentage of time individual schools spend in using each of the models reviewed.

REFERENCES

Bents, R. H., & Howey, Ken R. (1981). Staff development: Change in the individual. In B. Dillon-Peterson (Ed.), *Staff development/organization development*. Alexandria, VA: Association for Supervision and Curriculum Development.

Calfee, R. (1981). Cognitive psychology and educational practice. In David C. Berliner (Ed.), *Review of research in education, 9*. Washington, DC: American Educational Research Association.

Carroll, J. G. (1981). Faculty self-evaluation. In Jason Millman (Ed.), *Handbook of teacher evaluation*. Beverly Hills, CA: Sage.

Cawelti, Gordon, & Reavis, Charles. (1980, December). How well are we providing instructional improvement services? *Educational Leadership, 38*, 236–240.

Cogan, Morris. (1973). *Clinical supervision*. Boston: Houghton Mifflin.

Eisner, Elliott. (1982). An artistic approach to supervision. In Thomas Sergiovanni (Ed.), *Supervision of teaching*. Alexandria, VA: Association for Supervision and Curriculum Development.

Fenstermacher, Gary D. (1978). A philosophical consideration of recent research in teacher effectiveness. In David C. Berliner (Ed.), *Review of research in education, 6*. Washington, DC: American Educational Research Association.

Fuller, Frances. (1969). Concerns of teachers: A developmental conceptualization. *American Educational Research Journal, 6*, 207–226.

Glatthorn, Allan. (1984). *Differential supervision*. Alexandria, VA: Association for Supervision and Curriculum Development.

Glickman, Carl. (1981). *Developmental supervision: Alternative practices for helping teachers improve instruction*. Alexandria, VA: Association for Supervision and Curriculum Development.

Goldhammer, Robert. (1969). *Clinical supervision: Special methods for the supervision of teachers*. New York: Holt, Rinehart & Winston.

Gould, R. (1972). The phases of adult life: A study in developmental psychology. *The American Journal of Psychiatry, 129*, 521–531.

Hall, Gene E., & Loucks, Susan. (1978, September). Teacher concerns as a basis for facilitating and personalizing staff development. *Teachers College Record, 80*, 36–53.

Kerman, Sam. (1979, June). Teacher expectations and student achievement. *Phi Delta Kappan, 6*, 716–718.

Lawrence, Gordon, & Branch, J. (1978, June). Peer support as the heart of inservice education. *Theory Into Practice, 17*, 245–247.

Levinson, Daniel. (1978). *The Seasons of a Man's Life.* New York: Knopf.

Liu, Ching-Jen, & Daresh, John C. (1985). Instructional Leadership Behavior of High School Principals. Paper presented at the Annual Meeting of the American Educational Research Association, Chicago.

Loevinger, J. (1976). *Ego development.* San Francisco: Jossey-Bass.

Lovell, John T., & Phelps, M. S. (1976). *Supervision in Tennessee: A study of perceptions of teachers, principals, and supervisors.* Murfreesboro: Tennessee Association for Supervision and Curriculum Development.

Maslow, Abraham. (1960). *Motivation and personality,* New York: McGraw-Hill.

McNeil, J. D. (1971). *Toward accountable teaching.* New York: Holt, Rinehart & Winston.

Peterson, Penelope P. (1979). Direct instruction reconsidered. In Herbert J. Walberg (Ed.), *Research on teaching.* Berkeley, CA: McCutchan.

Redfern, George B. (1980). *Evaluating teachers and administrators: A performance objectives model.* Boulder, CO: Westview.

Ritz, W. C., & Cashell, J. G. (1980, October). 'Cold war' between supervisors and teachers? *Educational Leadership, 38,* 77–78.

Russell, D., & Hunter, Madeline. (1980). *Planning for effective instruction.* Los Angeles: University Elementary School.

Sergiovanni, Thomas J. (1982). Toward a theory of supervisory practice: Integrating scientific, clinical, and artistic views. In T. Sergiovanni (Ed.), *Supervision of teaching.* Alexandria, VA: Association for Supervision and Curriculum Development.

Sheehy, Gail T. (1976). *Passages: Predictable crises of adult life.* New York: Dutton.

Sturges, A. W. (1978). *The roles and responsibilities of instructional supervisors.* Alexandria, VA: Association for Supervision and Curriculum Development.

Young, J. M. & Heichberger, R. L. (1975, Fall). Teacher perceptions of an effective school supervision and evaluation program. *Education, 96,* 10–19.

ADDITIONAL READINGS

Eisner, Eliott. (1979). *The educational imagination.* New York: Macmillan.

Glickman, Carl D. (1985). *Supervision of instruction: A developmental approach.* Boston: Allyn & Bacon.

Rubin, Louis. (1985). *Artistry in teaching.* New York: Random House.

CHAPTER 17

Supervision as Effective Staff Development and Inservice Education

Educational reform requires that we pay more attention to discovering how classroom teachers increase the effectiveness of the learning process for children. For the past few years the specific practices and behaviors of teachers related to student achievement, particularly in the basic skills areas of reading, language arts, and mathematics, have been the focus of considerable research. We are learning more about how teachers organize their classrooms, interact with students, and deliver instruction to elicit positive results. Still, many teachers are not aware of those practices that may have the greatest potential for improving their schools. Staff development and inservice education—the traditional systems that support professional development in teachers and other educators—are typically viewed as relatively ineffective. This perceived ineffectiveness hinders our judgment of a potentially valuable contribution to school improvement. And as we have stressed throughout this text, the effective practitioner of proactive supervision always focuses on one ultimate goal: the enhancement of school effectiveness for the improvement of student learning.

One of the proactive supervisor's most important ongoing responsibilities is to promote the continuous professional growth and development of all those who are working toward achieving the goals and objectives of the school. In short, supervisors need to be aware of effective practices associated with staff development and inservice teacher education. We generally accept the notion that inservice education and staff development must be improved if schools are to improve. We also believe that, in many ways, the responsibilities of supervisors are those of staff development. But efforts to make staff development and inservice education more effective tend to be

251

sporadic. Little attention is normally paid to the relationship between professional development for teachers and the improvement of instruction for students. As we noted in Chapter 6, research on school effectiveness has shown that the ability of school supervisors and administrators to provide instructional leadership in their schools and districts is an important factor in the improvement of instruction. Yet few educators seem to recognize that positive change occurs when school leaders accept the responsibility of working with their staffs to plan, carry out, and ultimately evaluate inservice and staff development activities.

In this chapter we will consider a number of issues related to the supervisor's ability to provide more effective professional development. We will begin by defining educational staff development and examining some of the more positive trends in the design of more effective staff development and inservice education programs. We will pay particular attention to recent research findings that focus on the determination of desirable content and delivery in development programs. Finally, we will examine two issues associated with more effective staff development and inservice programs: adult learning theories and individual differences among learners.

FINDING A DEFINITION

Staff development and inservice education have become hot topics of discussion for educators in the 1980s. Increased attention to an important topic is generally a good thing, but the downside of this phenomenon is that many people talk without always knowing what they are talking about. All sorts of schemes have appeared on the market promising to increase the effectiveness of staff development overnight. We cannot rid the field of professional education of all those profitable quick-fix packages for staff development and inservice education, but we do suggest that educators can take a big step toward improving the *quality* of staff development and training by more clearly defining just what staff development is.

The distinction between staff development and inservice education is normally based on whether an activity has been designed primarily to address a perceived deficit in professional knowledge or performance level, or to stimulate long-term improvement and on-the-job growth. The accepted view is that *inservice education* covers those activities directed toward remediating a perceived lack of skill or understanding; and *staff development* refers to an ongoing process that promotes professional growth, rather than remediation.

This distinction makes inservice education sound somehow "bad," and staff development "good." The fact is that, in certain situations, each activity may be effective and enhance the quality of education. Inservice education, generally perceived as something done "to" people to "fix them," is in fact necessary and appropriate in some settings, and is an entirely positive process. There are times when people need special training to correct deficits in their skills. Consider, for example, the number of very good teachers who have recently taken part in inservice education programs designed to provide skills in the use of microcomputers. Most teachers who graduated from college before 1980 had little or no training in computer technology; as a result, they were "deficient" in a very important area. Inservice education corrected that deficiency positively and appropriately. By contrast, developmental activities designed to engage teachers in process experiences to provide personal and professional insights are sometimes totally inappropriate. For example, engaging a beginning teacher who has few classroom survival skills in a developmentally focused, consciousness-raising staff development exercise is both pointless and potentially harmful. The young teacher may indeed grow, but at the cost of not acquiring some basic mechanical skills absolutely vital to teaching.

My preference is clearly to minimize the artificial distinctions that have been drawn between inservice education and staff development. Suggestions that one activity is better than the other, as we have seen, are false. And in the real world of schools, in any case, little difference is made in the use of the two terms.

Practitioners face daily problems in implementing more effective inservice and staff development; they are far more concerned with the quality of implementation than with subtle conceptual differences. If we must differentiate between inservice and staff development, I would suggest that staff development or the currently popular "professional development" is a broader term that includes inservice education as a subset. Whatever term we select, we are talking about a learning process designed to assist the professional staff of a school or district in carrying out their duties more effectively, to the end that children are able to learn better.

RESEARCH RELATED TO INSERVICE AND STAFF DEVELOPMENT

The complexities of current educational activities require staff to receive additional opportunities for learning. Simply stated, effective inservice and staff development are needed for effective schools; they may no longer be viewed as "extras" that are made available only if school systems have a few additional dollars to spend. Despite the critical need for effective approaches to inservice and staff development, however, these activities remain part of a field with few theoretical or conceptual roots (McLaughlin and Berman, 1977; Henderson, 1979), little respect from practitioners (Brimm and Tollett, 1975), and a generally meager research base (Swenson, 1981). Theorists suggest that both staff development and inservice education lack sufficient intellectual rigor, whereas practitioners often complain that what has been written has little practical value for addressing problems faced "here and now."

I recently reviewed research from the past 15 years on staff development and inservice education (Daresh, 1987) and found that from the many studies that have been conducted, primarily doctoral dissertations, two general observations can be made. First, the research techniques used to study inservice and staff development have been seriously limited. Most work has made use of survey questionnaires, for example. Second, and more relevant to our concerns in this text, most of the research has centered on only three targets: (1) the evaluation of specific inservice or staff development models, (2) the content of inservice and staff development activities, and (3) the delivery systems typically used.

Research on specific programs has consisted primarily of individual researchers studying the effectiveness of workshops, seminars, or other forms of inservice education that the researcher designed. Not surprisingly, a large number of these studies indicated that such efforts at providing inservice education were quite effective, but the studies added little to our goal of learning more about improving inservice education and staff development generally because of the difficulty of generalizing from a single setting to a larger sample.

Studies focused on content and delivery aspects of staff development and inservice education are of greater interest because their conclusions are more clearly applicable in helping supervisory personnel determine how they might make these activities more positive.

Content of Staff Development and Inservice Education

A review of recent studies on the nature of inservice and staff development content leaves us with four major observations:

1. Staff development and inservice education are perceived as more effective when content is based on the self-reported needs of participants.
2. Desired staff development and inservice education content reflects topics of immediate concern to practitioners. Great interest was expressed in how to implement externally mandated programs; for example, competency-based instructional programs; less interest was expressed in programs or activities designed to deal with less concrete, more conceptual, topics, such as building a more supportive organizational climate for student learning. At a mid-range of interest were topics concerning human relations skills development, such as how to enhance communication skills in the classroom.
3. Few strong relationships appeared to exist between teachers' demo-

graphic background characteristics and staff development and inservice education interests. In fact, the only characteristic repeatedly linked to desired content was length of service, or experience, as an educator. Beginning teachers (usually defined as those with one to three years' experience) sought activities that helped them deal with feelings of insecurity, frequent uncertainty, and limited knowledge concerning their immediate teaching environment and the larger field of professional education. Experienced teachers (more than 10 years in the classroom), who were generally less favorable toward staff development and inservice education, did express interest in topics focused upon increasing awareness of student instructional needs. In other words, the length of teacher experience was an important and accurate predictor of staff development and inservice education interests. Teachers' interests shifted gradually through their careers from teacher-centeredness to greater child-centeredness.

4. Teachers and other educators wanted to be involved in planning their own staff development and inservice education programs and activities.

Delivery of Staff Development and Inservice Education

Most recent studies addressed methods for planning and carrying out staff development and inservice education activities. Many of these studies were designed to examine the issue of content as well. My review of these studies produced the following four generalizations:

1. There is a general dissatisfaction with, or a least lack of interest in, existing procedures associated with most staff development and inservice education programs and activities. Studies did not always pinpoint the exact nature of the procedures causing the dissatisfaction; instead, such evaluations concerned the general ways in which staff development and inservice education are "usually" provided.

2. Staff development and inservice education participants want to be involved with planning, implementing, and evaluating their learning experiences. The general finding expressed in many studies was that participants do not wish to have someone "do" staff development "to" them. As we shall see later in this chapter, this finding is generally true of learning provided to adults, who want to play a primary role as sources of their own learning.

3. Staff development and inservice education participants prefer learning activities and programs that make them *active participants* in a process, not *passive observers* of presentations by others. Demonstrations were more highly valued than lecture presentations.

4. Both staff development and inservice education are viewed as more effective when they are part of training that continues over an extended period of time. Short-term, "one-shot" sessions were viewed negatively.

Supervisors need to recognize some general issues raised by recent research on staff development and inservice education. We might conclude, for example, that the skills most frequently sought by professional educators, as determined through the research, are knowledge-level skills. More often than not, those knowledge-level skills are related to issues of immediate interest and concern to practitioners. Thus, for a few years, staff development programs and related research were directed almost exclusively to the "hot topic" of mainstreaming handicapped students. Now the emphasis seems to be microcomputers and their use in classrooms. We can only wonder what the next wave of perceived need and interest will yield in terms of inservice focus.

Current research on staff development and inservice education seems unfortunately focused on collecting information of apparently limited benefit to the improvement of school practices, the ability of educators to be more successful in their roles, or the condition of staff development and inservice education. Despite these limitations, however, supervisory personnel may cull some important insights concerning the characteristics of effective staff development from the existing research. A number of researchers (Lawrence, 1974; Nicholson, Joyce, Parker, and Waterman, 1976; Paul, 1977; McLaughlin and Marsh, 1978; Hutson, 1981) have offered useful guidelines:

1. Effective inservice and staff development programs are directed toward local school needs.
2. Inservice and staff development participants are actively involved in effective programs.
3. Effective programs are based on participant needs.
4. Effective local school inservice and staff development programs are supported by a commitment of resources from the central office.
5. Effective programs provide evidence of quality control and are delivered by competent presenters.
6. Programs that enable participants to share ideas and provide assistance to one another are viewed as successful.
7. Rewards and incentives, both intrinsic and extrinsic, are evident to participants in programs that are viewed as successful.
8. Inservice and staff development activities are viewed more positively when provided during school time.
9. Effective inservice education and staff development activities are accompanied by ongoing evaluation.

These guidelines are general, but they should prove useful to supervisors and others charged with designing, developing, and implementing an effective inservice or staff development program. Other useful research includes that of Sprinthall and Thies-Sprinthall (1983) who also described effective practice for continuing professional development programs to improve educational practice:

Collaboration between participants and program sponsors: Building- or districtwide professional development councils can foster collaboration and cooperation in planning effective inservice programs.

Learning needs identified by participants: Professional development programs responsive to the needs of participants will maximize the probability of success. A comprehensive assessment of needs should be undertaken before planning specific programs.

Programs offered at convenient locations: Sites are easy to get to.

Intrinsic and extrinsic rewards provided: Intrinsic rewards are derived by gaining competence (self-esteem) or success (self-actualization). Extrinsic rewards could include certificates, enhanced promotional opportunities, or increments in pay.

Modeling by experts of skills and concepts: Demonstrations by skillful practitioners should be an integral part of professional development programs.

Utilization of participants' talents and abilities: Independent study, role-play exercises, or presentations by participants can be used to draw upon participants' talents and abilities.

Synthesis of content and adaptation to diverse situations: Case analyses, site visits, or guided group discussions may be employed to achieve synthesis of content and to explore its adaptation to diverse situations.

Individualized learning activities: Small-group discussions, private counseling, or case studies written and analyzed by participants may be useful.

Significant and challenging role-playing experiences: Role-play can be an integral part of many professional development programs, particularly those dealing with interpersonal relationships or instructional procedures.

Opportunities for reflection: Time for reading and reflection is essential; programming must provide time for this to occur.

Continuity and logical sequencing of activities: All presentations and activities should be carefully planned and coordinated to build on previous learning.

Both personal support and personal challenge: Participants grow through confrontation with challenges; they must have freedom to try, to fail, and to try again without penalty.

Assessment of results: The program should be evaluated in terms of its objectives, which might be cognitive, affective, or psychomotor development, or a combination thereof.

Knowledge of useful and effective practices regarding inservice education and staff development is clearly available. However, school districts and other agencies engaged in those activities too often tend to be unresponsive to the practices and guidelines we have noted here. Consequently, professional development efforts are not as effective as they might be. Attitudes are frequently quite negative. Those negative perceptions result in part from lack of attention to two important features of staff development that have traditionally been ignored by school personnel, as we shall see in the next section.

IMPORTANT MISSING INGREDIENTS

After listening to many teachers voice their frustrations about the quality of staff development activities, we have identified two basic ingredients of "good" programs.

Good staff development programs:

1. Recognize that adults have specialized learning needs.
2. Reflect an understanding of the individual differences among learners.

Characteristics of Adult Learning

Intuition has long suggested that adults have different learning needs or characteristics from those of children. Malcolm Knowles (1970), a major contributor to the field of adult education, is generally credited with coining the word *andragogy* (the art and science of teaching adults) as distinct from *pedagogy* (the art and science of teaching children). More important, Knowles identified four critical characteristics of adults and their patterns of learning:

1. As a person matures, his or her self-concept moves from one of dependency to one of self-direction.
2. The mature person tends to accumulate a growing reservoir of experience that provides a resource for learning.
3. The adult's readiness to learn becomes increasingly oriented toward the developmental tasks of his or her assigned social roles.
4. The adult's time perspective changes from postponed application of

knowledge to immediate application, and accordingly his or her orientation toward learning shifts from subject-centeredness to problem-centeredness.

Predictably, Knowles's work encouraged others to research and write in the field of adult education, and some researchers' work is useful for us in seeking to improve staff development in schools. Wood and Thompson (1980), for example, reviewed some salient aspects of adult learning:

1. Adults will learn when the goals and objectives of a learning activity are considered *by the learner* to be realistic, related, and important to a specific issue at hand.
2. Adults will learn, retain, and use what they perceive as relevant to their immediate personal and professional needs.
3. Adults need to see the results of their efforts and have frequent and accurate feedback about progress that is being made toward their goals.
4. Adult-learning is highly ego-involved. When a person is unsuccessful at a given learning task, it is likely that he or she will take it as an indication of personal incompetence and failure.
5. Adults always come to any learning experience with a wide range of previous experiences, knowledge, skills, and competencies.
6. Adults want to be the origins of their own learning, and they wish to be directly involved in the selection of learning objectives, content, activities, and so forth.
7. Adults will tend to resist any learning experience that they believe is either an open or implied attack on their personal or professional competence.
8. Adults reject prescriptions by others for their learning.
9. Adult motivation comes from the learner and not from any external source. While this may generally be said of motivation of all individuals, it is true that, as a person matures, efforts to motivate from outside the individual will decrease in probable effectiveness.

Taken together, these characteristics of adult learning should provide practitioners of supervision who design and lead staff development experiences with some important insights into how such experiences should be planned and carried out. First, the fact that adults want (and learn best from) experiences that address immediate problems suggests that supervisors should direct activities toward answering the perennial question, What should I do on Monday morning? Presentations of the latest research on teacher behavior and school effectiveness, no matter how carefully prepared, will be exercises in futility unless staff members clearly understand how this research relates to what needs to be done now in their school. There is, of course, a danger in trying to narrow the staff development focus too directly on issues of immediate importance to a school or district; such a practice might, in fact, be equally futile because adults, as we saw above, tend to reject prescriptions—quick fixes—to complex problems. Those planning staff development need to understand what the *real* problems are in a school or district and to avoid the temptation to provide "band-aid" responses to current problems and ignore more serious ones.

The study of adult learning or andragogy also provides some important clues about adult self-concept needs. Teachers frequently complain that staff development and inservice education experiences seem threatening—that participants often feel incompetent. The implication here is that as people become more mature and fixed in their ways, they become increasingly self-conscious in situations where they believe they might experience failure (and perhaps ridicule) in front of others. Staff development and inservice education activities must therefore be planned so that teachers and other staff will not be put in situations where their performance might be compared publicly with that of their co-workers. Thus, we might question the wisdom of using activities such as role-playing, which require people to "perform" in front of others to demonstrate particular techniques, especially when people have not clearly volunteered to do so.

Finally, the literature in adult learning clearly shows that as people mature, they tend to accumulate additional learning experiences, and supervisory personnel involved with adult learning experiences should recognize the potential richness of this previous learning. Nothing is more frustrating to teachers than being asked to participate in activities designed to send everyone "back to square one." Practices that do this not only ignore an important resource for teaching adults but also violate a basic rule of effective staff development, namely that individual differences among learners must be taken into account.

Individual Learning Differences

Although educators constantly affirm the belief that every learner is different, they seem to forget this principle when they plan staff development activities. A recurring message from critics of "bad" staff development is that teachers do not like to be treated as if they were a herd of sheep—a sort of amorphic blob known collectively as "the staff." Supervisors and others who plan development activities often seem to overlook the fact that, within the staff, many different needs, interests, learning styles, and abilities exist. Time and again, teachers report that staff development and inservice sessions are a waste of time because no effort was made to match learning activities with learning needs.

Fortunately, a considerable amount of information is now coming from the research community concerning differences among teachers. This information has much to offer supervisors and other planners of staff development and inservice education. For example, Unruh and Turner (1970) defined four stages of professional growth reflected within most school staffs. These categories should be useful to the supervisor in determining broad groupings of teachers who might be interested in different staff development activities and learning opportunities:

1. *The preservice period.* Within the school, this period is represented by student teachers and interns. Although this is not a period with great immediate implications for staff development, general interest is usually high because much of what happens in education is actually a supplement to what took place (or should have taken place) as part of college training.
2. *The initial training period.* Teachers in this period, who generally have one to five years' experience, often have "beginner" problems such as discipline, routine organizational and administrative chores, and general class planning and curriculum development. The supervisor aware of the unique concerns of staff in this period might design activities to address these problems particularly for teachers in this category.
3. *The building-security period.* Teachers with 5 to 15 years' service might be most interested in increasing their personal knowledge and skills. The supervisor needs to make certain that inservice and staff development experiences are appropriately designed to promote individual growth for teachers in this category.
4. *The maturing period.* "Master teachers" have an undefined number of years of experience but a clear depth of professional expertise. The supervisor would do well to tap into the knowledge and skills possessed by these teachers as additional resources in promoting professional growth.

Although these stages of professional growth suggest differentiated patterns for staff development and inservice education, their usefulness is somewhat limited by the fact that right now the vast majority of teachers in most schools belong to the "building security" period. We need finer definitions of individual or staff needs to assist in devising more effective strategies.

Promising work in this area has been done by Gene Hall and his associates at the Texas Research and Development Center for Teacher Education (Hall and Loucks, 1978). Building on the earlier work of Frances Fuller (1969), Hall and his colleagues suggest that an important way to differentiate needs of staff members is according to their levels of concern about a particular educational practice. Hall indicates that teachers might be classified according to the following descending order of "Levels of Concern":

6. *REFOCUSING:* The teacher believes he or she has some ideas about making good practices even better.
5. *COLLABORATION:* The teacher is interested in combining his or her good ideas with the ideas of co-workers.
4. *CONSEQUENCE:* The teacher is concerned with the extent to which there will be a positive impact on student learning.
3. *MANAGEMENT:* The teacher is concerned with getting materials ready for instruction.
2. *PERSONAL:* The teacher is most interested in what personal effect a school practice will have on him or her.
1. *INFORMATIONAL:* The teacher is most concerned with finding out basic information about a practice.
0. *AWARENESS:* The teacher is not interested in a particular issue or practice.

This classification system is in no sense evaluative. In other words, we should assume that, at any given time, a school's staff will be distributed across all seven levels of concern, *depending on the issue at hand.* Teachers are not automatically better than their co-workers simply because they are at the "refocusing" level; conversely, virtually all teachers may legitimately be classified at the "awareness" level from time to time. In fact, shifting from one level to another depending on the issue may indicate a healthy professional environment, where staff members feel free to act in an honest and open fashion.

The implications of this work for staff development and inservice education should be fairly obvious. For one thing, it makes clear that not every staff member will be interested in every topic, and this does not constitute a negative evaluation of the school's total staff development plan. A second implication is that the design of any staff development or inservice education activity must be flexible enough so that staff members can approach an issue according to their own levels of concern, without feeling anxious or threatened if they are not interested in a particular issue at a particular time.

Hall and Loucks (1978) summarize the most crucial lessons to be learned in the area of staff development, according to the "Levels of Concern" categories:

1. The staff development leader must attend to the teachers' concerns as well as to the content to be covered.
2. It is all right to have personal feelings.
3. Change cannot be accomplished overnight.

4. Teachers' concerns might not be the same as those of the staff developers.
5. Within any group, there is a variety of concerns.

Finally, Gordon Lawrence (1982) has suggested the analysis of psychological types as a fruitful path for supervisors and other planners of inservice and staff development to explore. Lawrence's work is based on the original premise of the Swiss psychologist C.G. Jung (1923), who suggested that people's behavior could be best explained through the extent to which they followed certain patterns, or "psychological types." Jung based these types on how people prefer to make and perceive judgments. Lawrence (1982) noted that in Jungian psychology, "all conscious mental activity can be classified into four mental processes—two perception processes (sensing and intuition) and two judgement processes (thinking and feeling). What comes into consciousness, moment by moment, comes either through the senses or through intuition. To remain in consciousness, perceptions must be used. They are used—sorted, weighed, analyzed, evaluated—by the judgment processes, thinking and feeling" (p. 6).

Sixteen different psychological types have been identified, and measures such as the Myers-Briggs Type Indicator (MBTI), designed by Isabel Briggs Myers and Katherine Briggs (1962), help us determine the extent to which individuals fall into one or another of the different types by looking at relative strengths in four areas: extroversion (E) versus introversion (I); gathering information through sensing (S) versus intuition (N); making judgments as a product primarily of thinking (T) versus feeling (F); and a desire to live in a world defined mostly through judgment (J) versus perception (P). The possible combinations of these different descriptors, along with typical behaviors associated with each of the 16 possible types, are shown in Figure 17.1.

For our purposes, the value of the psychological types as noted by Lawrence is that they provide important clues about the individualized concerns of teachers and enable us, once again, to avoid the trap of assuming that all teachers have the same needs interests. "Staff" development, then, becomes increasingly involved with defining and meeting individual developmental needs and concerns of members of the staff.

In this section, we presented two concepts—adult learning characteristics and differentiation of individual needs—that are often ignored in current staff development programs. It is tempting to suggest that adding these two ingredients will improve all that ails staff development and inservice education in schools, but to do so would be to suggest a quick-fix solution to a complex problem. The comments of many teachers today reflect other and deeper concerns. However, designing staff development that recognizes both adult needs and differences among staff members will certainly address two major clusters of individual complaints.

ENTJ

Intuitive, innovative ORGANIZER; aggressive, analytic, systematic, more tuned to new ideas and possibilities than to people's feelings.

ESTJ

Fact-minded, practical ORGANIZER; aggressive, analytic, systematic, more interested in getting the job done than in people's feelings.

INTP

Inquisitive ANALYZER; reflective, independent, curious, more interested in organizing ideas than situations or people.

ISTP

Practical ANALYZER; values exactness, more interested in organizing data than situations or people, reflective, a cool and curious observer of life.

ESTP

REALISTIC ADAPTER in the world of material things; good natured, tolerant, easy going, oriented to practical, first-hand experience, highly observant of details of things.

ESFP

REALISTIC ADAPTER in human relationships; friendly and easy with people, highly observant of their feelings and needs, oriented to practical, first-hand experience.

ISTJ

Analytical MANAGER OF FACTS AND DETAILS; dependable, decisive, painstaking and systematic, concerned with systems and organization, stable and conservative.

ISFJ

Sympathetic MANAGER OF FACTS AND DETAILS; concerned with people's welfare, dependable, painstaking and systematic, stable and conservative.

ISFP

Observant, loyal HELPER; reflective, realistic, empathic, patient with details, gentle and retiring, shuns disagreements, enjoys the moment.

INFP

Imaginative, independent HELPER; reflective, inquisitive, empathic, loyal to ideals, more interested in possibilities than practicalities.

ESFJ

Practical HARMONIZER and worker-with-people, sociable, orderly, opinioned, conscientious, realistic and well tuned to the here and now.

ENFJ

Imaginative HARMONIZER and worker-with-people; sociable, expressive, orderly, opinioned, conscientious, curious about new ideas and possibilities.

INFJ

People-oriented INNOVATOR of ideas; serious, quietly forceful and persevering, concerned with the common good, with helping others develop.

INTJ

Logical, critical, decisive INNOVATOR of ideas; serious, intent, highly independent, concerned with organization, determined and often stubborn.

ENFP

Warmly enthusiastic PLANNER OF CHANGE; imaginative, individualistic, pursues inspiration with impulsive energy, seeks to understand and inspire others.

ENTP

Inventive, analytical PLANNER OF CHANGE; enthusiastic and independent, pursues inspiration with impulsive energy, seeks to understand and inspire others.

Figure 17.1. Brief descriptions of the 16 possible psychological types derived from the Myers-Briggs Personality Type Indicator.

PROMISING PRACTICES

One promising development is not truly a new practice per se, but is nevertheless an important improvement in the area of inservice education and staff development; that is, the way in which this topic is defined. We do appear to be coming closer to developing a clear conceptualization of what both inservice and staff development are supposed to be and do—a goal that we noted as critical earlier in this chapter. Kenneth Howey (1985) suggested, for example, the following six critical functions to be served:

1. *Continuing pedagogical development.* Learning about more effective instructional techniques in the classroom, such as classroom management skills and teacher presentation skills.
2. *Continuing understanding and discovery of self.* Learning more about developmental needs; for example, in interpersonal skills.
3. *Continuing cognitive development.* Determining the level of cognitive ability and development of teachers so that future staff development and inservice schemes might be able to address potential differences more completely.
4. *Continuing theoretical development.* Contributing to the attainment of goals set forth in a selected educational theory.
5. *Continuing professional development.* Increasing the competence levels of teachers in a way that would enable these individuals to contribute to a knowledge base which would, in turn, also contribute to the development of teaching as a profession.
6. *Continuing career development.* Creating greater leadership skills and other competencies that might lead teachers eventually to greater career development opportunities.

Other valid assessments of the purposes for staff development and inservice education are no doubt possible; I offer Howey's primarily to indicate that this field has become increasingly sophisticated in recent years. We no longer view staff development as a "chore" that must be done periodically in schools, or a "frill" carried out only in wealthy districts. A look at the multiple purposes for staff development and inservice education suggests how critical a responsibility it is for those who provide leadership in schools. The effective practitioner of proactive supervision must not only be well-versed in the techniques for implementing staff development, but must also settle upon a clear personal understanding of purpose.

A second promising development in inservice education has appeared in an area often overlooked throughout most of professional education: program evaluation. Bruce Joyce and Beverly Showers (1988) suggest a useful conceptual framework for the evaluation of staff development, derived from a review of responses to questions in three categories:

1. *Questions related to the human resource development system as such.* The purpose of these questions is to determine generally how a system is doing. Is it in good health? Does it succeed in its purposes? How well does it provide for individuals, schools, and district initiatives?
2. *Questions related to the major dimensions of the system and the health of those dimensions.* How well are individuals, schools, and system initiatives being served? What can be done to improve each identified dimension within a system?
3. *Questions related to the study of specific programs and events within each dimension of a system.* A number of specific questions can be asked here, but only a few may be addressed in a formal evaluation system: Are programs that give teachers the opportunity to study teaching skills and strategies succeeding? Are school improvement programs being implemented and affecting the lives of students in a positive way? Are school district initiatives being implemented, and are they improving the performance of students? (p. 118)

Once again, I do not suggest that this analytic framework must be followed; I offer the work of Joyce and Showers as one example of what is being done in one critical area. Staff development and inservice education programs *must* be evaluated intensively to determine if they are truly worth the effort of maintaining them. Past staff development programs have too often been attempts to provide simple answers to complex organizational problems, and they have not been adequately evaluated according to schemes such as the one presented here. This lack of evaluation contributes greatly to the perception of many teachers that programs are ineffective, or at least that they are "snake oil remedies" that promise more than they deliver. Supervisory personnel need to direct their attention to ongoing evaluation if they truly want their efforts to be successful.

SUMMARY

Effective staff development and inservice education programs are critically important to the development of good schools. As a result, the planning, the implementing, and the eventual evaluation of formal professional development programs are particularly important responsiblities for the practitioner of proactive supervision, whose ultimate goal is always to make schools more effective.

In this chapter we considered the distinction—conceptual as well as practical—that theorists often draw between staff development and inservice education, and we pointed out that, although the differences between the two can be both subtle and real, practicing educators rarely make such fine distinctions. We reviewed recent research and defined the characteristics that are typically part of those development programs considered effective; and we noted that recent studies have primarily focused on content and delivery of effective programs.

We explored the two areas in which, in the broadest terms, staff development programs are viewed as experiencing their greatest problems: the extent to which adult learning and development principles are ignored; and the lack of attention to individual learner differences. We then suggested some useful studies that supervisors might consult to remedy these persistent problems. Finally, we presented some promising recent developments in the areas of definition and evaluation that may lead to eventual refinement and improvement of staff development and inservice education.

SUGGESTED ACTIVITIES

1. Interview a group of teachers to determine their perceptions of the strengths and weaknesses of inservice and staff development programs in which they have recently participated. Compare your list of findings with the issues related to individual differences and adult learning that we reviewed in this chapter.
2. Using the Levels of Concern descriptor presented here, review how a group of five or more teachers react to the implementation of some new practice in their school. Chart the number of people found at each level as you carry out your interviews.

REFERENCES

Brimm, J. R., & Tollett, D. J. (1975). How do teachers feel about inservice education? *Educational Leadership, 30*(7), 60–62.

Daresh, John C. (1987). Research trends in staff development and inservice education. *Journal of Education for Teaching, 13*(1), 3–11.

Fuller, Frances F. (1969). Concerns of teachers: A developmental conceptualization. *American Educational Research Journal, 6,* 207–226.

Jung, C. G. (1923). *Psychological types.* In Jolande Jacob (Ed.) (1970), *Psychological reflections: A new anthology of the writings of C. G. Jung.* Princeton, NJ: Princeton University Press.

Hall, Gene E., & Loucks, Susan. (1978, September). Teacher concerns as a basis for facilitating and personalizing staff development. *Teachers College Record, 36–53.*

Henderson, E. S. (1979). The concept of school-focused inservice education and training. *British Journal of Teacher Education, 5*(1), 17–25.

Howey, Kenneth. (1985). Six major functions of staff development: An expanded imperative. *Journal of Teacher Education, 58–64.*

Hutson, H. M. (1981). Inservice best practices: The learnings of general education. *Journal of Research and Development in Education, 14*(2).

Joyce, Bruce, & Showers, Beverly. (1988). *Student achievement through staff development.* White Plains, NY: Longman.

Knowles, Malcolm S. (1970). *The modern practice of adult education.* New York: Association Press.

Lawrence, Gordon. (1974). *Patterns of effective inservice.* Tallahassee: Florida Department of Education.

———— (1982). *People types and tiger stripes: A practical guide to learning styles.* Gainesville, FL: Center for Applications of Psychological Type.

McLaughlin, Milbrey, & Berman, Paul. (1977). Retooling staff development in an era of decline. *Educational Leadership, 34,* 21–28.

McLaughlin, M. W., & Marsh, D. D. (1978). Staff development and school change. *Teachers College Record, 80*(1): 69–94.

Myers, Isabel Briggs, & Briggs, Katherine. (1962). *The Myers-Briggs Type Indicator.* Princeton, NJ: Educational Testing Service.

Nicholson, A. M., Joyce, B. R., Parker, D. W., & Waterman, F. T. (1976). *The Literature of inservice education: An analytic review.* Palo Alto, CA: Stanford Center for Research and Development in Teaching.

Paul, Douglas. (1977). Change processes at the elementary, secondary, and postsecondary levels. In Jack Culbertson & Nicholas Nash (Eds.), *Linking processes in educational improvement.* Columbus, OH: University Council for Educational Administration.

Sprinthall, N. A., & Thies-Sprinthall, L. (1983). The need for a theoretical framework in educating teachers: A cognitive developmental perspective. In Kenneth R. Howey & W. E. Gardner (Eds.), *The education of teachers: A look ahead.* White Plains, NY: Longman.

Swenson, Thomas L. (1981). The state of the art in inservice education and staff development. *Journal of Research and Development in Education, 15*(1), 2–7.

Unruh, A., & Turner, H. E. (1970). *Supervision for change and innovation.* Boston: Houghton-Mifflin.

Wood, Fred, & Thompson, Steven R. (1980). Guidelines for better staff development. *Educational Leadership, 37,* 374–378.

CHAPTER 18

Future Trends and Issues in Supervision

In this final chapter I want to explore briefly some issues that serve as a basis for analyzing the field of educational supervision and that I believe suggest the important directions that analysis will take in the future.

CONTINUED CALL FOR REFORMS

I have suggested throughout this book that an effective supervisor is one who can anticipate and plan for situations rather than reacting to pressures and demands from outside the school. But these pressures and demands will no doubt continue to exist in the foreseeable future of our nation's educational environment. We will hear not fewer calls for improvement in our schools but more and more calls for educational reform.

Supervisors and other educational leaders need to be prepared for these continued calls for reform. To be unprepared will suggest that schools are *not* functioning well and are, in fact, apologizing for their performance. Most people who work in and around schools on a continuing basis realize that, although problems exist, good things are happening as well.

Unfortunately, much of the American public lacks that same daily awareness of what goes on in schools. Instead, most people base their assumptions on what is taking place through the airing of public criticisms and reports on the evening news. When professional educators ignore criticisms and respond instead to the critics, we appear to be making excuses. Supervisors who engage in proactive leadership practices are more likely to know the true nature of the strengths and weaknesses of educational programs and to be ready for the expectations for reform that may arise. When public criticisms are made, the proactive leader is able to respond from a knowledge base that is more wide-ranging than many critics expect.

INCREASED PROFESSIONALISM OF SUPERVISORS

As was pointed out in Chapter 3, one of the continuing controversies in educational supervision is that supervisors often function in a vaguely defined middle area. Neither administrators nor teachers, supervisors are often perceived as relatively unimportant people. This, I suggest, will change.

Increasingly, we are recognizing that the main business of school is instruction, and that the main business of educational leaders is instructional practices. Traditional discussions of educational leadership have not always made that clear. A glance through educational administration textbooks of the past suggests, for instance, that "administrative tasks" include such things as maintenance of the physical plant, student discipline, staff and community relations, fiscal management, and, occasionally, the development of curricula and overseeing instruction. Generally, these various tasks are presented as if they were all of equal importance and value. They are not. The absence of high-quality instruction and effective curriculum development is much worse than a leaky roof or a nonfunctioning furnace. The supervision of staff and instruction is a critical, and perhaps the most critical, responsibility of any principal or school administrator.

As a result of this increasing recognition of the importance of instruction, we can fairly assume that those who serve officially as "supervisors" will less and less be viewed as people who "want to escape the classroom, but don't have what it takes to be administrators," as one of my colleagues once suggested. Instead, many school systems will be moving to ensure that supervisory personnel have training and background skills equivalent to the challenges they will face in their newly identified critical roles. This is in fact already happening in some state departments of education. For instance, Ohio until very recently certified people as supervisors who had only a few courses related to supervision. Until 1987, a person could be licensed as a supervisor by having three years of teaching experience, a masters degree in any field, one course in general curriculum, one in basic supervision, and a practicum. Now Ohio expects future supervisors to have training in the analysis of instruction, evaluation of staff and students, staff development, and adult learning, and advanced training in supervisory models. Certification now implies that the holder possess an advanced degree in the study of supervision itself. Although more university courses do not always imply better training, the fact is that an official movement seems to be underway toward increased preparation and professionalization for educational supervision.

MORE PROFESSIONAL OPPORTUNITIES

Historically, supervisory positions in school systems have been filled almost exclusively by "in-house" applicants. People are assigned to supervisory slots while they await placement in "more important" jobs, such as school principals, for example. Supervisory positions in some school systems are "limbo" territory, to which people are sent briefly in anticipation of something else.

As recognition of the uniqueness of supervisory skills and responsibilities increases, I predict that there will be more professional opportunities for individuals who have deliberate and focused supervisory skills. A good example, I believe, can be found in the emergence of staff development specialists in many districts; educators are increasingly realizing that inservice and staff development are not "frills." A few years ago, some of my students conducted a study in a large metropolitan area to determine who, if anyone, was in charge of staff development for given districts. In most cases, particularly in the suburban communities, we were surprised to find that the responsibility was assigned to one of the high school principals—if it was assigned at all. Staff development was not even a targeted duty of the district personnel office. This situation has begun to change. More and more districts are employing people with special skills in human resources and staff development as members of the typical leadership team. I believe that we will see more of this in the future.

SUMMARY

Educational supervision will continue to be a field with unclear boundaries and expectations. It will never be defined as precisely as teaching or administration. Nevertheless, I believe that supervision will play an increasingly important role in schools in years to come and that one way in which those who go into supervision can guarantee that increasing importance is deserved is to approach their responsibilities *proactively,* rather than as after-the-fact, "fix-it" specialists. Professionalism is on the rise in many educational roles. Supervision will be part of that movement.

Index

Abstraction, 236–237
Academic community, 134
Accommodation, 162–163
Accountable supervision, 240–241
Acheson, Keith A., 208–209, 217,
    219–220, 222–223
Achievement tests, 205
Action plan, 29–36, 74, 111–112, 143,
    235, 236
Action and theory, 53–54
Adaptiveness, 65, 68–69, 77. *See also*
    Innovation
Administration, 42–45, 47, 83, 129,
    148–149. *See also* Administrative
    monitoring; Administrators
Administrative monitoring, 239, 246–248
Administrators, 44–45, 178, 207, 242,
    270
Adult learning/learners, 191–192, 232–237,
    246, 255, 258–260
Age of teachers, 180, 192
Aggression, 161–162
Agricultural model of change, 131–133
Aiken, Michael, 140
Aims of education, 30
Analysis in clinical supervision, 217, 219,
    225, 227, 230
Analytical observers, 237
Analyzers as leaders, 95–97

Anderson, Robert, 216
Andragogy, 258–259, 260
Anecdotal records, 223
Anticipatory set, 239–240
Appraisal contracts, 220, 221, 245
Argyris, Chris, 75
Armstrong, David G., 183
Artistic supervision/teachers, 205–206, 241
Art, teaching as an, 187–188, 241
Assessment, 196, 239–240, 247–248,
    257, 258. *See also* Evaluation
Association for Supervision and Curriculum
    Development (ASCD), 99–100, 102,
    237
Attitudes
    and action plans, 29–36
    and administrative monitoring, 247
    and beliefs, 25
    and change, 138, 140–141
    and clinical supervision, 217
    and communication, 124–125, 127
    definition of, 25
    and evaluation, 203, 209
    importance of analyzing, 24, 36
    and personal philosophy, 24–29
    and staff development/inservice education,
        258, 262
    and values, 25–26
Authentic behavior, 20–21, 23

Authority, 44, 45–47, 73, 85, 146–153
Autonomy, 77, 78–79, 142, 225
Avoidance, 162–163, 171
Awareness, 140–142, 262
Axiomatic Theory of Organizations (Hage), 60, 63–69, 79, 81

Bass, Bernard, 175
Behavior/behaviorism, 26, 78–79, 81, 89, 95–97. *See also name of specific type of behavior*
Beliefs
  and action plans, 29–36
  and attitudes, 25
  and developmental supervision, 232–237
  importance of analyzing, 24, 36
  and metaphors of organizational analysis, 74
  and organizations as cultures, 73
  and personal philosophy, 24–29
  of supervisors, 232–237
  and values, 24–25
Benne, Kenneth D., 173–174
Bennis, Warren, 85, 100, 101, 128, 130
Berliner, David, 203–205
Bhola, H. S., 136
Biases, 59, 189
Blake, Robert, 91–93, 162
Blumberg, Arthur, 178
Borich, Garry, 202
Boulding, Kenneth, 155
Bowers, D. G., 90
Brains, organizations as, 73
Branch, J., 244
Briggs, Katherine, 263
Briggs, Thomas H., 14–15
Burns, James McGregor, 101

Calfee, R., 240
Career choice of teachers, 160–161, 180, 182–184, 192–193
Cartwright, Dorian, 173
Cashell, J. G., 237
Cawelti, Gordon, 237
Centralization, 63–64, 68–69
Certification, 39–40, 44–45, 178, 215, 270

Change. *See also name of specific model of change or researcher*
  and action plans, 143
  and administration, 129
  and attitudes, 138, 140–141
  and authority, 152
  and autonomy, 142
  and awareness, 140–142
  barriers to, 137–140, 141–142
  and climate, 138–139
  and clinical supervision, 217, 226
  common characteristics of models of, 137
  and communication, 131–132, 136–137
  and contact, 133
  and control, 131
  and decision making, 141
  and development, 133–136
  and dissemination, 133–136
  and effectiveness, 129
  and evaluation, 132, 140–142, 211
  fears of, 139, 142
  and feedback, 138, 142
  and goals, 137
  and implementation, 140, 141
  and initiation, 140
  and innovation, 131–132
  and interest, 140–142
  and interpersonal relations, 133
  and knowledge, 138, 140–141
  and leadership, 83, 84, 85, 87, 102, 129, 139–140
  and levels of use, 130–131
  and morale, 138
  and networking, 131
  organizations as emblems of, 74
  and perceptions, 142
  and personal philosophy, 143
  phases of, 140–142
  and planning, 133
  and power, 152
  and predictability, 130
  and problem solving, 130–131, 136, 139
  and rationality, 131, 133
  and research, 133–136
  and rewards, 138, 140
  and roles, 139
  and routine, 140
  and satisfaction, 138

Change (*continued*)
  and skills, 138
  and staff development/inservice education, 262
  and support, 138, 142
  trial and adoption phase of, 140–142
  and trust, 142
  and values, 138, 142, 143
Charisma, 102, 149, 151
Clark, David L., 133
Classroom visits, 10, 13, 17–18, 99, 246–248. *See also* Clinical supervision; Evaluation
Climate
  and administrative monitoring, 247–248
  and autonomy, 78–79
  and behavior, 81
  and change, 138–139
  and clinical supervision, 218–219, 227, 230
  and control, 78–79
  and educational platform, 30, 32–33
  and evaluation, 202
  and human relations, 16, 78–79
  and innovation, 79
  and leadership, 99
  and morale, 78–79
  and motivation, 109
  and organizational analysis, 73, 78–79, 81
  and organizations as organisms, 73
  and personality, 81
  and productivity, 78–79
  and staff development/inservice education, 262
  types of, 78–79
Clinical supervision
  and accountable supervision, 240–241
  and activities for evaluation, 209
  and analysis, 217, 219, 225, 227, 230
  and appraisal contract, 220, 221
  and artistic supervision, 241
  and assessment, 239–240
  assumptions of, 215–218
  and attitudes, 217
  and autonomy, 225
  and change, 217, 226
  and climate, 218–219, 227, 230
  and communication, 220, 227

  and competency, 218–219, 242
  and conferencing, 217, 219–220, 226–227, 230
  and conflict, 242
  and decision making, 217, 229
  and diagnosis, 239–240
  as differentiated supervision, 239–243
  and diversity, 228, 229
  evaluation of, 227
  and expectations, 220
  fears of, 228–229
  and feedback, 216, 217–218, 219–220, 226, 227, 229–230
  and follow-up, 220
  as a formative evaluation, 208, 215, 230
  and goals/purposes, 216, 217–218, 220, 226, 240
  and the inspection view of supervision, 18
  and learning, 226, 240–241
  limitations of, 217–218, 228–230
  and modeling, 240
  and motivation, 220, 228
  and objectives, 239–240
  and observation, 219–220, 221–225, 227, 230
  and outcomes, 226, 240–241
  and peer programs, 218, 228, 242, 243–244
  and perceptions, 225
  and planning, 219–220
  potential pitfalls of, 218–219
  and principals/administrators, 242–243
  and problem solving, 217
  providers of, 242
  and reality, 225
  receivers of, 241–242
  recording data in, 222–225
  and reinforcement, 217
  as a resource, 218
  and resources, 219
  responsibility for, 216–217, 227
  and rewards, 219, 226
  role of supervisors in, 218, 226–227, 242
  and satisfactions, 226
  and scientific supervision, 239–240, 241
  and self-evaluation, 217, 226–227
  and skill development, 216–217, 242
  and staff development, 216–217, 225

and staff evaluation, 217, 225, 229
stages of, 219–227, 230
and student achievement, 240–241
teacher-directed, 217–218, 235
and teacher-supervisor relationships, 217,
   219, 226, 230
and teaching style, 217
and time, 219, 228
and trust, 218–219, 226, 227, 230
and values, 217, 225
Coercive power, 148–149
Cogan, Morris, 216, 219
Cognitive development, 236–237, 265
Cohesion, 77, 88, 119–120
Collaboration, 162–163, 178, 233, 235,
   257, 262
Collectivities, 168
Commitment, 85, 236–237
Communication
   and attitudes, 124–125
   barriers to, 125–127
   and change, 131–132, 136–137
   and clinical supervision, 220, 227
   and cohesion, 119–120
   and conflict, 155, 163
   and control, 124–125
   and decision making, 122
   definition of, 117–118
   and effectiveness, 128
   and evaluation, 202, 206, 207–208
   and feedback, 118–119, 121–122, 127
   forms of, 123–125
   functions of, 118–120
   and goals of organization, 118
   and health of organization, 76, 81
   and identity, 118, 119
   importance of, 117
   improvement of, 127
   and leadership, 100
   nonverbal, 124–125
   one-way, 120–122
   and outcomes, 118
   and perception, 127
   and roles, 126
   and rules/procedures, 118
   two-way, 122–123
   types of, 120–123
   verbal, 123
   written, 124

Competency
   and administrative monitoring, 246
   and adult learning, 259
   and clinical supervision, 218–219, 242
   and evaluation, 200
   and the inspection view of supervision, 8,
      9, 10, 17–18
   and proactive supervision, 20
   and the scientific view of supervision,
      13
   and staff development/inservice education,
      256, 257, 259, 260
   of supervisors, 41–42
Competition, 162–163
Complexity, 12, 64–65, 68–69, 85,
   236–237
Compliance theory, 150
Compromise, 162–163, 171
Concern, levels of, 261–263
Concerns-Based Adoption Model (Hall and
      Loucks), 130–131
Conferencing, 217, 219–220, 226–227,
      230, 243, 245
Conflict, 71, 72, 73, 96, 112, 154–163,
      170–171, 172, 175, 242
Consistency, 20–21, 23, 113, 206
Construct theory, 29
Contact, 133, 190, 192
Content of staff development/inservice
      education, 254–255, 257
Continuation theme, 182
Continuous evaluation. See Formative
      evaluation
Control
   and change, 131
   and climate, 78–79
   and communication, 124–125
   and developmental supervision, 233,
      235
   and effectiveness of supervisors, 45–47
   and leadership, 84, 95–97, 102
   and organizations as instruments of
      domination, 74
   and power, 148–149
   and the scientific view of supervision,
      11–13
   in supervisory encounter, 233, 235
   by teachers, 183–184, 228
   and teaching, 186, 187, 188

Cooley, Charles M., 169
Cooperation, 161–162
Cooperative professional development, 239, 243–244
Cox, Philip W. L., 14
Creative groups, 171, 175
Crisis orientation, 76
Criteria for evaluation, 203–206, 211
Croft, Donald, 78–79, 81
Cultures, organizations as, 73
Cumulative learning, 59
Curriculum, 30, 31, 199, 211, 216–217

Decision making, 45–46, 63, 91, 99, 122, 141, 211, 217, 229
Delivery systems for staff development/ inservice education, 254, 255–258
Democratic process, 14
Dependent groups, 171, 175
Descriptive theories, 63, 86
Deutsch, Morton, 155
Developmental supervision, 232–237
Diagnositicians, supervisors as, 78
Diagnostic evaluation, 196–197, 198–199, 200, 211
Differentiated supervision
    and administrative monitoring, 246–248
    approaches to, 237, 239
    and clinical supervision, 239–243
    and cooperative professional development, 243–244
    and self-directed development, 244–246
Direct instruction model, 240
Directive supervision, 233, 235, 246
Discursive treatment of a topic, 54–55, 59, 63, 86
Disengagement, 78–79
Dissemination of change, 133–136
Diversity, 89, 191, 228, 229, 232, 257, 259, 260–264
Domination, organizations as instruments of, 74
Dropouts, teachers as, 236
Due process, 207–208
Duke, Daniel, 191–192
Dwight, Theodore, 9
Dynamic organizations, 66–68, 79, 81

Educational connoisseurship, 205
Educational platform, 29–35, 36, 111–112, 113, 237
Effectiveness
    and administrative monitoring, 247–248
    and authority, 45–47, 152
    and change, 129
    and communication, 128
    and conflict, 157–161
    and control, 45–47
    and evaluation, 196, 202, 203–205, 208
    and groups, 171, 175–176
    and health of organization, 75–76
    and human resource development, 19
    and interaction, 171, 175–176
    and leadership, 84, 88, 92–93, 97, 98–99, 129, 252
    and learning, 251
    and line officers, 45–46
    and motivation, 109, 113
    and personality styles, 46
    and power, 152
    research about, 252
    and social systems theory (Getzels), 71, 81
    and staff development/inservice education, 251–252, 253, 254, 256, 258
    and staff members, 45–46
    task, 171, 175–176
    and teachers, 191
    and values, 47
Efficiency, 11–13, 65–66, 68–69, 188, 206
Egocentricism, 126
Eisner, Elliott, 18, 205, 241
Eliot, E. C., 12
Empowerment, 85, 101, 102
Environment. See Climate
Equitable/equal, 110
Equity theories of motivation, 109–110, 111
Etzioni, Amitai, 150
Evaluation. See also Assessment; Clinical supervision; name of specific type of evaluation
    and achievement, 205, 206
    and artistic supervision/teachers, 205
    and attitudes, 203, 209

and change, 132, 140–142, 211
and climate, 202
and communication, 202, 206, 207–208
and competency, 200
and consistency, 206
criteria, 196, 203–206, 211
curriculum, 199, 211
and decision making, 211
definition of, 195–196, 211
and due process, 207–208
and effectiveness, 196, 202, 203–205, 208
and effective teacher behaviors, 203–205
and efficiency, 206
evaluations of, 210–211
and expectations, 198, 199, 206, 207
and expertise, 206–207
and feedback, 197, 200, 202, 208–210
and follow-up, 207, 208–210
function of, 195
and goals, 206, 208
importance of, 211
and improvement, 197, 200, 202, 210, 211
and interest, 206
and interpersonal skills, 200–201
and leadership, 97–99
and learning, 203, 206
monitoring, 197
and motivation, 112
objectives of, 198–201
and objectivity, 206
and outcomes, 205
and predictability, 209
problems/issues concerning, 201–211
purposes of, 196, 197, 198, 202, 208, 210–211
and quality education, 211
recording of data for, 208–209
and reinforcement, 209–210
and research, 206
responsibility for, 211
and routine, 206
stages of, 211
and teacher involvement, 202
and trust, 202, 205
types of, 196–198, 211
Expectancy theories of motivation, 111–112

Expectations
  and clinical supervision, 220
  and conflict, 159–160
  and cooperative professional development, 244
  and developmental supervision, 235
  and evaluation, 198, 199, 206, 207
  and motivation, 111–112
  and organizations as machines, 72
  and social systems theory (Getzels), 70–72, 81
  and teaching, 188
Expediters, supervisors as, 15
Experience of teachers, 180, 192, 254–255
Expertise and evaluation, 206–207
Expert power, 149–150
Experts. *See* Specialists
Explanation, theory, 57, 60

Facilitators, 90, 97–99, 136, 235
Feedback
  and administrative monitoring, 247–248
  and adult learning, 259
  and change, 138, 142
  and clinical supervision, 216, 217–218, 219–220, 226, 227, 229–230
  and communication, 118–119, 121–122, 127
  and evaluation, 197, 200, 202, 208–210
  and motivation, 110–111
  and staff development/inservice education, 259
Fight groups, 171
Flanders Interaction Analysis scale, 223
Followership, 85, 101
Follow-up, 207, 208–210, 220, 226–227, 243
Formal groups, 170–171
Formative evaluation, 197, 198, 199, 200–201, 202, 208, 211. *See also* Clinical supervision
French, J. R. P., 148
Fullan, Michael, 130
Fuller, Frances, 236, 261
Functional principle, 11–13

Gall, Meredith D., 208–209, 217, 219–220, 222–223

Garman, Noreen, 216
Geer, Blanche, 179
Gender, 87, 88, 180
Generalizations, 57, 59, 60
Gestalt psychology, 16
Getzels, Jacob, 26, 69–72, 82, 157, 160
Glatthorn, Allan, 237–243, 244–245, 246
Glickman, Carl, 232–237
Goals
  and adult learning, 259
  and change, 137
  and clinical supervision, 216, 217, 220, 226
  and communication, 118
  and conflict, 158
  and developmental supervision, 244–245
  and evaluation, 206, 208
  and groups, 168, 169–170, 175, 176
  and health of organization, 75, 76, 81
  and leadership, 90, 99–100
  and metaphors, 81
  and motivation, 112
  and organizational analysis, 66, 68, 71, 75, 76, 81
  and power, 150
  and social systems theory (Getzels), 71
  and staff development/inservice education, 259
  and teaching, 186, 188
Goldhammer, Robert, 216, 220–227, 230
Gorton, Richard, 127, 148, 149
Gould, R., 236
Great person approach to leadership, 86–87, 89, 101–102
Gross, N., 131
Groups, 159–160, 167–177, 185
Guba, Egor G., 133
Guditus, Charles, 66
Guided practice, 240

Hage, Gerald, 60, 63–69, 79, 81, 140
Hall, Gene E., 130–131, 137, 236, 261–262
Halpin, Andrew W., 78–79, 81, 90, 91, 138–139
Happiness, 15–16, 19, 77
Hare, Paul, 168, 169–170
Harris, Ben, 42, 228–229

Harvard-Newton Summer School project, 216
Havelock, Ronald G., 132, 133, 134, 136, 141
Health of organizations, 75–78, 81, 262, 266
Heichberger, R. L., 237
Hemphill, John K., 88
Herzberg, Frederick, 108–109
Hidden agendas, 73, 125
Hierarchy of needs, 106–109, 236
Hoeh, James, 85
Holmes Group, 180
House, Ernest R., 133
House, Robert J., 91
Howey, Kenneth, 265
Hoy, Wayne K., 52
Hughes, Larry, 158–159
Human relations, 14–16, 18–19, 78–79, 93
Human resource development, 17, 18–19, 77, 266
Hunter, Madeline, 239–240
Hygiene factors (Herzberg), 108–109

Identity, 118, 119
Idiographic dimension (Getzels), 70–72, 81, 90, 157
Image of the teacher/learner, 30, 31–32
Improvement. See Clinical supervision; Evaluation; Staff development/inservice education
In-between people, supervisors as, 16
Informal groups, 170–171
Innovation, 65, 77, 79, 131–132, 139. See also Adaptiveness; Change
Insecurity, 191
Inservice education. See Staff development/inservice education
Inspection, supervision as, 8–11, 17–18, 178
Institution (social systems theory), 70–72, 81
Instruction, direct/indirect, 97–99, 240
Instructional leadership, 97–101
Instrumental leadership, 91
Interaction. See also Groups
  and change, 131–133, 136

and effectiveness, 171, 175–176
and leadership, 90, 102
Interest, 140–142, 188, 206, 236, 254, 255, 256
Interpersonal relations, 133, 182, 200–201
Interreference groups, 159–160
Intrareference groups, 159
Involvement, 255, 256, 259

Job description, 8, 39–40, 41–42, 64–65, 112, 158, 159–160
Job satisfaction, 65–66, 68–69
Joyce, Bruce, 265–266
Judgement, 263
Jung, C. G., 263
Justman, Joseph, 14–15

Kelly, G. A., 29
Kerman, Sam, 244
Knowledge, 138, 139, 140–141, 186, 241
Knowles, Malcolm, 258–259
Krajewski, Robert, 216
Kunkel, Richard C., 210

Lawler, E., 111
Lawrence, Gordon, 244, 263
Leadership. *See also name of specific researcher or type of leadership*
and administrators, 83, 129, 207
and authority, 85
and behavior/behaviorism, 89, 95–97, 99–100, 102
and change, 83, 84, 85, 87, 102, 129, 139–140
and charisma, 102
and classroom visits, 99
and climate, 99
and cohesion, 88
and communication, 100
and complexity, 85
and conflict, 96
and consideration, 90
and control, 84, 95–97, 102
and decision making, 91, 99
definitions of, 84–85, 89, 173
descriptive views of, 85–86, 89, 90–91, 102
and diversity, 89

and effectiveness, 84, 88, 92–93, 97, 98–99, 129, 252
and empowerment, 85, 101, 102
and evaluation, 97–99
and facilitation, 90, 97–99
and followership, 85, 101
frequency of, 89
and gender, 87, 88
and goals, 90, 99–100
and groups, 173
historical development of, 86–90
and homogeneity, 88
and human relations, 93
importance of, 85
and instructional leadership, 97–101
and interaction, 90, 102
and intimacy, 88
locus of, 89
and manipulation, 102
and monitoring, 99
and morale, 93
myths of, 101–102
normative views of, 85–86, 89, 91–97, 102
participative, 91, 99
and people dimension, 91–93
and personality, 86–87, 102
and personal philosophy, 23
potency of, 89–90
and predictability, 85, 100
and problem solving, 97–99
and productivity, 91–93
and professionalism, 270
and quality of instruction, 99
and resources, 97–99
and responsibility, 85
and satisfaction, 88
and scientific management, 93
scope/range of, 90
and self-concept, 100
sexism, 87, 88
situational approach to, 88, 89, 93–95
and skills, 101
and staff development, 97–99
strategies for successful, 100
and structure, 90
and success, 100
and support, 90, 91, 95–97, 99

Leadership (*continued*)
and tasks, 91–93, 95–97
and teachers, 97–99
and titles, 101
traitist approach to, 87–88, 89
and trust, 90, 100
and the Wallenda factor, 100
Learning. *See also* Adult learning/learners
and administrative monitoring, 247
adult patterns of, 258–259
and clinical supervision, 226, 240–241
cumulative, 59
and educational platform, 30, 31, 32
and effectiveness, 251
and evaluation, 206
excitement of, 184
and individual differences, 260–264
knowledge about, 138
and staff development/inservice education,
257, 262
and teaching, 185–186, 188, 192
Legal authority, 151
Legitimate power, 149
Levels of concern, 261–263
Levinson, Daniel, 236
Lieberman, Ann, 185–187
Line officers, 42–46
Linkage model of change, 136–137
Lipham, James, 85, 89, 102, 129
Lippitt, G., 131
Lippitt, R., 130
Listing of characteristics for a theory, 63, 86
Liu, Ching-Jen, 97–99
Loevinger, J., 236
Lortie, Dan, 179–180, 182–183
Loucks, Susan, 130–131, 236, 262–263
Lovell, John T., 105, 137–140, 218–219,
226, 229–230, 237

McGregor, Douglas, 27–29, 113
Machines, organizations as, 72–73
McLaughlin, Milbrey, 132
McNeil, J. D., 240–241
Management-by-objective programs, 245
Managerial Grid (Blake and Mouton),
91–93
Manipulation, 19, 20, 74, 102, 109,
110–111, 151–152
Maslow, Abraham, 106–109, 236

Master teachers, 216, 261
Material benefits of teaching, 182–183
Mechanistic organizations, 66–68, 79, 81
Metaphors, 72–75, 81, 185–186
Miles, Matthew B., 75–78, 81, 132
Miller, Lynne, 185–187
Miskel, Cecil G., 52
Mixed groups, 171
Modeling, 23, 56, 87, 240, 257
Monitoring, 99, 197, 239, 246–248
Morale, 77, 78–79, 93, 138, 247
Morgan, Gareth, 72–75, 81
Mosher, Robert L., 219
Motivation
and action plans, 111–112
and adult learning, 259
and authority, 152
and career choice, 160–161, 182–184
and climate, 109
and clinical supervision, 220, 228
and conflict, 112, 155
and consistency, 113
definition of, 105–106
and educational platform, 111–112, 113
and effectiveness, 109, 113
equity theories of, 109–110, 111
and evaluation, 112
expectancy theories of, 111–112
and feedback, 110–111
and goals, 112
and job descriptions, 112
and manipulation, 109, 110–111
need-satisfaction theories of, 106–109
and outcomes, 111–112
and perceptions, 109–110, 111–112
and personal philosophy, 111–112
and power, 152
and predictability, 108–109
reinforcement theories of, 110–111, 113
responsibility for, 113
and rewards, 110, 112
and roles, 112, 113
and rules/procedures, 110–111
and staff development/inservice education,
259
and teaching, 187
and values, 111–112
Mouton, Jane, 91–93, 162
Myers-Briggs Type Indicator (MBTI), 263

Myers, Isabel Briggs, 263
Myths of leadership, 101–102

Nanus, Burt, 85, 100, 101, 128
National Education Association, 14
Needs, 106–109, 236, 254, 256, 257, 259
Need-satisfaction theories, 106–109
Networking, 131
Nomothetic dimension (Getzels), 70–72, 82, 90, 157
Nondirective orientation, 233, 235
Nonverbal communication, 124–125
Normative theory, 86
Normative view
   of leadership, 85–86, 89, 91–97, 102
   of power, 150
Norms, 172–173, 186, 189
Northwest Regional Laboratory for Educational Development (Portland, OR), 95–97

Oberg, Antoinette, 29
Objectivity, 58, 59–60, 127, 206
Observation
   and clinical supervision, 216, 219–220, 221–225, 227, 230
   and cooperative professional development, 243, 244
   and the discursive treatment of a topic, 54–55, 59, 63, 86
Oliva, Peter, 220, 222
Olmsted, Michael, 168, 169–170
One-way communication, 120–122
Operational values, 26
Organisms, organizations as, 73
Organizational analysis. *See also name of specific theory or researcher*
   formal, 62, 63–75, 79, 81
   informal, 62, 75–81
Organizational Climate Description Questionnaire (Halpin and Croft), 78–79
Organizational health (Miles), 75–78, 81
Organization development (OD) model of change, 132
Organization. *See* Line officers;
   Organizational analysis; Staff members
Orientations of supervisors, 233–237

Outcomes
   and the Axiomatic Theory of Organizations (Hage), 63, 65–66, 68–69, 79, 81
   and clinical supervision, 226, 240–241
   and communication, 118
   and evaluation, 205
   and motivation, 111–112
   and theory, 53
Owens, Robert, 76, 92, 134, 155, 156, 162–163

Palonsky, Stuart, 187, 189
Paradoxes, 74
Paraphrasing, 127
Participative leadership, 91, 99
Paul, Douglas, 130, 131–132, 135
Payne, William, 12
Peabody, Robert, 151
Pedagogy, 30, 32, 258
Peer program
   and clinical supervision, 218, 228, 242, 243–244
   and cooperative professional development, 243
People dimension, 69–72, 81, 91–93, 173–175
Perceptions
   and artistic supervision, 241
   and change, 142
   and clinical supervision, 225
   and communication, 127
   and developmental supervision, 233
   and metaphors of organizational analysis, 74
   and motivation, 109–110, 111–112
   and power, 149–150
   and staff development/inservice education, 263
Personality, 46, 70–72, 81, 86–87, 102, 126, 160–161, 217
Personal philosophy, 23–36, 58–60, 74, 111–112, 143, 157, 160, 237
Phelps, M. S., 237
Piece-rate principle, 11–13
Planning, 11–13, 133, 158, 217, 219–220, 246–247, 255, 260
Political systems, organizations as, 73
Porter, L. W., 111

Power, 73, 76, 146–153
Practicality, 189
Predictability
  and change, 130
  and evaluation, 209
  and leadership, 85, 100
  and motivation, 108–109
  and organizations as machines, 72
  and proactive supervision, 20
  and the scientific view of supervision,
    11–13, 18
  and social systems theory (Getzels), 72
  and teaching, 188–189
  and theory, 54, 56, 60, 86
Preservice tryouts, 161
Primary groups, 169–170
Principals, 38–40, 42, 78–79, 81,
  139–140, 242–243, 246–248
Privacy, 189–190
Proactive supervision. *See also name of
  specific topic*
  characteristics of, 2, 8, 20–21, 23
  definition of, 8
  example of, 1, 2
  holistic aspect of, 2–3
Problem solving
  and change, 130–131, 136, 139
  and clinical supervision, 217
  and conflict, 162–163
  and developmental supervision, 233,
    236–237
  and groups, 171
  and health of organization, 77
  and leadership, 97–99
  and organizations as machines, 72–73
Procedural groups, 171
Process, supervision as a, 21, 30, 33–34,
  41–42, 44, 47, 71, 217
Productivity
  and Axiomatic Theory of Organizations
    (Hage), 65–66, 68–69
  and climate, 78–79
  and conflict, 158–159
  and groups, 171
  and the human relations era, 15–16
  and human resource development, 19
  and leadership, 91–93
  and scientific management, 18
  and social systems theory (Getzels), 71

Professional development, 239, 261. *See
  also* Staff development/inservice
  education
Professionalism of supervisors, 270–271
Professional opportunities for supervisors,
  271
Professionals, teachers as, 237
Profiles of teachers, 236–237
Promoters, 95–97
Psychic prisons, organizations as, 73–74
Psychological types, 263
Purpel, D. E., 219
Purposes. *See name of specific topic*

Quality
  and evaluation, 211
  and the human relations era, 15–16
  and the inspection view of supervision,
    10–11
  and leadership, 99
  and the scientific view of supervision, 13
  and staff development/inservice education,
    252, 256

Race of teachers, 180
Rationality, 73, 131, 133
Raven, B., 148
Reactive supervision, 1–2, 21, 74
Reality, 60, 73–74, 225
Reavis, Charles, 237
Recording of data, 208–209, 222–225
Reddin, W. J., 93–95, 171–172
Redfern evaluation plan, 245
Referent power, 149
Reflection-in-action concepts, 29
Reform, calls for, 269–270
Regulation. *See* Rules/procedures
Reinforcement, 110–111, 113, 188,
  209–210, 217, 233
Religion, 8–9, 10
Remediation, 252
Research. *See name of specific topic or
  researcher*
Research and development centers, 134
Research-Development-Diffusion Model of
  Change, 133–136
Resources, 97–99, 219, 244–245, 256
Responsibility
  and clinical supervision, 216–217, 227

and conflict, 155
for evaluation, 211
and leadership, 85
for motivation, 113
for staff development/inservice education,
    216–217, 251–252, 271
of students, 203
Resser, Clayton, 147
Rewards
and the Axiomatic Theory of
    Organizations (Hage), 64–65
and change, 138, 140
and clinical supervision, 219, 226
and motivation, 110, 112
and power, 148
and staff development/inservice education,
    256, 257
of teachers, 185
Ritz, W. C., 237
Rogers, E. M., 131, 140
Rokeach, Milton, 24, 25
Roles
and adult learning, 258
and change, 139
and communication, 126
and conflict, 160–161
and groups, 173–174
maintenance, 174
and motivation, 112, 113
and personalities, 71–72, 160–161
and social systems theory (Getzels),
    70–72, 81
and tasks, 174
of teachers, 71–72, 113
Routine, 140, 183, 188, 206
Rubin, Louis J., 18, 186, 187–188,
    205–206
Rules/procedures, 110–111, 118, 171,
    189–190
Ryan, B., 131

Sanders James, 195–196, 197
Satisfaction, 88, 106–109, 138, 226
Schmuck, Richard A., 132
Schon, Donald, 29
School boards, 18, 237
Scientific management, 11–13, 14, 18, 19,
    72–73, 93, 187, 237, 241
Scriven, Michael, 197

Seashore, S. E., 90
Secondary groups, 169–170
Secular values, 26
Self-concept, 100, 126, 258, 260, 265
Self-directed development, 239, 244–246
Self-evaluation, 203, 210, 217, 226–227,
    235
Sergiovanni, Thomas J., 29–35, 36, 52,
    65, 94, 241
Service theme in career choice, 182
Sexism and leadership, 87, 88
Shakeshaft, Charol, 87
Sheats, Paul, 173–174
Sheehy, Gail T., 236
Shoemaker, F. F., 131
Showers, Beverly, 265–266
Simon, Herbert, 147
Simplified listing, theory, 63, 86
Situational dimension of leadership, 88, 89,
    93–95
Skills development, 216–217, 242,
    252–253, 256, 261
Skills. See name of specific topic
Skinner, B. F., 110
Social interaction model of change,
    131–133, 136
Social systems theory (Getzels), 69–72, 81,
    90, 157, 160
Specialists, 11–13, 16, 43, 257
Spillman, Russell, 120, 123
Sprinthall, N. A., 257
Staff development/inservice education
and assessment, 257, 258
and attitudes, 258, 262
and awareness, 262
and change, 262
and climate, 262
and clinical supervision, 225
and cognitive development, 265
and collaboration, 257, 262
and competency, 256, 257, 259, 260
and content, 254–255, 257
and cooperative professional development,
    244
definition of, 252–253
delivery systems for, 254, 255–258
and diversity, 257, 259, 260–264
and effectiveness, 251–252, 253, 254,
    256, 258

Staff development/inservice education
(*continued*)
evaluations of, 255, 256, 265–266
and experience of teachers, 254–255
and experts, 257
and feedback, 259
functions of, 265
and goals, 259
and health of organization, 262, 266
and human resource development, 266
importance of, 266
and improvement, 251–252
and instructional leadership, 97–99
and interest, 254, 255, 256
and involvement, 255, 256, 259
and learning, 255, 257, 258–260,
   262
and levels of concern, 261–263
and modeling, 257
and motivation, 259
and needs, 254, 256, 257, 259
and perceptions, 263
and planning, 255, 260
promising developments in, 265–266
and psychological types, 263
and quality, 252, 256
research related to, 253–258
and resources, 256
responsibility for, 216–217, 251–252,
   271
and rewards, 256, 257
satisfaction with, 255
and self-concept, 260, 265
and skill development, 252–253, 256,
   261
and success, 256, 257, 259
and support, 257–258
and teacher characteristics, 254–255
and theoretical development, 265
Staff evaluation, 199–201, 202, 203–206,
   207–208, 211, 217, 225, 229
Staff members, 42–46
Starratt, Robert J., 29–35, 36, 52, 65, 94
Stratification, 64–65, 68–69, 126
Structure
   and the Axiomatic Theory of
      Organizations (Hage), 63–65, 66–68,
      79, 81
   components of, 63–65

and the social systems theory (Getzels),
   69–72
Student achievement, 30–31, 188, 206,
   240–241, 244, 251
Student evaluation, 198–199, 211
Students, responsibility by, 203
Students. *See* Learning; Student
   achievement; Student evaluation;
   Teachers
Sturges, A. W., 242
Success, 100, 175, 240, 256, 257, 259
Summative evaluation, 198, 199, 201, 202,
   207–208, 211, 245
Superintendents, 12
Supervision
   administration compared with, 42–45,
      47, 83
   artistic, 205
   and clinical supervision, 217
   controversies about, 38–47
   definition of, 21
   fluid nature of, 7–21, 38–42
   historical stages of, 8–16
   importance of, 3, 270, 271
   as inspection, 8–11, 17–18, 178
   institutionalization/professionalization
      of, 12
   as a process, 21, 30, 33–34, 41–42,
      44, 47, 71, 217
   and scientific management, 11–13, 18
Supervisors
   ambiguity of role of, 38–42
   certification of, 44–45, 178, 215,
      270
   competency areas of, 41–42
   definition of, 44
   as diagnositicians, 78
   effectiveness of, 45–47
   as facilitators, 90, 97–99, 136, 235
   generic tasks/responsibilities of, 41–42
   as in-between people, 16
   of instruction, 39–40
   job description for, 39–40, 41–42
   orientations of, 233–237
   principals compared with, 38–40
   professionalism of, 270–271
   professional opportunities for, 271
   and size of school system, 40
   titles for, 40

Supervisory orientation, 233–237
Support. *See also* Facilitators; Staff
    development/inservice education
    and change, 138, 142
    and developmental supervision, 233
    and leadership, 90, 91, 95–97, 99
    and staff development/inservice education,
        257–258
    and teaching, 186–187

Tasks
    of administrators, 270
    and effectiveness, 171, 175–176
    and groups, 174
    and leadership, 91–93, 95–97
    and the Managerial Grid (Blake and
        Mouton), 91–93
    and roles, 174
Taxonomies, 54, 55–56, 86
Taylor, Frederic W., 11–12, 18
Teacher Expectations and Student
    Achievement (TESA) model, 244
Teacher involvement, evaluation, 202
Teachers. *See also name of specific topic*
    activities of, 184–190
    and the administration/supervision
        controversy, 42–45
    age level of, 180, 192
    as analytical observers, 237
    behavior of, 78–79, 81, 203–205
    characteristics of, 179–181, 232–237,
        254–255
    commitment of, 236–237
    diversity among, 191
    as dropouts, 236
    experience of, 180, 192, 254–255
    gender of, 180
    isolation of, 186–187, 190, 192, 243
    master, 261
    material benefits of, 182–183
    as professionals, 237
    profiles of, 236–237
    race of, 180
    rewards of, 185
    roles of, 71–72, 113
    student relationships with, 30, 32,
        240–241

    supervisors' relationships with, 178,
        190–193, 217, 219, 226, 230
    as unfocused workers, 237
Teaching
    as an art, 187–188, 241
    disadvantages of, 190
    importance of, 184
    metaphor about, 185–186
    nature of, 184–190, 191
    as practical, 189
    as private, 189–190
    skills of, 191
    styles of, 185, 217
Team teaching, 244
Texas Research and Development Center
    for Teacher Education, 261–262
Thelen, Herbert, 173
Theoretical development, staff
    development/inservice education,
    265
Theory
    and biases, 58, 189
    characteristics of a, 52, 56–57
    definition of, 51–53, 60
    descriptive, 63, 86
    and discursive treatment of a topic,
        54–55, 59, 63, 86
    and explanation, 57, 60
    formal/informal, 58–60
    functions of, 53–54
    future aspects of a, 52, 53, 57
    and generalizations, 57, 59, 60
    importance of, 57
    and the integration of knowledge, 53
    and the listing of characteristics, 54, 55,
        63, 86
    and model building, 56
    normative, 86
    and objectivity, 58, 59–60
    and outcomes, 53
    and personal philosophy, 58–60
    and predictability, 54, 56, 57, 60, 86
    and reality, 56–57, 60
    and research, 53
    restrictions on the use of, 58, 60
    steps in the development of a, 54–56,
        60, 86
    and taxonomies, 54, 55–56, 86

Theory (*continued*)
  and values, 51–52
  verification of a, 53, 57, 59–60
Theory X/Y (McGregor), 27–29, 113
Thies-Sprinthall, L., 257
Thomas, Kenneth, 161–163
Thompson, Steven R., 259
3–D Theory of Leadership (Reddin),
  93–95
Tikunoff, W., 203–205
Time
  and clinical supervision, 219, 228
  and developmental supervision, 236
Time compatibility theme of career choice,
  183
Timeline coding, 223
Time-management activities, 158–159
Time-study principle, 11–13
Titles, 40, 101
Tom, Alan, 185–186
Top-down orientation, 13, 14
Traditional authority, 150–151
Traitist approach to leadership, 87–88, 89
Transformative leadership, 101
Trial and adoption phase of change,
  140–142
Trust
  and change, 142
  and clinical supervision, 218–219, 226,
    227, 230
  and conflict, 163
  and evaluation, 202, 205
  and the inspection view of supervision,
    10, 17–18
  and leadership, 90, 100
Tucker, Susan, 210
Turner, H. E., 261
Two-way communication, 122–123

Unfocused workers, 237
Unions, 45–46, 139
Unruh, A., 261
Use, levels of, 130–131

Values
  as abstract ideals, 26
  and action plans, 29–36

  analysis of, 36
  and attitudes, 25–26
  and behavior, 26
  and beliefs, 24–25
  and change, 138, 142, 143
  and clinical supervision, 217, 225
  and communication, 127
  and conflict, 157
  definition of, 25
  and effectiveness, 47
  and groups, 172–173
  importance of analyzing, 24, 25–26,
    36
  and McGregor's assumptions, 27–29
  and motivation, 111–112
  operational, 26
  and organizations as cultures, 73
  and personal philosophy, 24–29
  secular, 26
  and theory, 51–52
Verbal communication, 123
Videotaping, 246

Wallenda factor, 100
Waller, Willard, 179
Watson, Goodwin, 142
Weber, Max, 147, 150–151
Weller, Richard, 216–217
Wickerman, James, 9–10
Wide-lens techniques, 223
Wiles, Kimball, 15, 105, 137–140,
    218–219, 226, 229–230
Winer, J. A., 90, 91
Women as teachers, 180, 192
Wood, Fred, 259
Working conditions of teachers, 183
Worthen, Blaine, 195–196, 197
Written communication, 124
Wynn, Richard, 66

Young, J. M., 237
Yukl, Gary, 84

Zaltman, Gerald, 140–141
Zander, Alvin, 173